Production and Logistics

Titles in this Series

Erwin Pesch
*Learning in Automated
Manufacturing*
1994. XIV, 258 pages.
ISBN 3-7908-0792-3

Rainer Kolisch
*Project Scheduling under
Resource Constraints*
1995. X, 212 pages.
ISBN 3-7908-0829-6

Armin Scholl
*Balancing and Sequencing
of Assembly Lines*
1995. XVI, 306 pages.
ISBN 3-7908-0881-4

Dirk C. Mattfeld

Evolutionary Search and the Job Shop

Investigations on
Genetic Algorithms for
Production Scheduling

With 62 Figures
and 30 Tables

Physica-Verlag

A Springer-Verlag Company

Dr. Dirk C. Mattfeld
University of Bremen
Department of Economics
D-28334 Bremen, Germany

ISBN 3-7908-0917-9 Physica-Verlag Heidelberg

Die Deutsche Bibliothek – CIP-Einheitsaufnahme

Mattfeld, Dirk C.:
Evolutionary search and the job shop: investigations on
genetic algorithms for production scheduling ; with 30 tables /
Dirk C. Mattfeld. – Heidelberg: Physica-Verl., 1996
  (Production and logistics)
  ISBN 3-7908-0917-9

Preface

Production planning and control systems suffer from insufficient computational support in the field of production scheduling. Practical requirements dictate highly constrained mathematical models with complex and often contradicting objectives. Therefore scheduling even in computerized manufacturing systems still relies on simple priority rule based heuristics. Thus, we can expect a great so far unexploited optimization potential in manufacturing environments.

Within the last decade academic research in scheduling has gained a significant progress due to modern Local Search based heuristics. Much effort has been put into suitable neighborhood definitions which go for the key feature of Local Search. However, it remains questionable whether this work can be transferred in order to fit the flexible requirements of production scheduling.

Evolutionary Algorithms can be formulated almost independently of the detailed shaping of the problems under consideration. As one would expect, a weak formulation of the problem in the algorithm comes along with a quite inefficient search. Nevertheless, for practical requirements the advantage of constraint and objective independence is most obvious.

Dirk Mattfeld applies Evolutionary Algorithms to the Job Shop Scheduling Problem. He analyzes the problem and gives a survey on conventional solution techniques and recent Local Search approaches. He covers Evolutionary Algorithms and their appliance to combinatorial problems. Then, he performs a search space analysis for the Job Shop Problem before he develops a Genetic Algorithm. Finally he refines this algorithm resulting in a parallel genetic search approach.

The benefit of this book is twofold. It gives a comprehensive survey of recent advances for both, production scheduling and Evolutionary Algorithms in the didactic way of a textbook. Moreover, it presents an efficient and robust optimization strategy which can cope with varying constraints and objectives of real world scheduling problems.

Bremen, November 1995   Herbert Kopfer

Acknowledgement. This research is embedded in the PARNET project supported by the Deutsche Forschungsgemeinschaft in their Research Program of Emphasis: **Distributed Systems in Management Science**.

The project was founded by Prof. Dr. S. Stöppler back in 1991 at the former Institute for Business Informatics and Production at the University of Bremen. After the early death of Siegmar Stöppler the research activities were integrated at the Chair of Logistics, governed by Prof. Dr. H. Kopfer.

I thank Siegmar Stöppler for attracting my attention towards production scheduling and my advisor Herbert Kopfer for supporting my work.

Klaus Schebesch at the University of Bremen read the thesis carefully and gave critical response in many fruitful discussions.

Martina Gorges-Schleuter at the Forschungszentrum Karlsruhe refereed an early version of the attitude inheritance model with valuable comments.

Rob Vaessens at the Eindhoven University of Technology provided most of the benchmark material including up to date lower- and upper bounds.

I owe a great debt of gratitude to my close friend and colleague Christian Bierwirth, who continuously guided my (re)search and helped me to escape from local entrapments many, many times.

Bremen, November 1995   Dirk Christian Mattfeld

Table of Contents

1. **Introduction** 1
   1.1 Production Planning 1
   1.2 Production Scheduling 3
   1.3 Heuristic Search 4
   1.4 Overview of the Thesis 5

2. **Job Shop Scheduling** 7
   2.1 Representation of the JSP 7
       2.1.1 Gantt-Chart Representation 8
       2.1.2 Acyclic Graph Representation 11
       2.1.3 The Critical Path 15
   2.2 Schedule Generation Techniques 17
       2.2.1 Temporal Scheduling of Operations 17
       2.2.2 Semi-Active versus Active Scheduling 19
       2.2.3 Schedule Generation Control 21
   2.3 Enumeration Methods 22
       2.3.1 Implicit Enumeration 23
       2.3.2 Partial Enumeration 24

3. **Local Search Techniques** 27
   3.1 Neighborhood Definitions 28
       3.1.1 The First Neighborhood 29
       3.1.2 The Second Neighborhood 32
       3.1.3 Makespan Estimation 34
       3.1.4 The Third Neighborhood 35
   3.2 Local Hill Climbing 37
       3.2.1 Applying a Neighborhood Move 38
       3.2.2 A Hill Climbing Framework 40
       3.2.3 Comparing Search Strategies 42
   3.3 Local Search Extensions 44
       3.3.1 Iterated Search 44
       3.3.2 Simulated Annealing 44
       3.3.3 Tabu Search 45
       3.3.4 Variable Depth Search 47

4. Evolutionary Algorithms 49
   4.1 The Evolutionary Metaphor 49
      4.1.1 Evolutionary Strategies 50
      4.1.2 Genetic Algorithms 51
      4.1.3 Why Does Adaptation Work? 52
   4.2 Adaptation in Epistatic Domains 54
      4.2.1 Crossover Procedures 54
      4.2.2 Fitness Contribution 58
   4.3 Genetic Hybrids 60
      4.3.1 Evolution versus Learning 61
      4.3.2 Hybridization Approaches 62
      4.3.3 Incorporating Local Search 63

5. Perspectives on Adaptive Scheduling 65
   5.1 Configuring the Solution Space 65
      5.1.1 Heuristic Search Space 66
      5.1.2 Problem Search Space 67
      5.1.3 Solution Search Space 68
      5.1.4 Which Representation Fits Best? 74
   5.2 Properties of the Search Space 75
      5.2.1 Fitness Landscape 76
      5.2.2 Distance Metric 78
      5.2.3 Configuration Space Analysis 79
      5.2.4 Population Entropy 82
      5.2.5 Fragile Arcs 86
      5.2.6 Correlation Length 87
   5.3 Summary of Perspectives 89

6. Population Flow in Adaptive Scheduling 91
   6.1 Genetic Algorithm Template 93
   6.2 Inheritance Management 94
      6.2.1 Mutation Operators 94
      6.2.2 Crossover Operators 96
      6.2.3 Crossover- and Mutation Rate 102
   6.3 Population Management 102
      6.3.1 Population Size 103
      6.3.2 Selection Scheme 103
      6.3.3 Termination Criterion 104
      6.3.4 Local Search Hybridization 104
   6.4 Applying Adaptive Scheduling 106

7. Adaptation of Structured Populations 111
   7.1 Finite and Structured Populations 112
       7.1.1 Structured Population GAs 113
       7.1.2 Incorporating the Diffusion Model 115
       7.1.3 Population Flow in the Diffusion Model 116
   7.2 Inheritance of Attitudes 121
       7.2.1 Metaphor of Learned Behavior 121
       7.2.2 Model of Attitude Inheritance..................... 123
       7.2.3 Operation Frequencies 124
       7.2.4 Inbreeding Coefficients 127

8. A Computational Study 131
   8.1 Survey of the GA-Approaches 131
       8.1.1 Overview of Parameters 131
       8.1.2 Comparison of Results 133
   8.2 Benchmark Study 134
       8.2.1 Available Benchmark Suites 134
       8.2.2 Computational Results........................... 136
       8.2.3 Limitations of Adaptive Scheduling 142

9. Conclusions and Outlook 143
   9.1 The Real World is Different............................. 143
   9.2 GAs and Real World Scheduling......................... 145

References 147

1. Introduction

Scheduling allocates resources over time in order to perform a number of tasks. Typically resources are limited and therefore tasks are assigned to resources in a temporal order. From an economic point of view limited resources are scarce goods and consequently the problem of task scheduling is of more than just academic relevance.

Following Van Dyke Parunak (1992) scheduling is circumscribed by asking **what** has to be done **where** and **when**. A task (what) occupies a dedicated resource exclusively (where) for some period of time (when). A group of task primitives may form a complex, in which several tasks have to pass resources in a certain order. In this way the temporal order of resource allocations is restricted by dependencies among the task primitives. Any process that defines a subset of what×where×when can be said to execute scheduling.

1.1 Production Planning

Scheduling in a manufacturing environment allocates machines for processing a number of jobs. This function is embedded in the the domain of production planning and control (PPC), compare e.g. Scheer (1989). The purposes covered by a PPC system are outlined best by considering the information flow in a manufacturing system. Figure 1.1 is taken from Pinedo (1995) and sketches a simplified information flow while neglecting the interfaces to other functions of a manufacturing environment.

Demand forecasts and customer orders are input to the medium- to long-term production planning. A master schedule is built resulting in the demand of end product quantities and their desired due dates. On the basis of quantities and due dates the material required for production is planned according to volume and period. This process results in material requirements of forthcoming production periods which have to be supplied in time.

The material requirements planning is highly interwoven with the capacity planning. Here, temporal assignments of orders to the available processing capacity are shifted such that capacity bottlenecks are avoided and due dates are kept. Up to this stage coarse grained production planning is performed on the basis of customer orders. Now shop orders (jobs) and their release times are introduced as an outcome of the capacity planning.

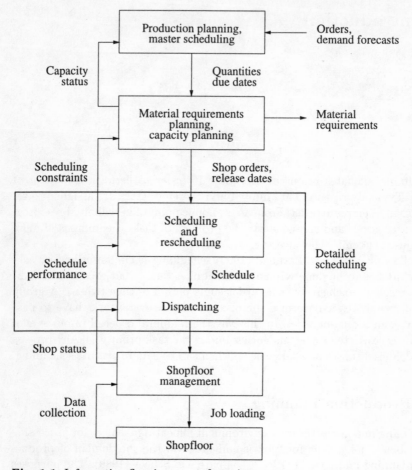

Fig. 1.1. Information flow in a manufacturing system.

The jobs are input to the scheduling engine of the PPC system. Production scheduling performs lot sizing, keeps capacity constraints and finally produces a detailed schedule, i.e. determines the periods of processing some job on its dedicated machines. Thereby scheduling pursues an economically motivated objective. Typically, a reduction of the work in-process inventory is pursued by increasing the throughput of jobs. Moreover, scheduling aims to avoid delivery delays of customer orders and tries to make full use of the available production capacity.

Production planning finishes with dispatching already scheduled jobs to the shop floor management. The organizing of the schedule engine is subject to the following considerations.

1.2 Production Scheduling

In manufacturing systems operations (tasks) are processed by machines (resources) for a certain processing time (time period). Typically, the number of machines available is limited and a machine can process a single operation at a time. Often, the operations cannot be processed in arbitrary orders but obey to a prescribed processing order. Jobs often follow technological constraints which define a certain type of shop floor. In a flow shop all jobs pass the machines in an identical order. In a job shop technological constraints may differ from job to job. In an open shop exists no technological restriction and therefore the operations of jobs may be processed in arbitrary orders.

Apart from technological constraints of the three general types of shop floors, a wide range of additional constraints may be taken into account. Among those, job release times and due dates as well as order dependent machine setup times are the most common ones.

Production scheduling determines starting times of operations without violating technological constraints such that processing times of identical machines do not overlap in time. The resulting time table is called a schedule. Thereby scheduling pursues at least one economic objective. Typical objectives are the reduction of the makespan of an entire production program, the minimization of mean job tardiness, the maximization of machine load or some weighted average of many similar criteria.

When neglecting technological constraints the solution space of a scheduling problem can be approximated by the cardinality of the product of what × where × when. For reasonably sized problems the computational time needed for solving the problem can be from very long up to intractable.

Expert systems offer solutions to the problem of tractability. Knowledge based reasoning makes production scheduling tractable by either a simplification or a decomposition of the overall problem. A comprehensive survey on expert systems for scheduling is given by Kusiak and Chen (1988).

Production scheduling problems can be subject to extremely many and/or complicated constraints so that, in some cases, it is difficult to even find a feasible solution. A simplification of the overall problem is obtained by relaxing conflicting constraints in a way that feasibility of the resulting solutions is still assured. In order to achieve feasibility, the consequences of constraint relaxations are controlled by the inference machine of the expert system. This process requires a detailed knowledge of the production system itself.

In practice, a manufacturing system typically deals with a large number of tasks. The size of the problem is reduced by decomposing it in such a way that the problem still retains its original properties. Typically, a hierarchical decomposition of a multi-level problem is proposed by taking detailed knowledge of the production system into account. Both, simplification by relaxation and hierarchical decomposition, for instance is used in the constraint-directed search approach of Fox (1990).

Manufacturing is typically a "sustained pursuit", hence the character of scheduling is less of static than of dynamic type. Considering release times and due dates of jobs in a dynamic production environment, a temporal decomposition of the overall problem suggests itself. Here, the size of the actual problem may be reduced by neglecting operations whose jobs have not yet been released or whose due dates are non-critical in time. Such a decomposition approach is reported in Raman et al. (1989).

1.3 Heuristic Search

Expert systems are well suited for breaking down the complexity of scheduling problems, but they do not always succeed in generating competitive operational schedules. Even the use of human expert knowledge (e.g. production rules) may lead to poor results in the face of an increasing problem size, compare Glover (1989). Thus, we can expect that a reasonable solution quality can be obtained in polynomial time whereas a better performance requires an iterative search process.

Since uninformed search by enumeration methods seems computational prohibitive for large search spaces, heuristic search receives increasing attention, see Morton and Pentico (1993). Instead of searching the problem space exhaustively, modern heuristic techniques concentrate on guiding the search towards promising regions of the search space, compare Reeves (1993).

A wide range of different heuristic search techniques have been proposed which all have some basic component parts in common. A representation of partial- and complete solutions is required. Next, operators are needed which either extend partial solutions or modify complete solutions. An objective function is needed which either estimates the costs of partial solutions or determines the costs of complete solutions. The most crucial component of heuristic search techniques is the control structure which guides the search. Finally, a condition for terminating the iterative search process is required.

Prominent heuristic search techniques are, among others, Simulated Annealing, Tabu Search and Evolutionary Algorithms. The first two of them have been developed and tested extensively in combinatorial optimization. To the contrary, Evolutionary Algorithms have their origin in continuous optimization. Their theoretical foundation is not well suited for discrete search spaces. Although numerous approaches to combinatorial problems exists, this research still lacks comparability with other heuristic search techniques.

This might be hindered by the biologically inspired language which has been adopted by the evolutionary research community. Nevertheless, the components of Evolutionary Algorithms have their counterparts to other heuristic search techniques. A solution is called an individual which is modified by operators like crossover and mutation. The objective function corresponds to the fitness evaluation. The control structure has its counterpart in the selection scheme of Evolutionary Algorithms.

In Evolutionary Algorithms, the search is loosely guided by a multi-set of solutions called a population, which is maintained in parallel. After a number of iterations (generations) the search is terminated by means of some criterion. A careful evaluation of the suitability of Evolutionary Algorithms for production scheduling is subject of this thesis. Thereby particular attention is paid to the conditions which must be fulfilled so that guiding the search succeeds.

We have chosen the general Job Shop Problem as a representative of the scheduling domain, because it is known to be extremely difficult to solve, it is strongly motivated by practical requirements, and a good deal of previous research has been done and therefore many benchmarks exist, compare e.g. Błażewicz et al. (1995). This enables us to compare Evolutionary Algorithms with other approaches proposed.

Nevertheless, the standard Job Shop Problem is an oversimplification of practical requirements in scheduling. In the real world we often follow several objectives simultaneously even though different objectives may mathematically contradict each other. At least the objective of minimizing the makespan rarely meets the requirements of manufacturing systems.

Unlike other heuristics proposed, Evolutionary Algorithms offer the opportunity to formulate the algorithm almost independently of an objective pursued. This degree of freedom is achieved at the expense of a relatively inefficient search compared to more tailored techniques. Nevertheless, the advantage of objective independence is most obvious.

1.4 Overview of the Thesis

In Chap. 2 we give a formulation of the Job Shop Problem in terms of the graph representation. A subset of the arcs of the problem graph represents a schedule for which we give a procedure for the calculation of the objective value. Next, we turn to schedule generation techniques, which incrementally construct feasible schedules by inserting arcs into the graph. Finally, enumeration techniques for the Job Shop Problem are sketched.

In Chap. 3 we discuss Local Search techniques which may improve the solution quality once a schedule is built. Local Search techniques modify a candidate solution by means of neighborhood moves. First, several neighborhood definitions are introduced. Then, hill climbing techniques for the Job Shop Problem are evaluated. Finally, Local Search extensions are described which tentatively guide the search.

In Chap. 4 we introduce the paradigms of Evolutionary Algorithms and outline their previous applications to combinatorial problems. Here, particular attention is paid to the phenomenon of epistasis and its effects on genetic operators like crossover. This Chapter finishes with a discussion of hybridization, i.e. the incorporation of Local Search into Evolutionary Algorithms.

In Chap. 5 we give an outlook on the perspectives of Evolutionary Search for the Job Shop Problem. First, different ways of representing a schedule for genetic adaptation are discussed. We end up with the definition of a representation for which the notion of the fitness landscape is introduced. Based on this notion several perspectives of genetic adaptation for the Job Shop Problem are evaluated.

In Chap. 6 we propose a hybrid Genetic Algorithm. First, we outline a Genetic Algorithm template. Then we constitute an inheritance management as well as a population management. The various parameters are either evaluated separately or their setting is drawn from arguments of plausibility. Finally, we present computational results of the algorithm.

In Chap. 7 we enhance the Genetic Algorithm by a model of a structured population. This model introduces a limited dispersal between the individuals of a population. The population flow of the resulting algorithm is discussed in detail. Finally a model of inherited attitudes of individuals is proposed and investigated in the following.

In Chap. 8 we compare the approaches considered throughout the thesis. Then we present an extensive computational study on 162 benchmark problems for the most efficient approach. Thereby particular attention is paid on the suitability of Evolutionary search for either very difficult or very large problem instances.

Finally we conclude in Chap. 9 with an outlook on the perspectives of Evolutionary Search for real world production scheduling.

2. Job Shop Scheduling

Within the great variety of production scheduling problems the general job shop problem (JSP) is the probably most studied one by academic research during the last decade. It has earned a reputation for being notoriously difficult to solve. It illustrates at least some of the demands required by a wide array of real world problems.

2.1 Representation of the JSP

Consider a shop floor where jobs are processed by machines. Each job consists of a certain number of operations. Each operation has to be processed on a dedicated machine and for each operation a processing time is defined. The machine order of operations is prescribed for each job by a technological production recipe. These technological constraints are therefore static to a problem instance. Thus, each job has its own machine order and no relation exists between the machine orders (given by the technological constraints) of any of two jobs[1]. The basic JSP is a static optimization problem, since all information about the production program is known in advance. Furthermore, the JSP is purely deterministic, since processing times and constraints are fixed and no stochastic events occur.

The most widely used objective is to find a feasible schedule such that the completion time of the total production program (i.e. the makespan) is minimized. Feasible schedules are obtained by permuting the processing order of operations on the machines (operation sequence) but without violating the technological constraints. Accordingly we face a combinatorial minimization problem with constrained permutations of operations. More specifically, the operations to be processed on one machine form an operation sequence for this machine. A schedule for a problem instance consists of operation sequences for each machine involved. Since each operation sequence can be permuted independently of the operation sequences of other machines, we have a maximum of $(n!)^m$ different solutions to a problem instance, where n

---

[1] The case of identical machine order for all jobs involved defines the class of flow shop problems (FSP) as a subset of the JSP. The FSP is referred to as line processing in production scheduling.

denotes the number of jobs and m denotes the number of machines involved. According to Garey and Johnson (1979) the JSP is an *NP*-hard problem and among those optimization problems it is one of the least tractable known. The complete restrictions of the basic JSP are listed informally below, compare e.g. French (1982).

1. No two operations of one job may be processed simultaneously.
2. No preemption (i.e. process interruption) of operations is allowed.
3. No job is processed twice on the same machine.
4. Each job must be processed to completion.
5. Jobs may be started at any time, no release times exist.
6. Jobs may be finished at any time, no due dates exist.
7. Jobs must wait for the next machine to be available.
8. No machine may process more than one operation at a time.
9. Machine setup times are negligible.
10. There is only one of each type of machine.
11. Machines may be idle within the schedule period.
12. Machines are available at any time.
13. The technological constraints are known in advance and are immutable.

The set of constraints involved in real world applications is much more complex. In practice, only a few assumptions of the basic JSP may hold. In spite of the restrictive assumptions stated above, the JSP is already a notoriously hard scheduling problem. The JSP is popular in academic research as a test-bed for different solution techniques to combinatorial problems. Furthermore, benefit from previous research can only be obtained if a widely accepted standard model exists.

Typical extensions of the basic JSP are the consideration of parallel machines, multi purpose machines, machine breakdowns and time windows introduced by release times and due dates of jobs. Dynamic scheduling is considered when jobs are released stochastically throughout the production process. Finally, in non-deterministic scheduling processing times and/or processing constraints are evolving during the production process (e.g. order dependent setup times).

2.1.1 Gantt-Chart Representation

In the following a closer look at the basic JSP is given which leads to the Gantt-Chart representation. A problem instance consists of n jobs and m machines, where J_j denotes the j-th job ($1 \leq j \leq n$) and M_i denotes the i-th machine ($1 \leq i \leq m$). The machine order (technological constraints) for job J_j is given by $\varphi_j = (M_{\varphi_{jh}})_{(1 \leq h \leq m)}$, where h denotes the h-th operation of J_j. The processing time of an operation of job J_j to be performed on machine M_i is given by p_{ji}. The technological constraints φ as well as processing times p are given problem data.

The processing order (machine sequences) for machine M_i is given by $\vartheta_i = (J_{\vartheta_{ik}})_{(1 \leq k \leq n)}$, where k denotes the k-th operation to be processed on M_i. A solution to the JSP can be formulated as a matrix ϑ. The problem data of a JSP instance and one possible solution are given in Tab. 2.1 for a JSP consisting of 3 jobs and 3 machines. Recall, that φ contains machine numbers, p contains processing times and ϑ contains job numbers.

Table 2.1. Matrix representation of a JSP. The two matrices on the left side represent given problem data, the right hand side matrix represents one solution of the problem.

$$\varphi_{jh} = \begin{bmatrix} 1 & 2 & 3 \\ 2 & 3 & 1 \\ 2 & 1 & 3 \end{bmatrix} \quad p_{ji} = \begin{bmatrix} 3 & 3 & 2 \\ 3 & 2 & 3 \\ 3 & 4 & 1 \end{bmatrix} \quad \vartheta_{ik} = \begin{bmatrix} 1 & 2 & 3 \\ 2 & 3 & 1 \\ 2 & 1 & 3 \end{bmatrix}$$

The processing unit of a job on a machine[2] is denoted as operation o_{jh}. Every operation o has at most two direct predecessor operations, a job predecessor PJ_o and a machine predecessor PM_o. Note that the first operation of a machine sequence has no PM_o whereas the first operation of a job has no PJ_o. Analogous every operation has at most two direct successor operations, a job successor SJ_o and a machine successor SM_o. The last operation of a machine sequence has no SM_o and the last operation of a job has no SJ_o. An operation is called schedulable if both, PJ_o and PM_o (as far as they are defined) are already scheduled.

The objective is to find a processing order ϑ such that the total makespan is minimized. A schedule is built successively by assigning starting times $r_{o_{jh}}$ to schedulable operations. The starting time of an operation is determined by the maximum completion time $C_{o_{jh}}$ of both of its predecessors.

$$C_{o_{jh}} = r_{o_{jh}} + p_{j,\varphi_{jh}}, \quad r_{o_{jh}} \geq \max(C_{PJ_{o_{jh}}}, C_{PM_{o_{jh}}}). \tag{2.1}$$

The completion time of o_{jh} is calculated by (2.1) with $r_{o_{jh}} = 0$ for undefined $PJ_{o_{jh}}$ and $PM_{o_{jh}}$. After all operations are scheduled, the makespan is given by the maximum of all completion times $C_{\max}$.

An intuitive way of representing a JSP schedule is the Gantt-Chart. An example is given in Fig. 2.1 for the matrices of Tab. 2.1. The Gantt-Chart shows time units at the abscissa and machine numbers at the axis of ordinate.

– Each ordinate row i consists of the operations to be processed on M_i in the order given by ϑ_i. E.g. the machine sequence of machine M_1 determines J_1 to be processed first, followed by J_2 and J_3.

---

[2] Problem instances, where each job is to be processed on each machine are called rectangular because the number of operations is determined by $n \cdot m$. As a special case we consider quadratic problem instances with $n = m$. Although our JSP model does not restrict to rectangular problems, all benchmarks considered throughout this thesis are of rectangular type.

- The operations are depicted in the length of their processing time. As an example we consider the third operation to be processed on machine M_1. Its job number J_3 is obtained from ϑ_{13} and then its processing time 3 is obtained from p_{31}.
- We determine the position of operations in the technological order of their job. E.g. the third operation to be processed on M_1 is J_3, compare ϑ_{13}. Now we scan φ_3 for M_1 and find φ_{32} with $h = 2$. Thus, the operation considered is o_{32} which is to be processed as the second operation of J_3.
- We rearrange the operations in the Gantt-Chart in such a way that an operation with a lower index h of some job precedes an operation with a higher index h. E.g. o_{23} is to be processed as the third operation of J_2, compare φ_{23}. Hence, operation o_{22} has to precede o_{23} in order to avoid a simultaneous processing of operations of one job.
- Starting times and completion times of operations can now be taken directly from the abscissa. Job and machine predecessor dependencies are outlined explicitly by machine idle times (in gray shade). The completion time of the rightmost operation in the Gantt-Chart gives the makespan achieved. In the example $C_{o_{33}}$ defines the $C_{\max}$ value.

The operation o_{11} in Fig. 2.1 could be started at time unit 2 without influencing the starting time of any other operation. Considering operation starting times after the earliest possible starting times is known as passive scheduling. Throughout this thesis we define the earliest possible starting times as the actual starting times of operations. Scheduling all operations at their earliest starting time is known as semi-active scheduling, i.e. a schedule cannot be improved in terms of makespan without changing operation sequences of machines.

A schedule is called active, if makespan improvement cannot be gained even by changing any of the processing orders ϑ_i. In terms of the Gantt-chart representation shown in Fig. 2.1 one can say that any permissible left shift of an operation cannot improve the makespan. A non-delay schedule is given, if no machine is kept idle when it could start processing some operation. We can state that the class of passive schedules includes semi-active schedules whereas the class of semi-active schedules includes active ones. Furthermore the class of active schedules includes non-delay schedules. Concerning a minimal makespan, at least one optimal schedule is an active schedule but not

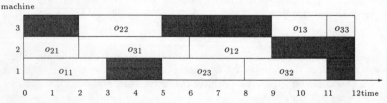

Fig. 2.1. Example of a Gantt-Chart representation of a 3×3 job shop problem.

necessarily a non-delay schedule. The solution considered in Fig. 2.1 is semi-active as well as active. Actually, it is an optimal one.

If the starting time of an operation cannot be delayed without causing a deterioration of the makespan, it is called a critical operation. In the example all operations apart from o_{11} are critical, since their starting time cannot be delayed without worsening the makespan given by $C_{o_{33}}$. A critical operation cannot start delayed, since it has no buffer time available. At least one operation, the job- or the machine successor starts immediately after a critical one. Thus, the completion time of a critical operation is equal to the starting time of at least one of its successor operations, e.g. $C_{o_{22}} = r_{o_{23}}$ in Fig. 2.1.

The buffer time is given by the minimum time span between the completion time of an operation and the starting time of its job- and machine successor. For instance consider o_{23} and o_{12} which are direct successors of operation o_{11}. Here the buffer time is calculated $\min(5, 6) - 3 = 2$. The earliest starting time of an operation is sometimes referred to as head. A head of an operation determines the amount of time needed before the operation can be started. Analogous, a tail $q_{o_{jh}}$ gives the time needed for the rest of the production program after the completion of the operation considered. For all critical operations head, processing time and tail adds up to $C_{\max}$.

$$C_{\max} = r_{o_{jh}} + p_{j,\varphi_{jh}} + q_{o_{jh}}, \quad \text{if } o_{jh} \text{ is critical.} \tag{2.2}$$

Informally one can say that a tail indicates the amount of time needed to complete the production program from the viewpoint of an operation. For non-critical operations the tail gives a lower bound regarding the makespan.

2.1.2 Acyclic Graph Representation

Thus far an introduction to the JSP has been given by a simple example based on the Gantt-Chart representation. In the following we give a problem formulation based on a graph representation due to Roy and Sussman from 1964. This representation is described in Adams et al. (1988). The graph representation of the JSP is used throughout this thesis.

Let $\mathcal{V}$ be the set of operations. Since operations are considered as members of the set $\mathcal{V}$ from now on, we can drop the operation indices introduced in the beginning of this chapter. Additionally to the operations $\mathcal{V}$ contains two dummy operations b and e with processing times $p_b = p_e = 0$ denoting the "begin" and "end" of the entire production program.

In order to express the precedence of operations regarding jobs and machines, the sets $\mathcal{A}$ and $\mathcal{E}$ are introduced.

– Set $\mathcal{A}$ denotes the technological constraints as pairs of successive operations $v, w \in \mathcal{V}$, such that $v = PJ_w \wedge w = SJ_v$.
– The set $\mathcal{E}$ consists of m subsets $\mathcal{E}_i$ denoting pairs of operations to be processed on M_i, such that $v = PM_w \wedge w = SM_v$.

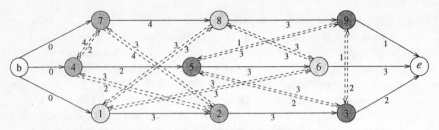

Fig. 2.2. Graph representation for a simple problem instance.

Problem Representation. In the following a problem is represented as a disjunctive graph $\mathcal{G} = (\mathcal{V}, \mathcal{A} \cup \mathcal{E})$ with the node set $\mathcal{V}$, the conjunctive arc set $\mathcal{A}$ and the disjunctive arc set $\mathcal{E}$. The set $\mathcal{E}$ is decomposed into subsets $\mathcal{E}_i$ with $\mathcal{E} = \bigcup_{i=1}^{m} \mathcal{E}_i$, such that there is one $\mathcal{E}_i$ for each machine M_i. The terms 'node' and 'operation' and the terms 'arc' and 'constraint' are used synonymously depending on the context from now on.

The arcs in $\mathcal{A}$ and $\mathcal{E}$ are weighted with the processing time of the operation representing the source node v of the arc (v, w). Hence, arcs starting at operation v are identically weighted. Within $\mathcal{A}$ the dummy operation b is connected to the first operation of each job. These arcs are weighted with zero. The last operation of each job is incident to e and consequently weighted with the processing times of the last operation in each case.

The graph representation of a JSP instance is shown in Fig. 2.2. The different gray shadings denote the various machines on which the operations are to be processed. In the following $\mathcal{G}$ is described in detail by referencing the matrices φ and p of Tab. 2.1.

- Node b on the left side of the figure is the source of $\mathcal{G}$ and represents the start of the entire production program. The sink e is placed on the right side of the figure. The node e denotes the end of the production program. Both, b and e have a zero processing time.
- The solid arcs of set $\mathcal{A}$ represent technological constraints between operations of a single job. E.g. the operations 1, 2 and 3 belong to job J_1 and have to be processed in the technological order given by the solid arcs $(1, 2)$ and $(2, 3)$. Furthermore, the arcs $(b, 1)$ and $(3, e)$ connect the first and last operation of J_1 with the dummy operations denoting the begin and end of the entire production program.
- The dashed arcs of set $\mathcal{E}$ represent machine constraints which are obtained from matrix φ. E.g. operation 2 is the second operation of J_1 and operations 4 and 7 are the first operations of J_2 and J_3. These three operations have to be processed on M_2 as given by φ_{12}, φ_{21} and φ_{31}. In this example subset $\mathcal{E}_2$ consists of all dashed arcs which fully connect operations 2, 4 and 7. Theoretically, each of the three operations can precede all other operations of M_2, such that arbitrary machine sequences ϑ_2 can be obtained for M_2.

– The arc weights stand for the processing times obtained from matrix p. They are used as costs of a connection between two incident operations. E.g. operation 7 is the first operation of J_3. According to φ_{31} its related machine is M_2. The matrix element p_{32} contains its processing time 4. Thus, arcs which have operation 7 as their source node are weighted with a processing time of 4 units.

Schedule Representation. All pairs of operations given by arcs in $\mathcal{A}$ and $\mathcal{E}$ cannot overlap in time. By taking up the processing times p_v and p_w and the starting times r_v and r_w of pairs of incident operations v and w, we can formulate the problem as a linear programming model.

$$\min r_e$$
$$
\begin{aligned}
r_w - r_v &\geq p_v, & (v,w) &\in \mathcal{A} \\
r_v &\geq 0, & v &\in \mathcal{V} \\
r_w - r_v \geq p_v \quad \vee \quad r_v - r_w \geq p_w, & & (v,w) &\in \mathcal{E}_i, i \in M.
\end{aligned}
\tag{2.3}
$$

The goal is to find a feasible schedule for which r_e is minimized. Since e denotes the end of the entire production program and a zero processing time is assigned to e, r_e is equivalent to C_e and C_e is equivalent to $C_{\max}$. The first inequality ensures the prescribed order (technological constraints) of operations within each job. The second condition restricts the earliest starting times of operations to non-negative numbers. The final constraints avoid the simultaneous processing of operations on one machine (machine sequences). Each solution obeying to the inequalities given in (2.3) is a feasible schedule.

In order to identify a feasible schedule we transform each $\mathcal{E}_i$ into a machine selection $\mathcal{S}_i$. Therefore we consider the inequalities in the last line of (2.3). For each pair of disjunctive arcs (v,w) and (w,v) in $\mathcal{E}_i$ we discard the one for which either $r_w - r_v \geq p_v$ or $r_v - r_w \geq p_w$ does not hold. This results in $\mathcal{S}_i \subset \mathcal{E}_i$, such that $\mathcal{S}_i$ contains no cycle and a Hamiltonian path exists among the operations to be processed on M_i. A selection $\mathcal{S}_i$ corresponds to a valid processing sequence of machine M_i. Hence, obtaining $\mathcal{S}_i$ from $\mathcal{E}_i$ can be seen in equivalence to sequencing machine M_i.

A complete selection $\mathcal{S} = \bigcup_{i=1}^{m} \mathcal{S}_i$ represents a schedule (i.e. a solution to a problem instance) in the digraph $\mathcal{D}_\mathcal{S} = (\mathcal{V}, \mathcal{A} \cup \mathcal{S})$. The acyclic selections $\mathcal{S}_i \in \mathcal{S}$ have to be chosen in a way that the first inequality of (2.3) holds. In

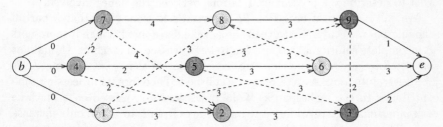

Fig. 2.3. Graph representation for one selection $\mathcal{S}$ carried out.

this case $\mathcal{D}_S$ remains acyclic and therefore corresponds to a feasible solution. Figure 2.3 gives an example of $\mathcal{D}_S$ for the solution formerly presented as a Gantt-Chart in Fig. 2.1.

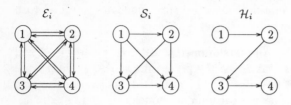

Fig. 2.4. A machine selection and the appropriate Hamiltonian selection carried out for a machine sequence of 4 operations.

For computational purpose we consider in each machine selection just arcs which establish the Hamiltonian path $\mathcal{H}_i \subseteq \mathcal{S}_i$. An example of a Hamiltonian selection $\mathcal{H}_i$ for machine M_i with four operations is shown in Fig. 2.4. The arcs in $\mathcal{S}_i$ are chosen from $\mathcal{E}_i$ such that $\mathcal{S}_i$ is acyclic and all nodes can be visited following a single path $\mathcal{H}_i = \{(1,2),(2,3),(3,4)\}$.

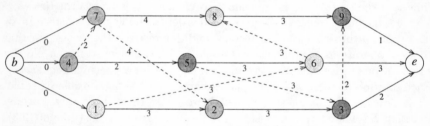

Fig. 2.5. Graph representation for one Hamiltonian selection $\mathcal{H}$ carried out.

A complete Hamiltonian selection $\mathcal{H} \subseteq \mathcal{S}$ is shown in Fig. 2.5. It has the same properties as $\mathcal{S}$ with respect to the precedence relation of operations. Thus, for our purpose $\mathcal{D}_S = (\mathcal{V}, \mathcal{A} \cup \mathcal{S})$ and $\mathcal{D}_H = (\mathcal{V}, \mathcal{A} \cup \mathcal{H})$ are equivalent. Both sets, $\mathcal{S}$ and $\mathcal{H}$ determine the complete set of machine constraints and therefore represent the same schedule of a problem instance. Opposite to $\mathcal{S}$ which requires $m \cdot \frac{n(n-1)}{2}$ arcs, $\mathcal{H}$ is defined by $m(n-1)$ arcs only. For instance, the 4 nodes of Fig. 2.4 require 6 arcs for $\mathcal{S}_i$ and 3 arcs for $\mathcal{H}_i$ in order to describe the precedence relations between the nodes involved.

We call a union of arcs $\mathcal{P} \subset \mathcal{H}$ a partial selection. Note that a partial schedule $\mathcal{D}_P = (\mathcal{V}, \mathcal{A} \cup \mathcal{P})$ is already an acyclic digraph, although it represents an incomplete solution. An operation to be processed on machine M_i and not connected by any arc from the set $\mathcal{E}_i$ can be viewed as not yet sequenced. Its job constraints from $\mathcal{A}$ are already established. Therefore its processing time contributes to the makespan as if the operation is processed on a machine with infinite capacity. Adding any further arcs from $\mathcal{E}$ to $\mathcal{P}$ can only increase $C_{\max}$. Therefore $C_{\max}$ of $\mathcal{D}_P$ can serve as a lower bound of the makespan.

2.1.3 The Critical Path

The makespan of a schedule is equal to the length of a longest path in $\mathcal{D}_H$. Thus solving a JSP is equivalent to finding a complete Hamiltonian selection $\mathcal{H}$ that minimizes the length of the longest path in the directed graph $\mathcal{D}_H$.

An advantage of the graph representation is the opportunity to use well-known graph algorithms. Graph representations similar to the one introduced by Adams et al. (1988) are used in Project-Management since the sixties. We use a longest path method adopted from a standard algorithm described in Christofides (1975) in order to calculate the makespan.

1. In the first step a node array $\mathcal{T}$ of length $l = |\mathcal{V}|$ is filled with the topological sorted $v \in \mathcal{V}$ with respect to the arcs in $\mathcal{A} \cup \mathcal{H}$ defining a complete schedule. For any arc (v, w) node v is sorted prior to w. This can be achieved by the labeling algorithm proposed by Kahn (1962).

2. In the next step we determine the heads of all nodes in $\mathcal{T}$ defining the starting times r_v. In the beginning all r_v are set to zero.

$$r_{T_1} = \max(r_{PJ_{T_1}} + p_{PJ_{T_1}}, r_{PM_{T_1}} + p_{PM_{T_1}})$$
$$\vdots \qquad\qquad\qquad\qquad\qquad\qquad (2.4)$$
$$r_{T_l} = \max(r_{PJ_{T_l}} + p_{PJ_{T_l}}, r_{PM_{T_l}} + p_{PM_{T_l}})$$

The makespan is given by $C_{\max} = r_e$. The node e is the last element of $\mathcal{T}$ because e denotes the sink of the graph $\mathcal{D}_H$.

3. Optionally, we may calculate the tails $q_v, v \in \mathcal{V}$, which are given by the longest path from v to e. All tails q_v are initialized to zero.

$$q_{T_l} = \max(q_{SJ_{T_l}} + p_{T_l}, q_{SM_{T_l}} + p_{T_l})$$
$$\vdots \qquad\qquad\qquad\qquad\qquad\qquad (2.5)$$
$$q_{T_1} = \max(q_{SJ_{T_1}} + p_{T_1}, q_{SM_{T_1}} + p_{T_1})$$

Node v is critical if $r_v + p_v + q_v = r_e$ holds, otherwise $r_v + p_v + q_v$ gives a lower bound for makespan with respect to v.

4. If we are interested in one longest path itself, we trace backwards from the sink of the graph towards the source following critical operations. Any arc (v, w) is critical for which $r_v + p_v = r_w$ holds. Actually there may exist more than one critical path in $\mathcal{D}_H$, although we concentrate on an arbitrary one in the following.

Step 1–4 evaluates the objective function f for a schedule $\mathcal{D}_H$. Since $\mathcal{D} = (\mathcal{V}, \mathcal{A}$ is fixed and $\mathcal{D}_H = (\mathcal{V}, \mathcal{A} \cup \mathcal{H})$ is determined by the complete Hamiltonian selection $\mathcal{H}$ only, we use the shorthand $f(\mathcal{H})$ in the following. The result of f is referred to as makespan or as $C_{\max}$ in the following.

An example for the calculation of the heads r, the tails q and the critical path itself is given in Fig. 2.6. This figure shows a feasible solution in the acyclic graph representation. The three machines involved are given in different gray shades of the nodes.

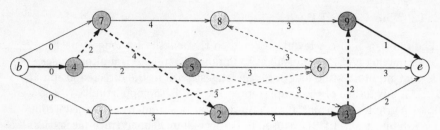

Fig. 2.6. One critical path shown for the acyclic JSP graph.

First $\mathcal{T}$ is obtained by sorting the nodes $v, w \in \mathcal{V}$ such that for any arc (v, w) node v is sorted prior to w. Table 2.2 shows the topological sorted nodes of $\mathcal{T}$ in the first line. The corresponding processing times p are given in the second line. Now, the heads r are calculated. Finally the tails q are calculated and now critical nodes can be determined by testing $r_v + p_v + q_v = r_e$. In the example, only operation 1 is non-critical. For all other operations r_v, p_v, q_v add up to $r_e = 12$. One resulting critical path is shown in Fig. 2.6 with bold face arcs.

$\mathcal{T}$	b	1	4	7	2	5	3	6	8	9	e
p_v	0	3	2	4	3	3	2	3	3	1	0
r_v	0	0	0	2	6	2	9	5	8	11	12
q_v	12	7	10	6	3	7	1	4	1	0	0

Table 2.2. Processing times, heads, and tails.

Figure 2.7 shows the corresponding job-oriented Gantt-Chart. Again, the gray scale of operations refers to the machines like shown in Fig. 2.6. Different to the machine-oriented Gantt-Chart of Fig. 2.1 where the axis of ordinate depict machines, here jobs of the problem instance are depicted by the axis of ordinate. In this way successive operations along the abscissa correspond to a path of solid arcs in Fig. 2.6 denoting a job.

The length of the blocks correspond to the processing time of the operations. Consequently, the white blocks give the waiting times of jobs in the production process. Here, the longest path is given by bold face operations.

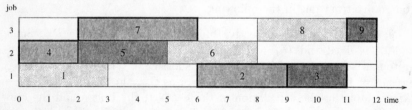

Fig. 2.7. Job oriented Gantt-Chart representation of the 3×3 JSP example.

2.2 Schedule Generation Techniques

Since the JSP is known to be *NP*-hard, in general suboptimal solutions built by heuristics[3] receive increasing attention beside optimal ones built by enumeration algorithms. Only smaller problem sizes in terms of machines and jobs can be solved in polynomial time by construction algorithms as reported by Błażewicz et al. (1993):

– JSP of two jobs.
– JSP of two machines where all operations have identical processing time.
– JSP of two machines where jobs do not have more than two operations.

In other cases the JSP remains *NP*-hard. In the first place an algorithm for building semi-active schedules is presented. Next, an enhanced version of this algorithm is described which always produces active schedules. Third, we discuss the incorporation of priority relations among operations into the presented algorithms. Then we turn to enumeration algorithms and sketch the ideas of Branch and Bound. Finally the Shifting Bottleneck heuristic is described.

2.2.1 Temporal Scheduling of Operations

A simple framework for building $\mathcal{D}_H$ from the scratch, i.e. from $\mathcal{D}$ as shown in Fig. 2.8, is presented. This framework schedules operations in a temporal order independently of their assigned machine.

Generally, we start with $\mathcal{D}$, as shown in Fig. 2.8. At a first stage, we can schedule one operation from $\{1, 4, 7\}$. At further stages, an operation v is called schedulable if its predecessors PM_v and PJ_v are already scheduled. The number of stages t in the scheduling process is determined by the number of operations of the problem instance.

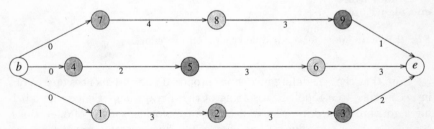

Fig. 2.8. Graph representation of technological constraints.

---

[3] A reasonable definition is given in Reeves (1993): A heuristic is a technique which seeks good (i.e. near-optimal) solutions at a reasonable computational cost without being able to guarantee either feasibility or optimality, or even in many cases to state how close to optimality a particular feasible solution is.

Let us define the set $R \subset \mathcal{V}$ of all schedulable operations at stage t of the scheduling process. Initially, R contains the first operation of each job, i.e. the successors of the 'start' operation b. We may reduce R by means of a reduction operator Ψ capable of discarding non promising candidates from R. We obtain the set $S{\subseteq}R$, such that $S = \Psi(R)$. In order to determine an operation v to be scheduled next we declare a choice operator Φ, choosing $v = \Phi(S)$. Summing up, we determine the candidate operation v by first reducing R into S and second choosing a node v from S. Thus we may write $v = \Phi(\Psi(R))$. Once a candidate v is chosen, we delete v from R. After v is scheduled, we update R by adding v's job successor SJ_v to R so far it exists.

Furthermore we define a set $K \subset \mathcal{V}$ consisting of the last operations scheduled on each machine. Initially K is empty, because no operations have been scheduled so far. Scheduling an operation v at stage t means to add the operation v to the Hamiltonian selection $\mathcal{H}_i$. This is done by constructing the machine constrained arc (w, v) such that $w \in K$ (w has been scheduled last on its machine) and $(w, v) \in \mathcal{E}_i$ (w and v are to be processed on the same machine M_i). If the first operation is scheduled on machine M_i, no arc is constructed. Each time an operation has been scheduled, w is replaced by v in K. The algorithm described is presented in Fig. 2.9.

algorithm schedule **is**
$\qquad R :=$ successors of b
$\qquad K := \emptyset$
$\qquad$ **while** $R \neq \emptyset$ **do**
$\qquad\qquad S := \Psi(R)$
$\qquad\qquad v := \Phi(S)$
$\qquad\qquad R := R\backslash\{v\}$
$\qquad\qquad w := k \in K, (k, v) \in \mathcal{E}$
$\qquad\qquad K := K\backslash\{w\}$
$\qquad\qquad$ **if** w exists **then** construct arc (w, v)
$\qquad\qquad$ **if** SJ_v exists **then** $R := R \cup \{SJ_v\}$
$\qquad\qquad K := K \cup \{v\}$
$\qquad$ **end while**
end algorithm

Fig. 2.9. Framework for a schedule generation procedure.

Note that the scheduling procedure proposed above sequences operations in accordance to a topological sorting of the digraph $\mathcal{D}_H$. Hence, the labeling algorithm needed in order to achieve a topological sorting of operations, compare p. 15, is superfluous. Therefore scheduling in a temporal order accelerates the evaluation of $C_{\max}$ considerably. The operators Ψ and Φ determine a control strategy of the scheduling algorithm. The operators Ψ and Φ are modeled throughout the remainder of this chapter. In particular, we show that introducing problem specific knowledge into Ψ and Φ can be used to formulate simple scheduling heuristics.

At any stage t an operation can be chosen from R or S respectively, such that the makespan of the partial selection built so far is least worsened. These procedures are called insertion heuristics. Once scheduled, an operation remains fixed up to the end of the insertion procedure. Generally, these algorithms perform excellent in early stages but suffer from a shrinking set of choices in later stages. For this reason, a bi-directional insertion procedure is proposed by Dell' Amico and Trubian (1993). The procedure schedules operations alternately from the source and the sink of $\mathcal{D}$ in order to avoid poor decisions for the last operations near the sink of the graph, i.e. the ending operations of jobs.

2.2.2 Semi-Active versus Active Scheduling

In the following we focus on semi-active scheduling and then continue with a closer look on active scheduling. Thereby we describe the algorithm due to Giffler and Thompson (1960). Semi-active as well as active scheduling can be described in terms of the (Ψ, Φ) framework shown in Fig. 2.9. We have already seen that the set of active schedules constitutes a subset of semi-active schedules. Since we know, that at least one of the optimal schedules is active, we may concentrate on generating active schedules only, compare French (1982). Anyway, the number of different active schedules of a moderate sized problem instance is already tremendous.

Semi-Active Scheduling. Semi-active schedules are generated by scheduling operations at their earliest starting times. Since we may schedule one operation of every job at any stage, it is not necessary to reduce the set R by the operator Ψ. In this first approach Ψ simply copies R into S. Since we do not incorporate preferences of choosing operations schedulable from R, the Φ operator randomly chooses an operation from S. Although the algorithm generates semi-active schedules, there is no reason to believe that it generates near-optimal solutions in terms of the makespan.

Active Scheduling. Again we use the (Ψ, Φ) framework from Fig. 2.9. The Giffler and Thompson algorithm (G&T) performs similar to the one described for semi-active scheduling, apart from that it generates active schedules. This feature can be achieved by using an operator Ψ in a way that scheduling is rather based on R than on the reduced set S. Scheduling one operation by the G&T algorithm is done in three steps.

1. The shortest completion time C^* of operations in R is calculated by $C^* = \min_{v \in R}(C_v)$. The operation $v \in R$ with completion time C^* determines a machine M^*. In case of a tie, M^* is chosen arbitrarily.
2. The set $S \subseteq R$ is derived such that the operations $v \in S$ require machine $M^*, (M_v = M^*)$ and have an earliest starting time $r_v < C^*$. Since the operations in S overlap in time, S is called the conflict set.
3. Now, one operation among the conflicting ones in S is chosen means of the Φ operator.

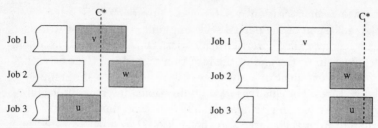

Fig. 2.10. Example of the Giffler and Thompson algorithm.

C^* gives the earliest possible completion time of the next operation to be added to the partial selection $\mathcal{D}_P$. The operations u, v, w in Fig. 2.10 are assumed to be processed on M^*. Operations ready to be scheduled appear gray. On the left hand side of the figure C^* is determined by operation u. The set S consists of the conflicting operations u, v only, because $r_w > C^*$. Note that $S \neq \emptyset$, since at least the operation for which C^* was calculated is a member of S. Assume operator Φ chooses operation v. The right hand side of the figure gives a situation we may meet at the next stage, if M^* remains the same machine. The operations u and w are still schedulable and C^* is determined by operation w this time.

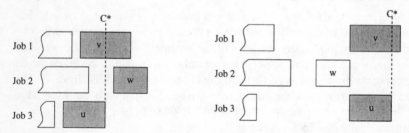

Fig. 2.11. Counterexample to the Giffler and Thompson algorithm. A semi-active schedule is obtained by scheduling a non-conflicting operation.

By examining a different Ψ operator we see that the G&T algorithm always produces active schedules. If Ψ still works on operations of M^* exclusively, but chooses operation w with $r_w \geq C^*$ this time, the starting time of operation u is delayed. This situation is sketched in Fig. 2.11, ending up with the situation shown on the right hand side. The schedule is semi-active because a left shift of u prior to w is permissible without delaying w, compare Sect. 2.1. Active schedules are typically better in terms of makespan than semi-active ones. Keeping in mind, that at least one optimal schedule is active, we may restrict the search to active schedules. So far, we did not care about which operation to choose from the conflict set S. This choice is subject of the following considerations.

2.2.3 Schedule Generation Control

We have considered the Ψ operator in combination with a Φ operator making random choices from the set S. Thereby we have neglected any preferences among the schedulable operations. In fact, there may be even strong preferences concerning either a prescribed scheduling order of operations or a guess about the "right" choice. To examine the first case we focus on explicit permutations of operations. The second case leads us to priority rules of choosing operations.

Scheduling Explicit Permutations. A permutation is given explicitly by an order of operations to be scheduled from left to right. Recall that scheduling an operation of which the predecessors are not already scheduled leads to an infeasible solution. Therefore we represent an operation v by its job identifier. The job identifier $j, (1 \leq j \leq n)$ occurs in a given permutation[4] as often as there are operations belonging to job j. The k'th occurrence of a job identifier refers to the k'th operation of this job. Since the permutation consists of all operations its length is $n \cdot m - 2$ because the operations b and e are not part of the permutation.

The solution of the JSP with $n = 3, m = 3$ shown in Fig. 2.1 can be represented by $(1, 2, 2, 3, 1, 3, 2, 3, 1)$. Reading it from left to right the first entry is a 1 and refers to the first operation of job 1. The next entry is a 2 and refers to the first operation of job 2. The third entry of the permutation is 2 again. This time it refers to the second operation of job 2. Then, 3 refers to the first operation of job 3 etc.

This permutation with repetition is introduced by Bierwirth (1995) in analogy to the natural permutation scheme of the traveling salesman problem (TSP) commonly used to represent this problem. The representation covers all feasible solutions of a JSP instance but no infeasible ones. Since we do not distinguish between different operations of a job (indeed, the scheduling procedure itself cannot), the number of different permutations is somewhat smaller than $(n!)^m$, see Sect. 2.1. Almost independently from the Ψ operator a more sophisticated Φ operator can schedule an explicit permutation. The Φ operator may be modeled as follows. Whenever a set of schedulable operations S is built, the operation v occuring first is picked while scanning the permutation from left to right. After choosing an operation, the related job identifier is deleted.

For the set up of a semi-active schedule always the first identifier in the permutation is chosen since at any stage of the scheduling process exactly one operation of every job may be scheduled. Hence we obtain a direct mapping of the permutation to the schedule built. For active scheduling the situation is slightly more difficult. We would find an appropriate operation for the

---

[4] In this context a permutation is extended to the term of a permutation with repetitions.

first identifier among the operations in R. But since we look for an appropriate operation in the conflict set S, we may have to skip some elements in the permutation before we find a suitable job identifier. Since a number of permutations (representing semi-active schedules) lead to the same active schedule, the mapping to active schedules is less direct. Anyway, we are not able to find a representation which is restricted to active schedules only, since we do not know the active schedules in advance.

Scheduling by Priority Rules. Again, we face a conflict among the schedulable operations in S. Only one operation can be chosen at a time and this operation may delay other operations not yet scheduled. The dilemma is obvious and well-known in other contexts too. We have to make a decision, but this decision has an unknown future outcome. Most simple remedies are rules of thumb known as priority rules in the context of scheduling. More than 100 of such rules have been developed, we name just a few very popular ones, listed in French (1982).

SPT   Shortest processing time. Select an operation with a shortest processing time among the operations in S.

FCFS   First come, first serve. Select an operation which has been in S for the largest number of stages.

MWKR   Most work remaining. Select an operation that belongs to the job with the most processing time remaining among the not yet scheduled operations.

LWKR   Least work remaining. Select an operation that belongs to the job with the least processing time remaining.

The reasons for applying these rules follow from arguments of plausibility. As we see for e.g. MWKR and LWKR, rules may contradict each other. Within the last decades a lot of research concerning priority rules has been done, see Haupt (1989) for a survey. Priority rule based scheduling is computationally fast, but the makespan improvement is generally still limited. Nevertheless priority rules are important and sometimes the only available procedures to fit the real time conditions of online scheduling.

2.3 Enumeration Methods

Let us consider an explicit enumeration of the search space. Starting from a digraph $\mathcal{D}$ with no operations scheduled and setting the search depth to the number of operations, we generate a complete enumeration tree. The leafs of the tree represent all feasible solutions. The path from the root to a leaf of minimal makespan represents an optimal solution. The remaining difficulty is the size of the search tree generated. Since we have a maximum of $(n!)^m$ solutions to consider, even moderately sized problems will keep any computer busy for a time period in excess of centuries. As a remedy implicit as well as partial enumeration methods have been proposed.

2.3.1 Implicit Enumeration

Branch and Bound (B&B) algorithms cut branches from the enumeration tree and therefore reduce the number of generated nodes substantially. B&B algorithms rely on a lower bound LB and an upper bound UB of the objective function value. The best solution generated so far determines the actual UB. An LB is calculated for each node of the enumeration tree starting from the root. A common way of generating nodes is the depth first search. The deeper a node is placed in the tree, the more constraints are taken into account in the resulting partial schedule. Only leaf nodes represent complete schedules and therefore express exact objective values. Figure 2.12 illustrates such an enumeration tree. Typically the LB calculated at a node becomes larger with the depth level in the enumeration tree. If $LB \geq UB$ becomes true, any deeper search is senseless. Then, the part of the enumeration tree below the current node is bounded from further search.

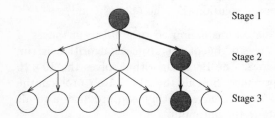

Stage 1

Stage 2

Stage 3

Fig. 2.12. A decision tree of depth 3 is shown. The gray nodes mark a single decision chain within the tree.

A low UB known from the start will accelerate the search process since branches are cut with respect to the present UB. Hence a good initial UB is provided by means of a heuristic before the B&B search actually begins. Furthermore, an appropriate branching procedure and a good LB calculation is needed. The branching procedure should follow promising nodes first, whereas the LB calculation should come up with almost reliable bounds.

A survey on B&B methods for the JSP is given in Błażewicz et al. (1993). The currently best B&B algorithm for the JSP has been developed by Brucker et al. (1994), The branching- and bounding schemes are sketched below as an example of B&B formulation for the JSP.

- The branching scheme is determined by longest path information. Brucker et al. start at the root node with the graph $\mathcal{D}$, such that only the conjunctive arcs representing the technological constraints exist, compare Fig. 2.8. At each node of the enumeration tree the longest path for the partial schedule $\mathcal{D}_P$ is calculated.
  A sequence of successive operations on the longest path to be processed on the same machine is called a block. It can be shown that an improvement may be gained by shifting an operation from the inside of a block to the first or to the last position of this block. At each node of the enumeration tree

two lists operations not yet scheduled is built. These lists contain candidate operations to be inserted "before" and "after" a block. Now the branching is performed by taking one operation of one of the two lists either in the first or in the last position of a block.

- The bounding scheme is based on a lower bound evaluation for the partial selection $\mathcal{P}$. At each depth level l of the enumeration tree one additional machine constraint from the set $\mathcal{E}$ is inserted to $\mathcal{P}$. Since $\mathcal{D}_P = (\mathcal{V}, \mathcal{A} \cup \mathcal{P})$, the technological constraints in $\mathcal{A}$ are always taken into account in $\mathcal{D}_P$ regardless of the actual $\mathcal{P}$ considered. The lower bound LB is calculated for $\mathcal{D}_P$ using a standard longest path algorithm like the one described in Sect. 2.1.3.

A partial schedule is a relaxation of original problem due to two different states for operations. Operations already sequenced contribute to the makespan with their starting time. Operations not yet sequenced contribute to the makespan with a conservative estimation of their expected starting time. The search is bound, e.g. if the lower bound obtained for $\mathcal{D}_P$ exceeds the currently best known solution (i.e. the upper bound).

Currently the use of B&B algorithms is limited to problem instances of a few hundred operations. In an experiment the Brucker algorithm is run for two problems listed in Chap 8. The B&B algorithm solves the 10×10 mt10 in about 20 minutes to optimality. Solving the 20×10 la27 problem the algorithm is interrupted after 20 000 minutes runtime and produces a result which is still more than 10% above the optimum.

2.3.2 Partial Enumeration

The Shifting Bottleneck heuristic is based on a problem decomposition. It has been proposed by Adams et al. (1988) and was the first heuristic able to solve the notorious mt10 problem to optimality. The result obtained could be proofed when Carlier and Pinson (1989) solved the problem with a B&B algorithm.

Again, we start with the digraph $\mathcal{D}$ without any machine constraints applied. In contradiction to techniques based on the framework in Fig. 2.9, the Shifting Bottleneck algorithm iteratively adds entire machine selections $\mathcal{H}_i (1 \leq i \leq m)$ to the partial schedule $\mathcal{D}_P$. At any stage $t (1 \leq t \leq m)$ a single $\mathcal{H}_i$ is added to $\mathcal{P}$, hence $\mathcal{D}_H$ is built from $\mathcal{D}$ in m stages.

1. The partial schedule $\mathcal{D}_P$ includes all machines scheduled so far. In the beginning of every stage the heads r_v and tails q_v are calculated for all $v \in \mathcal{V}$ in $\mathcal{D}_P$. Heads and tails of this temporary partial schedule indicate the makespan delay due to the constraints considered so far. In other words, for every v two points in time r_v and q_v are specified. r_v denotes the earliest starting time and q_v denotes the latest completion time allowed for operation v with respect to the constraints in the current $\mathcal{D}_P$.

2. For all machines not yet scheduled $\mathcal{H}_i$ is obtained for $\mathcal{E}_i$ by solving them as one machine problems with heads r and tails q. For each of these subproblems an optimal machine sequence is found under the conditions that an operation v cannot be started earlier than r_v and v must be completed until q_v. This sub-problem is already NP-hard, but there is an efficient B&B due to Carlier (1982) available.

3. In step 1 heads and tails for the one machine problem are calculated with respect to the current $\mathcal{D}_P$. Therefore each resulting $C_{\max}$ value of an optimized one machine problem defines a valid makespan for $\mathcal{D}_P$ plus one additional machine sequence $\mathcal{H}_i$. The machine which worsens $C_{\max}$ at most is chosen to be scheduled next. This machine is called bottleneck machine. Choosing the bottleneck machine is motivated by the conjecture that scheduling M_i at a later stage would worsen $C_{\max}$ even more.

The algorithm sketched above is named Shifting Bottleneck 1 (SB1). Its name is derived from the fact that the bottleneck machine is scheduled in step 3. This heuristic is based on the conjecture that an optimized isolated machine sequence has a large number of arcs in common with the optimal schedule. In order to obtain further improvements, local reoptimization cycles are applied after each insertion of a machine selection. The scheme of selecting a machine for insertion and the reoptimization cycles used have been subject to further refinements of the algorithm, compare e.g. Applegate and Cook (1991).

The quality of the schedules obtained by SB1 heavily depends on the order in which the one machine problems are solved and included into $\mathcal{D}_P$, as noted by Pesch (1994). Unfortunately, the results obtained by choosing the bottleneck machine at each stage are not really convincing. Therefore Adams et al. developed an enhanced version called Shifting Bottleneck 2 (SB2) which engages selective enumeration also know as beam search in other contexts.

In SB2 a search tree analogous to Fig. 2.12 is generated. At each node a set of machine selections not yet scheduled is obtained by an SB1 stage. Depending on depth l in the search tree, a number of successor nodes bounded by $\min(l, \lceil m^{1/2} \rceil)$ are generated. Again, the bottleneck criterion selects the machines which worsen $C_{\max}$ most. Instead of generating all possible successor nodes, SB2 relies on the bottleneck criterion and branches to the most promising nodes only. This feature cuts down the horizontal expansion of the search tree substantially.

Similar to B&B algorithms branches are bound by means of lower- and upper bounds. Furthermore, the lower bound obtained for a partial schedule is penalized by a value computed heuristically as a function of depth l. The more machines are included in the partial schedule, the less the lower bound will be penalized and vice versa. Hence branches are bound at early stages. In the remaining search tree a path from the root to a leaf of depth m determines the order in which the optimized machine selections are added to $\mathcal{D}$. Any path of length m corresponds to a feasible solution, since all m machine sequences are scheduled. Nevertheless, SB2 is still a heuristic, i.e. even an optimal order of sequencing machines does not necessarily lead to an optimal solution of the problem considered. SB2 is a fast heuristic for moderately sized problems. For these problems it comes up with excellent results.

3. Local Search Techniques

In recent research on combinatorics Local Search attracts increasingly attention, since the practical use of exact enumeration methods is restricted to problem sizes of a few hundred operations and most schedule generation techniques produce only reasonable solution quality. Local Search offers further improvements of solutions resulting from schedule generation heuristics.

Various Local Search algorithms have been developed sharing the basic idea of neighborhoods. A neighboring solution is derived from its originator solution by a predefined partial modification, called move. A move results in a neighboring solution which differs only slightly from its originator solution. We expect a neighboring solution to produce an objective value of similar quality as its originator solution because they share a majority of solution characteristics. One can say that a neighboring solution is within the vicinity of its originator. Therefore we concentrate on search within neighborhoods, since the chance to find an improved solution within a neighborhood is much higher than in less correlated areas of the search space.

The most simple deterministic iterative improvement is described e.g. in Vaessens et al. (1992). Starting from an initial (current) solution, the procedure continually searches the neighborhood of the current solution for a neighboring solution of better quality. Each time a neighboring solution gains an objective value improvement, the current solution is replaced by its neighbor. The procedure stops if no further improvement can be gained. The described procedure is known as hill climbing in discrete optimization. It can loosely be seen as the counterpart to gradient methods in continuous optimization.

Consider a multi modal objective function. A hill climbing procedure will accept a replacement of the current solution by a neighboring one as long as an improvement can be gained. The final solution is called a local optimum with respect to the neighborhood used. To the contrary a global optimum is a solution for which the objective value cannot be improved by any other solution of the entire search space. The chance that a local optimum is also a global optimum is very small for most difficult multi modal objective functions. The advantage of having a good chance to improve the objective value within a neighborhood comes along with the drawback of exploring only a small portion of the search space.

In order to avoid the short-come of getting trapped in a local optimum several extensions of the basic hill climbing principle are proposed.

- Instead of generating a single neighboring solution an entire neighboring set of solutions is generated. From this set the solution with the highest gain is accepted to replace its originator. This method is known as steepest descend strategy for minimization problems.
- A more intricate acceptance criterion can be used which allows a temporary worsening of the objective value. Such a feature allows the search process to escape from local optima. Examples for such methods are the well-known Simulated Annealing or the Tabu Search algorithms (described later on in Sect. 3.3.2 and 3.3.3).

The average solution quality obtained by Local Search strongly depends on the neighborhood definition since the neighborhood definition affects the number of local optima and their distribution in the search space. The search space properties obey to the neighborhood definition applied. Thus, using different neighborhoods leads to different appearances of the search space.

If there are only a few local optima present it's not unlikely that Local Search will run into a global optimum. On the other hand, if the search runs into a local optimum, the chance to escape is very small even for methods using temporary deterioration. To the contrary, if there are many local optima, hill climbing will perform poor and escape mechanisms are needed. If the local optima are widely spread across the search space, escape mechanisms will more likely fail as if the local optima are closely related.

In the following section we discuss several neighborhood definitions suitable for the JSP. Then different hill climbing strategies are introduced and compared in terms of their efficiency (i.e. the relation of solution quality and runtime demand). Finally, the principles of Simulated Annealing, Tabu Search and Variable Depth Search are sketched in terms of Local Search.

3.1 Neighborhood Definitions

The success of Local Search heavily depends on the properties of the neighborhood definition used. Therefore we first describe what can be fundamentally done in the JSP case in order to construct a neighboring move.

A basic move for the JSP is to rearrange the processing order of operations to be processed on the same machine. In terms of the graph representation introduced in Sect. 2.1.2 a move can be produced by permuting a Hamiltonian machine selection $\mathcal{H}_i$ for machine M_i. Thus, given a feasible schedule $\mathcal{D}_H$ (or $\mathcal{H}$ as a shorthand) its neighborhood set $\mathcal{N}(\mathcal{H})$ is obtained by slight perturbations (or moves) from $\mathcal{H}$.

Before we describe selected neighborhood definitions for the JSP, some considerations on desirable features of neighborhoods are addressed.

Correlation.   A neighboring solution $\mathcal{H}'$ should be highly correlated to its originator $\mathcal{H}$. Thus, a neighborhood $\mathcal{N}(\mathcal{H})$ of $\mathcal{H}$ should ensure a neighboring solution $\mathcal{H}'$ that differs only within a small spread from $\mathcal{H}$. This property takes care for a thorough exploration of the search space.

Feasibility.   Perturbations should always lead to feasible solutions. If possible, the search should be restricted to the domain of feasibility in order to avoid expensive repair procedures which in turn would lead to further modifications of $\mathcal{H}'$.

Improvement.   A move should have a good chance to obtain an improved $f(\mathcal{H}')$ value. In order to achieve this goal additional problem specific knowledge may be incorporated into the neighborhood definition.

Size.   The average size of a set $\mathcal{N}(\mathcal{H})$ should be within useful bounds. A small number of possible moves may halt the search process in early stages (at relatively poor local optima). To the opposite, a large number of moves in $\mathcal{N}$ may be computationally prohibitive if f itself is computationally expensive.

Connectivity.   It should be guaranteed that there is a finite sequence of moves (worsening ones included) leading from an arbitrary schedule to a global optimal one. Otherwise, promising areas of the search space may be excluded from the search. This is known as the connectivity property.

Some of the above considerations may contradict each other. Often these conflicts cannot be solved theoretically. At least some experience with applications is needed in order to develop appropriate neighborhood definitions. Summing up, the features above are desirable properties which can be used for developing efficient neighborhood definitions.

3.1.1 The First Neighborhood

Let us start with a somewhat naive neighborhood definition. Here, a move is performed by changing the precedence relation of one operation to be processed on machine M_i arbitrarily within its machine sequence $\mathcal{H}_i$. Unfortunately this neighborhood definition comes along with several drawbacks. An arbitrary change of a machine sequence can lead to a cycle in $\mathcal{D}_H$. Furthermore, if each job has to be processed on each machine the neighborhood is of size $m(n-1)$ and appears to be too large. A majority of feasible moves in $\mathcal{N}(\mathcal{H})$ does not change or, even worse, deteriorate $C_{\max}$.

These disadvantages can be avoided by restricting the moves to successive operations as reported by Van Laarhoven et al. (1992). Since their neighborhood definition meets a majority of desired features, a closer look on moves within successive operations is given in Lemma 3.1.1 and 3.1.2.

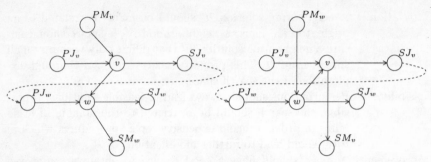

Fig. 3.1. Illustration of neighborhood definition $\mathcal{N}_1$.

Assume two successive operations v and w, $(v, w \in \mathcal{V})$ are given on a critical path as shown on the left hand side of Fig. 3.1. Their heads r_v and r_w are determined by the job predecessors PJ_v and PJ_w and by the machine predecessors PM_v and v. Note, that the machine predecessor of w is v. The tails q_v and q_w are determined by the job successors SJ_v and SJ_w and by the machine successors w and SM_w. These six adjacent operations are sufficient to explain a move carried out between v and w. The situation after the move is sketched on the right hand side of Fig. 3.1. Operation w has become the machine predecessor of v by reversing the arc (v, w) to the arc (w, v). In order to keep a Hamiltonian path in $\mathcal{H}_i$, two other machine sequence constraints incident to v and w are adjusted to the new situation.

Lemma 3.1.1. *Reversing one critical arc in $\mathcal{H}_i$ cannot lead to a cycle in $\mathcal{D}_H$ and therefore cannot result in an infeasible solution.*

Proof. Assume a path which leads to a cycle after reversing (v, w). Such a path is shown in Fig. 3.1 as a dashed curve from SJ_v to PJ_w. This path would lead to a cycle after reversing (v, w) as shown in the right hand side of the figure. Hence it has to be proved that the path from SJ_v to PJ_w cannot exist if arc (v, w) is critical. All operations have a well defined processing time $p_v > 0$. If the arc (v, w) belongs to a critical path, then $r_w = r_v + p_v$ holds. Hence we can state that $r_v + p_v + p_{SJ_v} + \ldots + p_{PJ_w} > r_v + p_v$. As long as the arc (v, w) is critical, no other path from v to w can exist. Hence the reversal of a critical arc (v, w) can never lead to an infeasible solution.

Lemma 3.1.2. *If the reversal of a non-critical arc in $\mathcal{H}_i$ leads to a feasible solution, then $f(\mathcal{H}') \geq f(\mathcal{H})$ holds.*

Proof. Obviously, reversing a non-critical arc does not affect the longest path. Hence the derived solution cannot shorten the $C_{\max}$ value of the new schedule. Note, that Lemma 3.1.1 does not hold if the reversed arc is non-critical. Reversing a non-critical arc may lead to an infeasible solution because of a cycle introduced by the move.

When moves are restricted to successive operations on a critical path in $\mathcal{D}_H$, feasibility of moves is preserved. Thus, the restricted neighborhood definition proposed by Van Laarhoven et al. (1992) meets most of the desirable features. An additional property reported by Matsuo et al. (1988) is of interest for an even more efficient neighborhood definition, since further non-improving moves are discarded from the neighborhood. This property is formulated in Lemma 3.1.3.

Lemma 3.1.3. *The reversal of a critical arc (v, w) can only lead to an improvement if at least one of PM_v and SM_w is non-critical.*

Proof. If (PM_v, v, w, SM_w) are successive operations on a critical path, a reversal of (v, w) does not change the starting time r_{SM_w} because $r_{PM_v} + p_v + p_w = r_{SM_w}$. Therefore these cases cannot not lead to an improvement. For an example refer to Fig. 3.1.

A machine sequence given in Lemma 3.1.3 is called a block. A block is defined as a chain of successive operations on a critical path which are to be processed on the same machine. An arc reversal of two successive operations inside a block cannot shorten $C_{\max}$.

Even two more moves can be discarded from being considered due to the following observation of Nowicki and Smutnicki (1995). Therefore we pay attention to the first block succeeding node b and last block preceding node e. A computational saving can be gained if one of the mentioned blocks consists of at least two operations.

Lemma 3.1.4. *Let v and w be the first two successive operations of the first block. Reversing the critical arc (v, w) cannot lead to a makespan improvement. Analogous let v and w be the last two successive operations of the last block. Again, no improvement can be gained by reversing v, w.*

The proof of lemma 3.1.4 is outside the scope of this thesis. Therefore the interested reader is referred to Nowicki and Smutnicki (1995). Now the foundations are laid for the definition of the first neighborhood $\mathcal{N}_1$.

Definition 3.1.1 ($\mathcal{N}_1$). *Given $\mathcal{H}$, the neighborhood $\mathcal{N}_1(\mathcal{H})$ consist of all schedules derived from $\mathcal{H}$ by reversing one arc (v, w) of the critical path with $v, w \in \mathcal{H}_i$. At least one of v and w is either the first or the last member of a block. For the first block only v and w at the end of the block are considered whereas for the last block only v and w at the begin of the block must be checked.*

The neighborhood $\mathcal{N}_1$ is extremely small and leads to slight perturbations only. It yields improved solutions with a relatively high probability and guarantees feasibility. The connectivity property does not hold for this neighborhood. For a counterexample refer to Dell' Amico and Trubian (1993).

3.1.2 The Second Neighborhood

A second neighborhood $\mathcal{N}_2$ is proposed by Dell' Amico and Trubian (1993), which can be used in conjunction with $\mathcal{N}_1$. So far we looked at operations placed at the border of blocks only. $\mathcal{N}_2$ takes precedence relations of operations inside a block into account. As stated in Lemma 3.1.3, the reversal of an arc inside a block cannot yield an improvement of the makespan. Therefore we focus on moves within a larger scope of operations.

Let operation v be a member of block b such that also PM_v and SM_v belong to $b = (b', v, b'')$. Solutions are considered as neighbors, if v is moved to the first or last position in b. For these cases we get (v, b', b'') or (b', b'', v). Actually such moves may lead to infeasible solutions. Since the operations affected by the move are not adjacent, Lemma 3.1.1 cannot be applied. Whenever a move to the first or the last position of a block leads to an infeasible solution, we consider the move closest to the first or last position as neighboring for which feasibility is preserved. In conjunction with $\mathcal{N}_1$ the benefits of $\mathcal{N}_2$ are twofold:

-- A new position for v in a block b may be found such that a move results in an improved coverage of the machine capacity to which v belongs. This can be seen as filling up a gap in the Gantt-Chart representation of the problem.
-- Moreover, moving v in the first or last position of its block may result in a schedule for which $\mathcal{N}_1$ allows a further shortage of the makespan in a next step.

The feasibility of a solution resulting from a block move can be tested with a standard labeling algorithm like the one described by Kahn (1962). Since this procedure is computational expensive, Dell' Amico and Trubian (1993) give an estimation for testing feasibility of solutions resulting from moves inside a block. The estimation ensures the feasibility at the expense of omitting a few feasible solutions. However, a standard labeling algorithm for each block move candidate is computationally prohibitive. Furthermore Dell'Amico and Trubian note, that only less promising moves are omitted by the estimation procedure. The estimation of feasibility is given by Lemma 3.1.5 and 3.1.6 below.

Lemma 3.1.5. *For a move inside block* $b = (b', v, b'')$ *closest to the first operation* w *of* b', *a cycle in the resulting digraph can exist if and only if there is a path from* SJ_w *to* PJ_v.

Proof. The path from SJ_w to PJ_v cannot exist if $r_{SJ_w} + p_{SJ_w} > r_{PJ_v}$ holds for each $w \in b'$ considered. Assuming non-negative processing times, the completion time of operation SJ_w must be later than the starting time of operation PJ_v. Thus, it is sufficient to test the inequality in order to ensure feasibility. A graphical example is given on the left hand side of Fig. 3.2.

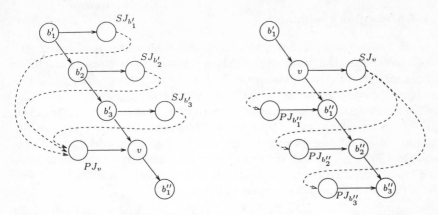

Fig. 3.2. Illustration of the neighborhood definition $\mathcal{N}_2$.

Lemma 3.1.6. *For a move inside block $b = (b', v, b'')$ closest to the last operation w of b'', a cycle in the resulting digraph can exist if and only if there is a path from SJ_v to PJ_w.*

Proof. The proof works similar to the one of Lemma 3.1.5. For each operation $w \in b''$ the condition $r_{SJ_v} + p_{SJ_v} > r_{PJ_w}$ has to be satisfied in order to ensure that a path from SJ_v to PJ_w does not exist. Again we assume non-negative processing times, thus the completion time of operation SJ_v must be later than the starting time of operation PJ_w. A graphical example is given on the right hand side of Fig. 3.2.

Note that the estimation for the direct predecessor and successor of v in Fig. 3.2 is not needed, since Lemma 3.1.1 already covers moves of successive operations. Following Lemma 3.1.2, moves of successive operations inside a block cannot lead to a shortage of the makespan anyway. Since feasibility is preserved in other cases by Lemma 3.1.5 and 3.1.6, we can state the neighborhood $\mathcal{N}_2$ as follows.

Definition 3.1.2 ($\mathcal{N}_2$). *Let operation v be a member of block b such that $b = (b', v, b'')$. In a neighboring solution v is moved closest to the first or the last operation of b for which feasibility is preserved.*

Now the desired connectivity property holds for the union of the neighborhoods $\mathcal{N}_1 \cup \mathcal{N}_2$. Unfortunately, the neighborhood size now increases. Although $\mathcal{N}_2$ contains promising moves, most neighbor candidates will not lead to improvements. Hence the computational time needed in order to detect improving solutions among the neighboring ones increases strongly. Recall, that each improvement trial requires the calculation of a longest path. Obviously, testing of the entire neighborhood seems computational prohibitive. Nevertheless it would be most useful to gain further makespan improvements.

3.1.3 Makespan Estimation

Since the exact calculation of the C_{max} values for all solutions of a neighborhood is computational prohibitive, Taillard (1993a) has developed a makespan estimation for the $\mathcal{N}_1$ neighborhood. Instead of comparing exact C_{max} values of neighboring solutions, Taillard uses estimated C'_{max} values in his Tabu Search algorithm. Using the proposed estimation, most non-improving moves can be omitted at constant computational cost. Only for moves accepted by the estimation the longest path is recalculated. Taillard's work has been extended by Dell' Amico and Trubian (1993) to a makespan estimation suitable for the $\mathcal{N}_2$ definition. First, Taillard's original estimation is described. Next, Dell'Amico and Trubian's extension is introduced.

$\mathcal{N}_1$ **estimation.** The calculation is based on the heads r_v and tails q_v of a solution. Recall that a head gives the earliest starting time of an operation. The calculation of the heads is part of the procedure determining the exact makespan, therefore no additional computational load arises. A tail q_v is defined by the longest path from v to the sink of the digraph. Roughly speaking, the tail expresses the – not yet started – rest of the entire production program from the viewpoint of the currently visited operation. The tail calculation requires an additional longest path algorithm starting at the graph's sink with all arcs reversed temporarily.

As stated previously in Sect. 2.1.3, a head is given by $r_v = \max(r_{PM_v} + p_{PM_v}, r_{PJ_v} + p_{PJ_v})$ whereas a tail is calculated by $q_v = \max(q_{SM_v} + p_{SM_v}, q_{SJ_v} + p_{SJ_v})$ with $p_v, r_v, q_v = 0$ for undefined v. No buffer time exists for any critical operation v, hence $C_{max} = r_v + p_v + q_v$. We keep these definitions in mind and recall the $\mathcal{N}_1$ illustration given in Fig. 3.1. Now we calculate r'_w, r'_v, q'_v, q'_w in a way as if the reversal of (v, w) has already taken place.

$$
\begin{aligned}
r'_w &= \max(r_{PM_v} + p_{PM_v}, r_{PJ_w} + p_{PJ_w}) \\
r'_v &= \max(r'_w + p_w, r_{PJ_v} + p_{PJ_v})
\end{aligned}
$$

$$
\begin{aligned}
q'_v &= \max(q_{SM_w} + p_{SM_w}, q_{SJ_v} + p_{SJ_v}) \\
q'_w &= \max(q'_v + p_v, q_{SJ_w} + p_{SJ_w})
\end{aligned} \tag{3.1}
$$

$$
C'_{max} = \max(r'_w + p_w + q'_w, r'_v + p_v + q'_v)
$$

The estimated makespan C'_{max} is given by the maximum makespan calculated at v and w. The estimation is exact, if at least one of the operations w and v belongs to a longest path after the reversal. Otherwise the estimated value is a lower bound for the new makespan.

$\mathcal{N}_2$ **estimation.** This more general approach offers an estimation also suitable for moves of non-successive operations within machine sequences. Therefore we view Taillard's (w, v) estimation as special case of an operation sequence of length 2. Let $L = (L_1, \ldots, L_l)$ be a machine sequence of successive operations on a longest path as it will appear in a neighboring solution. Furthermore let 'first' and 'last' be operations from L such that PM_{first} and SM_{last} are non-critical or do not exist. These nodes determine a maximal time span for the operations of sequence L. Therefore the operations 'first' and 'last' provide an embedding of L in the new graph. Since r_{first} and q_{last} will not change from the originator solution to a neighboring one the estimation of $C'_{\max}$ can be calculated similar to (3.1).

$$
\begin{aligned}
r'_{L_1} &= \max(r_{PM_{\text{first}}} + p_{PM_{\text{first}}}, r_{PJ_{L_1}} + p_{PJ_{L_1}}) \\
r'_{L_2} &= \max(r'_{L_1} + p_{L_1}, r_{PJ_{L_2}} + p_{PJ_{L_2}}) \\
&\vdots \\
r'_{L_l} &= \max(r'_{L_{l-1}} + p_{L_{l-1}}, r_{PJ_{L_l}} + p_{PJ_{L_l}}) \\[6pt]
q'_{L_l} &= \max(q_{SM_{\text{last}}} + p_{SM_{\text{last}}}, q_{SJ_{L_l}} + p_{SJ_{L_l}}) \\
q'_{L_{l-1}} &= \max(q'_{L_l} + p_{L_l}, q_{SJ_{L_{l-1}}} + p_{SJ_{L_{l-1}}}) \\
&\vdots \\
q'_{L_1} &= \max(q'_{L_2} + p_{L_2}, q_{SJ_{L_1}} + p_{SJ_{L_1}}) \\[6pt]
C'_{\max} &= r'_{L_1} + p_{L_1} + q'_{L_1} \\
C'_{\max} &= \max(C'_{\max}, r'_{L_2} + p_{L_2} + q'_{L_2}) \\
&\vdots \\
C'_{\max} &= \max(C'_{\max}, r'_{L_l} + p_{L_l} + q'_{L_l})
\end{aligned}
\tag{3.2}
$$

We have defined a fast estimation procedure for sequences of operations along a critical path which are processed on the same machine. Non improving moves within a neighborhood can be discarded at almost constant cost. Estimated makespan improvements are exact for most neighbors. The remaining estimation failures are assumed to correlate with the exact calculated makespan. I.e. we assume the deviation of the estimated makespan between solutions to correlate with the deviation of the exact calculated makespan although the values may differ.

3.1.4 The Third Neighborhood

In the following a third neighborhood definition is described, also proposed by Dell' Amico and Trubian (1993). Its goal is to extend $\mathcal{N}_1$ by taking the reversal of two arcs of one move into account. In certain cases a slight perturbation by reversing only one arc (v, w) does not yield an improvement, whereas a stronger perturbation by reversing two arcs simultaneously may succeed. These cases are addressed by the neighborhood definition $\mathcal{N}_3$.

Definition 3.1.3 ($\mathcal{N}_3$). *Let v and w be successive operations on a longest path. All possible permutations of $\{PM_v, v, w\}$ or $\{v, w, SM_w\}$ are considered as neighboring if v and w are reversed also.*

Table 3.1. Depending on a block's structure up to three permutations are regarded to be neighboring. If two precedence relations are changed, a conflicting path may lead to a cycle in the resulting digraph.

block structure	small block (v, w)	block begin (v, w, SM_w)	block end (PM_v, v, w)
permutations	$\{w, v\}$	$\{w, v\}$	$\{w, v\}$
		$\{w, SM_w, v\}$	$\{w, PM_v, v\}$
		$\{SM_w, w, v\}$	$\{w, v, PM_v\}$
conflicting path	—	(SJ_v, PJ_{SM_w})	(SJ_{PM_v}, PJ_w)

Depending on the block structure of the machine sequence three cases can be distinguished as shown in Tab. 3.1. The cases are denoted 'small block', 'block begin' and 'block end'. Note that a makespan improvement is possible only if one of PM_v and SM_w belongs to the longest path, compare Lemma 3.1.3. Thus, depending on the block structure at most three permutations are taken into consideration for a neighboring candidate. The possible permutations are illustrated in Fig. 3.3. The first graph shows a machine sequence as it appears in the digraph of the originator solution. The nodes u' and u'' represent further operations of the machine sequence which are not considered in this context. The gray nodes represent the part of the sequence where the $\mathcal{N}_3$ move takes place.

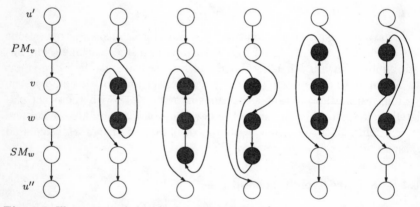

Fig. 3.3. Illustration of neighborhood definition $\mathcal{N}_3$.

For simplicity the job predecessors and job successors are omitted in Fig. 3.3. For the same reason conflicting paths are omitted from the figure. Nevertheless a second path may exist from PM_v to w or from v to SM_w in the machine sequence of the originator solution. Such a path will lead to a cycle when applying the permutations given in Tab. 3.1. Again, a labeling algorithm to detect a cycle can be avoided by evaluating the permutations considered in a certain order.

Lemma 3.1.7. *The estimated makespan of a (v, w) reversal is smaller or equal than any estimated makespan resulting from the reversal or two arcs if such a reversal leads to an infeasible solution.*

The proof of Lemma 3.1.7 is outside the scope of this thesis, the interested reader is referred to Dell' Amico and Trubian (1993). Following Lemma 3.1.7 a cycle in the resulting neighboring solution can be easily avoided by taking always the permutation with the smallest estimated makespan as the neighboring solution. If a (v, w) reversal and a more complicated reversal produce the same estimated makespan values, take the (v, w) candidate as the neighboring solution. The considerations above imply that only one candidate is regarded as a neighbor. Note, that it is impossible to calculate the makespan for an infeasible solution. Using the estimation introduced in (3.2) the C'_{max} of an infeasible solution is estimated by neglecting a possible cycle. Hence all estimations required for an $\mathcal{N}_3$ evaluation are directly comparable.

Three neighborhood definitions $\mathcal{N}_1$, $\mathcal{N}_2$ and $\mathcal{N}_3$ have been presented so far with $\mathcal{N}_1 \subseteq \mathcal{N}_3$ and $\mathcal{N}_2 \cap \mathcal{N}_3 = \emptyset$. Hence $\mathcal{N}_2$ may be used in conjunction with $\mathcal{N}_3$ in order to obtain an advanced neighborhood definition combining the advantages of $\mathcal{N}_2$ and $\mathcal{N}_3$.

Definition 3.1.4 ($\mathcal{N}_4$). $\mathcal{N}_4 = \mathcal{N}_2 \cup \mathcal{N}_3$.

We have seen that the definition of an efficient neighborhood is highly problem dependent and might be more difficult than Local Search literature implies. In this section four neighborhood definitions have been presented. They will be used throughout this thesis, first within Local Search algorithms and later on as a component of Evolutionary Search.

Other even more complex neighborhood definitions exist, compare e.g. Balas and Vazacopoulos (1994). Obviously, there is an efficiency tradeoff between the makespan improvement gained and the size of the neighborhood defined. We can finally decide whether a neighborhood definition fits the needs only in combination with the control structure of the heuristic search technique in which the neighborhood definition is embedded.

3.2 Local Hill Climbing

Hill climbing procedures iteratively perturb a solution by slight moves which improve the objective pursued (i.e. minimize the makespan). Before we are going to take a closer look at the properties of hill climbing for the JSP, we discuss an efficient way of implementing a neighborhood move.

Then different control structures which navigate the search are first described and then are used in combination with the neighborhoods defined throughout the previous section. Finally, the resulting strategies are applied to three arbitrarily selected benchmark problems. Some experiments carried out give us a qualitative impression of results we can expect from hill climbing for the JSP.

3.2.1 Applying a Neighborhood Move

After selecting $\mathcal{H}'$ from $\mathcal{N}(\mathcal{H})$ as a neighboring candidate due to estimation (see Sect. 3.1.3), the new digraph $\mathcal{D}_{H'}$ is established (i.e. the move is performed). Next, the topological sorting $\mathcal{T}'$ for $\mathcal{H}'$ is achieved, compare Sect. 2.1.3. Based on $\mathcal{T}'$ the heads $r_v \in \mathcal{V}$ are calculated in order to determine the new exact $C'_{\max}$ value. Anytime the estimation has failed in a way that $f(\mathcal{H}') \geq f(\mathcal{H})$ holds, we cancel the move and continue with choosing a next appropriate candidate (if any) from $\mathcal{N}(\mathcal{H})$. The critical path and the tails $q_v \in \mathcal{V}$ are calculated only if the move candidate $\mathcal{H}'$ is finally accepted to replace $\mathcal{H}$.

An entirely new calculation of the makespan as described in Sect. 2.1.3 requires a considerable computational effort. Therefore we face a strong demand for a fast recalculation procedure for the makespan of a neighboring solution. A slight perturbation of a solution $\mathcal{H}$ results in its neighboring solution $\mathcal{H}'$. These two neighboring solutions show a high similarity concerning their topological sorted nodes $\mathcal{V}$. We benefit from this similarity when calculating the makespan of a neighboring solution $\mathcal{H}'$.

Performing a Move. A simple move concerning $v, w \in \mathcal{V}$ as considered in $\mathcal{N}_1$ and $\mathcal{N}_2$ (see Definitions 3.1.1 and 3.1.2) can be expressed by the instruction: "schedule w prior to v". The implementation of a move instruction consists of the six statements shown in Fig. 3.4. Note that PM_v, PM_w and SM_w refer to the situation in $\mathcal{D}_H$ before any action has taken place. More complex moves as considered in $\mathcal{N}_3$ (see Definition 3.1.3) can be expressed by two instructions carried out subsequently. For instance, an inversion of the sequence (u, v, w) can be obtained by the instructions 1) schedule v prior to u, and 2) schedule w prior to v.

(1)	if PM_v delete arc (PM_v, v)
(2)	if SM_w delete arc (w, SM_w)
(3)	if PM_w delete arc (PM_w, w)
(4)	if $PM_w \wedge SM_w$ construct arc (PM_w, SM_w)
(5)	if PM_v construct arc (PM_v, w)
(6)	construct arc (w, v)

Fig. 3.4. Steps to be performed in order to schedule node w directly before v.

Achieving a Topological Sorting. We obtain the neighboring solution $\mathcal{H}'$ from $\mathcal{H}$ by performing a move as shown in Fig. 3.4. Now we establish a new topological sorting $\mathcal{T}'$ for $\mathcal{D}_{H'}$. Since the nodes v, w affected by a single move are closely related in $\mathcal{D}_H$, typically we will find them in a proximity within the old topological sorting $\mathcal{T}$. Therefore we keep most of the topological sorting previously done for $\mathcal{D}_H$ and obtain $\mathcal{T}'$ by adjusting $\mathcal{T}$ locally. We define $B_{v,w} \subseteq \mathcal{T}$ such that v is the first and w is the last node in B. A move of v and w affects the sorting of nodes in B exclusively, the topological sorting of nodes in A and C are not involved. The situation is sketched in Fig. 3.5.

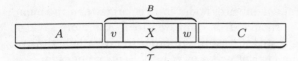

Fig. 3.5. A single move rearranges the nodes in B.

Now let us consider the nodes in $X = B \backslash \{v, w\}$, whose position obey to one of three distinct reasons.

1) A node in X occurs prior to w as a direct or indirect predecessor of w.
2) A node in X occurs after v as a direct or indirect successor of v.
3) A node in X is locally unrelated to v and w.

In $\mathcal{D}_{H'}$ node w is scheduled as a direct predecessor of node v. In order to achieve an identical order in $\mathcal{T}'$ we place w directly before v. Therefore we distinguish between 1) and 2) and split X into X' and X'' respectively. Nodes which obey to case 3) may occur arbitrarily in X' or X'' because the nodes in X are no successors of v or predecessors of w.

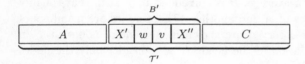

Fig. 3.6. B' is a valid sorting for the graph $\mathcal{D}_{H'}$.

In order to set up X' and X'' we label the nodes in X which are direct or indirect predecessors of w in $\mathcal{D}_{H'}$. The labeled nodes form X'. The nodes not labeled are either successors of v or unrelated to v and w forming X''. A valid topological sorting for the new digraph $\mathcal{D}_{H'}$ is given by $\mathcal{T}' = (A, B', C)$.

Figure 3.7 provides an example for the described procedure. The move considered schedules node 9 prior to 1. A valid topological sorting for the digraph $\mathcal{D}_H$ is $\mathcal{T} = (0, 4, 1, 7, 2, 5, 8, 3, 9, 6, 10)$ shown on the left side of the Fig. 3.7. We identify node 1 and 9 in $\mathcal{T}$ and extract $B = (1, 7, 2, 5, 8, 3, 9)$. In a next step we label node 7 and 8 as direct or indirect predecessors of node 9, illustrated by $B = (\boxed{1}, \underline{7}, 2, 5, \underline{8}, 3, \boxed{9})$ with labeled nodes underlined and nodes involved in the moved surrounded by boxes. Since we move node 9 directly before node 1, we have to move the nodes 7 and 8 before the new position of node 9 also. We end up with $B' = (\underline{7}, \underline{8}, \boxed{9}, \boxed{1}, 2, 5, 3)$ and $\mathcal{T}' = (0, 4, 7, 8, 9, 1, 2, 5, 3, 6, 10)$ which is a topological sorting for the digraph $\mathcal{D}_{H'}$ shown on the right hand side of Fig. 3.7.

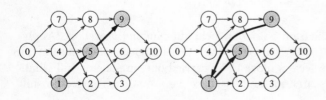

Fig. 3.7. Selection $\mathcal{H}_i = (1, 5, 9)$ of machine M_i is changed to $\mathcal{H}'_i = (9, 1, 5)$.

For this small example the number of nodes in B is larger than the number of nodes in $\mathcal{T} \cap B$. The smaller B is compared to $\mathcal{T}$, the more savings will be gained from the suggested procedure. In order to give a quantitative impression of the average number of nodes in B in percent of nodes in $\mathcal{T}$, a small experiment is carried out. The mean results of 1 000 runs are shown in Tab. 3.2 for three arbitrarily selected problems listed in Chap. 8.

name	size	A	B	C
mt10	10×10	45.4	5.9	48.7
la27	20×10	47.8	5.0	47.2
la35	30×10	46.9	4.5	48.5

Table 3.2. Nodes in A, B and C given in % of the no. of nodes in $\mathcal{T}$.

B consists of approximately 5% of the nodes in $\mathcal{T}$. In other words, 95% of all nodes are left untouched by restricting the recalculation of the topological sorting to B. For larger problem instance we expect even greater savings.

Recalculating Heads and Tails. Based on $\mathcal{T}'$ the new heads and tails can be calculated efficiently. In average, B is embedded in $\mathcal{T}$ such that roughly 47% of nodes are members of A and another 47% of nodes are members of C. The number of nodes observed are shown in percent of nodes in $\mathcal{T}$ in Tab. 3.2. For the recalculation of the heads r_v we consider only the nodes $v \in \{B' \cup C\}$, because the nodes in A are left unchanged. In turn, we recalculate the tails q_v for nodes $v \in \{B' \cup A\}$ only because nodes in C are left without modifications. Thus, we save roughly half of the computational amount needed for a recalculation of r_v and q_v. The new critical path in $\mathcal{D}_{H'}$ is unpredictable and therefore needs a completely new determination.

3.2.2 A Hill Climbing Framework

The neighborhood definition $\mathcal{N}$ and the navigation control $\mathcal{C}$, which selects a move candidate from $\mathcal{N}$, are parameters to a general hill climbing framework. A neighborhood $\mathcal{N}$ and a control $\mathcal{C}$ together define a search strategy.

1. Establish a solution $\mathcal{H}$ by a schedule generation technique.
2. Generate a set of neighborhood solutions $R := \mathcal{N}(\mathcal{H})$ for solution $\mathcal{H}$.
3. Discard the non improving solutions from R by applying $f(\mathcal{H}'), \mathcal{H}' \in R$.
4. If $R \neq \emptyset$, replace $\mathcal{H}$ by choosing $\mathcal{H}'$ from R subject to $\mathcal{C}$ and goto 2.
5. Terminate.

Fig. 3.8. Framework for a hill climbing procedure.

Figure 3.8 shows the framework of a local hill climbing procedure. Applying $\mathcal{N}$ to a solution $\mathcal{H}$ will result in the set of neighboring solutions $\mathcal{N}(\mathcal{H})$. The search control $\mathcal{C}$ selects a move to be carried out. In general, hill climbing is an irrevocable search method, because we are not permitted to shift attention back to previously suspended moves, see Pearl (1984). The search control is of particular importance to the success offered by hill climbing. In accordance with the literature we define three controls shown in Tab. 3.3.

Table 3.3. Three hill climbing control strategies.

strategy	abbr.	description
next	(nx)	The first improving neighbor found replaces $\mathcal{H}$.
steepest	(st)	The best of all improving neighbors replaces $\mathcal{H}$.
random	(rn)	A randomly chosen improving neighbor replaces $\mathcal{H}$.

Before we start an experimental investigation, we discuss what can be expected from neighborhoods and search controls within a hill climbing procedure for the JSP. We consider the neighborhood definitions $\mathcal{N}_1 \subseteq \mathcal{N}_3 \subseteq \mathcal{N}_4$ defined previously in this chapter[1]. We first argue, that the more effort we spend in setting up a neighborhood set, the more profit we expect to gain from a hill climbing procedure. Thus we expect the makespan improvements due to $\mathcal{N}_4$ to be superior to $\mathcal{N}_3$ which in turn should be of better quality than the improvements gained from $\mathcal{N}_1$. Of course, a higher effort is computationally more expensive. But is a better result worthwhile the longer computation time invested? Or can we neglect further limited improvement due to a more intricate neighborhood definition in order to obtain a fast hill climbing procedure?

The relation between the $\mathcal{C}_{nx}$, $\mathcal{C}_{st}$ and $\mathcal{C}_{rn}$ control is not clear from the advance. Intuitively, one would expect $\mathcal{C}_{st}$ to make larger steps of improvement than $\mathcal{C}_{rn}$. But will the latter control reach a similar solution quality compared with the former one?

In the context of scheduling $\mathcal{C}_{nx}$ has a special behavior. The operations along the critical path of $\mathcal{D}_H$ are successively investigated for improvements from the source to the sink. Thus the next descendant control $\mathcal{C}_{nx}$ always selects the move closest to the source of $\mathcal{D}_H$. Since the critical path changes after a move has taken place, another operation close to the source will be investigated in a next step. $\mathcal{C}_{nx}$ respects the temporal order of operations given by the technological constraints. Hence a thorough search can be expected, which rearranges operations with respect to the processing order of the jobs involved. In this way a hill climbing strategy using $\mathcal{N}_1$ works somewhat like the simple schedule generation techniques described in Sect. 2.2.1.

We conjecture that the results obtained from hill climbing depend on the characteristics (e.g. the problem size and the relation of n and m) of a JSP instance. We do not claim that general conclusions can be drawn from the results presented in the next section. However, comparisons with other benchmark problems carried out by sample come up with similar results.

---

[1] Recall, that $\mathcal{N}_2$ is part of $\mathcal{N}_4$ but does not appear solely in the following. Thus, only the neighborhood definitions $\mathcal{N}_1$, $\mathcal{N}_3$ and $\mathcal{N}_4$ are subject to the investigation.

3.2.3 Comparing Search Strategies

We pick three test problems from the benchmark suites described in Chap. 8. The mt10 is chosen as a small (10×10) but hard problem. The medium sized la27 (20×10) is also known to be hard to solve. The la35 (30×10) is considerably larger but quite easy to solve. For these problems hill climbers using all pairs resulting from the product of $\mathcal{N} \times \mathcal{C}$ are run $1\,000$ times each. We present the results obtained in Tab. 3.4, 3.5 and 3.6.

Table 3.4 shows the relative error calculated by $100(\text{mean} - \text{opt})/\text{opt}$ where 'mean' denotes the mean result obtained from $1\,000$ trials and 'opt' denotes the problem's optimum. In the first column the relative error of $1\,000$ randomly generated solutions is shown in parenthesis.

It can be clearly seen, that $\mathcal{N}_4$ dominates $\mathcal{N}_3$ which in turn dominates $\mathcal{N}_1$ for all strategies and all problems. $\mathcal{C}_{nx}$ is expected to perform best from the considerations on page 41. But for larger problems the benefit decreases and almost vanishes for the la35 problem. Additional experiments (not shown) with much larger problems (100×20) have resulted in a clear advantage of the $\mathcal{C}_{st}$ control compared to $\mathcal{C}_{nx}$ (26.3% to 33.89% relative error). $\mathcal{C}_{nx}$ seems to be superior only for small and/or quadratic ($n = m$) problems. Strategies which use $\mathcal{C}_{st}$ or $\mathcal{C}_{nx}$ control generally perform better than $\mathcal{C}_{rn}$. It is noticeable, that the quality of randomly generated solutions (given in parenthesis in the first column of Tab. 3.4) differ significantly for the three problems considered, and so do hill climbing results.

Table 3.5 shows the average number of moves performed in a single hill climb. Strategies which use $\mathcal{N}_1$ or $\mathcal{N}_3$ perform roughly the same number of moves, whereas the number of moves increases for the $\mathcal{N}_4$ neighborhood. For larger problems more moves are performed than for smaller ones. Hill climbing strategies using the $\mathcal{C}_{nx}$ control perform about twice the number of moves compared to $\mathcal{C}_{st}$ for all $\mathcal{N}$ considered. The $\mathcal{C}_{rn}$ control performs slightly more moves compared to the $\mathcal{C}_{st}$, but the latter produces better results as we have seen from Tab. 3.4. Recall from (3.2) that the estimated makespan is calculated at almost constant cost. In contradiction, a move requires two longest path calculations. Hence a large number of estimations in combination

problem	control	neighborhood		
		1	3	4
mt10	next	32.6	27.4	25.4
(84.2)	steepest	36.2	30.4	27.8
	random	36.3	31.0	28.5
la27	next	37.2	31.1	27.7
(95.7)	steepest	40.8	33.0	28.4
	random	40.9	34.3	31.2
la35	next	31.5	26.7	21.4
(74.2)	steepest	33.6	27.2	21.6
	random	33.5	28.6	24.4

Table 3.4. The average makespan found by different hill climb strategies is given in terms of the relative error.

problem	control	neighborhood		
		1	3	4
mt10	next	28.1	27.9	33.7
	steepest	16.2	15.1	16.9
	random	20.3	19.0	22.3
la27	next	55.9	59.1	79.1
	steepest	30.2	31.1	34.6
	random	36.5	36.9	45.5
la35	next	60.9	66.7	98.9
	steepest	34.2	34.1	40.5
	random	38.9	40.2	52.6

Table 3.5. The average number of moves performed until a local optimum is reached, shown for different hill climbing strategies.

with a small number of moves as used by C_{st} will outperform C_{nx} for larger problems.

The runtime performance of hill climbing is given in Tab. 3.6. The mean CPU time a single climb requires is shown in milliseconds. As expected, strategies using the N_1 neighborhood are faster than strategies using N_3 and (even more clearly) the N_4 neighborhood. While the runtime performance for strategies using N_1 or N_3 scale up moderately with the problem size, strategies using N_4 take about 0.4 sec. for a single run for the 30×10 sized problem. The C_{st} outperforms both other strategies for larger problems.

Note that control strategies using N_4 would not perform that worse for large quadratic problems. Recall that N_4 is defined as $N_2 \cup N_3$. Hence the dramatic increase of runtime for N_4 in Tab. 3.6 is due to N_2. This neighborhood definition searches within whole blocks, whereas strategies using N_3 searches at the "begin" and "end" of a block only. The fewer blocks a longest path contains, the more time will be spent for N_2 and vice versa. For example, a longest path of a quadratic 10×10 problem will consist of shorter blocks than a rectangular 20×5 problem. Additionally, the longest path itself will be shorter for quadratic problems compared with rectangular ones. Hence for large rectangular problems N_4 does not appear appropriate.

Summarizing, the advantage of the N_4 neighborhood is evident in terms of makespan improvements. Concerning the search control C_{st} and C_{nx} the results obtained are almost similar in terms of makespan. In terms of runtime

problem	control	neighborhood		
		1	3	4
mt10	next	9.7	16.3	31.8
	steepest	7.9	16.8	31.9
	random	9.9	21.4	38.9
la27	next	37.7	49.1	107.6
	steepest	24.7	46.2	108.1
	random	29.6	55.9	129.1
la35	next	65.3	85.1	428.1
	steepest	41.0	67.9	390.0
	random	49.6	78.8	423.5

Table 3.6. Average CPU time in milliseconds needed for a single run, shown for different hill climbing strategies.

performance C_{st} is clearly superior to C_{nx}. Hence the most effective strategy is to use $\mathcal{N}_4$ in connection with C_{st}. However, we should note the tradeoff between the results obtained and the runtime required. Whenever hill climbing is used in combination with an intricate control strategy of a heuristic guidance technique, we should examine whether the quality of solutions generated by $\mathcal{N}_3$ is sufficient in order to obtain an efficient algorithm.

3.3 Local Search Extensions

Local Search methods suffer from getting stuck in local optima. In this section Local Search techniques capable of escaping from local optima are described. Before we turn to Simulated Annealing, Tabu Search and Variable Depth Search, we first sketch Iterated Search as a most simple hill climbing extension.

3.3.1 Iterated Search

A simple approach of enhancing hill climbing is Iterated Search. As long as time is available start the best known hill climber from randomly generated solutions and store the best solution found so far. Neither the variance nor the best makespan of the solutions generated in the experiments of the last section are reported. Since the variance is quite high, some apparently good solutions were found during the 1 000 iterations. For the mt10 problem a makespan of 994 was found which is quite an impressive result even for more sophisticated heuristics. It was found by the C_{nx} control in combination with the $\mathcal{N}_4$ neighborhood. Recall from Tab. 3.6 that 1 000 runs just take about 30 seconds. Thus, if a problem is difficult to optimize by any method, iterated search is a serious alternative.

However, iterated search does not use information of former iterations in later trials. The usage of information of former trials in order to guide further search is subject of the techniques described in the following.

3.3.2 Simulated Annealing

Simulated Annealing was invented independently by Kirkpatrick et al. (1983) and by Černy (1985). The search process can be viewed in analogy to the cooling of a solid to its ground state. In physics a ground state is the state of the smallest energy level. The annealing process begins with a solid in a melted state and then gradually lowers its temperature.

In combinatorics the ground state is a (hopefully global) optimum. Starting from a random solution (melted state) non-improving moves are accepted with a relatively high probability which is gradually decreased over time. The cooling process is controlled by the temperature cooling parameter c.

Over the runtime of the algorithm c decreases continuously from the initial state 1 towards 0 in each iteration k. The lower c falls, the smaller the degree of deterioration allowed between $f(\mathcal{H})$ and $f(\mathcal{H}'), \mathcal{H}' \in \mathcal{N}(\mathcal{H})$ becomes. Typically the most improving move within a neighborhood is selected as the $\mathcal{H}'$ candidate. The solution $\mathcal{H}$ is replaced by a selected neighboring solution $\mathcal{H}'$ with the probability $\rho(k)$.

$$\rho(k) = \min \left\{ 1, \exp \left(\frac{-(f(\mathcal{H}') - f(\mathcal{H}))}{c_k} \right) \right\} \tag{3.3}$$

For improving moves the acceptance probability ρ is 1. For worsening moves, i.e. $f(\mathcal{H}) < f(\mathcal{H}')$, $\rho(k)$ determines if the move is accepted. Since c is lowered in each iteration k, the probability of accepting worsening moves is decreased exponentially over the runtime. The general idea of Simulated Annealing is to guide the search into promising areas of the search space in early stages while doing refinements in later stages.

At least two successful implementations for the JSP are reported in literature by Matsuo et al. (1988) and Van Laarhoven et al. (1992). The former uses a much more sophisticated neighborhood definition, whereas the latter uses a slower cooling procedure. Both publications present results of similar quality when comparable runtime is supposed.

A recent paper by Aarts et al. (1994) compares several Local Search techniques under the aspect of constant runtime. Simulated Annealing outperforms most other techniques, when time is of no concern. It took 2 to 15 hours runtime in order to solve the benchmarks listed in Tab. 8.10. However, 15 hours for problems with at most 300 operations seems a lot of time regardless of the implementation environment. These results are in accordance with Van Laarhoven et al. (1992).

This shortcoming might be due to the fact that Simulated Annealing uses no memory (apart from the current solution and the parameter c) about areas of the search space which have already been visited. Threshold Acceptance (a deterministic variant of Simulated Annealing) has been introduced by Dueck and Scheuer 1991. Aarts et al. (1994) present a JSP implementation of this technique, but obtain poorer results than the ones obtained by Simulated Annealing. The shortcoming described above for Simulated Annealing is at least also true for Threshold Acceptance.

3.3.3 Tabu Search

Tabu search was invented by Glover and Hansen independently in the eighties. An excellent survey is given in two parts by Glover (1989), Glover (1990) and in Glover and Laguna (1993). Similar to Simulated Annealing Tabu Search modifies one solution by means of a neighborhood definition $\mathcal{N}$. Typically the most improving move in $\mathcal{N}(\mathcal{H})$ is selected as the $\mathcal{H}'$ candidate. If no improving move is contained in $\mathcal{N}(\mathcal{H})$, the least worsening one is selected. Therefore Hansen called his technique: "Steepest descending, mildest ascending".

The link of modern heuristics to Artificial Intelligence is emphasized by Glover and Greenberg (1989). They state that the even most skilled 'expert knowledge' can sometimes make disastrous decisions in face of the combinatorial explosion. Therefore a framework is needed which guides the use of skill and knowledge in a flexible way. In this way Tabu Search guides the search process to explore new regions of the search space. Unlike Simulated Annealing, an explicit memory of recent moves is kept and evaluated later on for the choice of subsequent moves. Note that keeping moves in memory is not as restrictive as keeping a memory of solutions or parts there of. Not particular points of the search space, but subsets of the path into these points are kept in memory. Glover distinguishes between short- and long term memory.

Short term memory consists of the last k moves. Typically the short term memory is implemented as a list, called tabu list. Each time a move is performed, it is stored at the front end of the tabu list. At the same time the k'th entry of the list is discarded. If a selected move is part of the tabu list, this move is temporarily forbidden (or tabu in the notion of Tabu Search). This mechanism helps to prevent cycles in move sequences after a deterioration of the objective function value has taken place.

Long term memory consists of a data structure keeping track of all moves performed so far. Each time a move is carried out, an annotated counter is increased. The value of the move counter is the basis for a penalty function. The more a move has already be carried out in the past, the more this candidate is punished. In the long run this penalty avoids search of areas which already have been explored. Hence the search is directed into potentially unexplored regions of the search space.

Under certain circumstances the memory may prevent some substantial improvements because it currently forbids a potential good move. Therefore an aspiration criterion is introduced, which temporarily disables the memory function. A useful aspiration criterion is to allow a tabu move if an improvement beyond the best solution found so far can be achieved.

Tabu Search has been applied to a wide range of combinatorial problems. The technique seems to be generally well suited for highly constrained problems which allow a neighborhood definition. Various Tabu Search approaches for the JSP have been proposed. All implementations keep arcs inversions in a tabu list and use the makespan as a measure of improvement.

A basic implementation using an $\mathcal{N}_1$ like neighborhood definition is described by Taillard (1993a). Dell' Amico and Trubian (1993) extend his ideas leading to the neighborhood definition $\mathcal{N}_4$. Both approaches use makespan estimations for selecting the most improving neighboring move. Recently, Barnes and Chambers (1995) propose to calculate the exact makespan for an extremely small neighborhood definition. They obtain even better results compared with the former ones, which gives a hint on the possible misleading effect of makespan estimations for the algorithm's control structure.

A further approach of Hurink et al. (1994) concentrates on multi-purpose machine problems. The problems considered in this thesis can be seen as a specialized case there of. Hurink et al. use the $\mathcal{N}_2$ neighborhood (if only single-purpose machines are considered).

Apart from the neighborhood definition used, the approaches differ in the way of generating a good starting solution. Obviously, the properties of tabu search to exploit a portion of the search space are excellent. To the contrary, the properties to explore promising areas in a search space are limited since Local Search techniques generally tend to get trapped in a region around some local optimum. Therefore a good schedule generation technique (compare Sect. 2.2) is needed in order to set up a promising point in the search space from which Tabu Search can continue efficiently.

Another crucial aspect of Tabu Search is the maintenance of the tabu list. Advanced features like variable tabu list length or cycle detection mechanisms are needed in order to prevent cycling through a number of neighboring solutions. Barnes and Chambers (1995) simply discard the tabu list if no permissible move exists anymore in order to escape from local optima.

The currently best approach of Nowicki and Smutnicki (1995) uses the simple $\mathcal{N}_1$ neighborhood. Nowicki and Smutnicki gain even better results by controlling the Tabu Search with backtracking. In their approach a search tree is generated by adding a node (representing a solution) every time a new best solution is found. For each neighboring solution of such a node a limited Tabu Search is branched. The various search trajectories may generate further nodes themselves if they gain an improvement of the makespan. For some large and difficult benchmarks Nowicki and Smutnicki obtain the best known results although only short run times were needed.

Summing up, the various approaches can be classified by the neighborhood definition used and the way of maintaining the tabu list. Either a simple neighborhood definition and an intricate tabu list management is used or, the other way round, an intricate neighborhood definition is engaged by using a simple list management. Generally, the Tabu Search approaches described produce excellent results in a reasonable runtime.

3.3.4 Variable Depth Search

Variable Depth Search is due to Lin and Kernighan (1973) who applied this technique to the TSP. Variable Depth Search typically runs for a number of iterations starting from an initial solution. Each iteration performs a fixed number of neighborhood moves (worsening ones included). Thereby a move once carried out cannot be reversed by subsequent moves performed. Hence, different to Tabu Search, the list of forbidden moves grows dynamically within a Variable Depth Search iteration. At the end of an iteration the 'forbidden move' list is emptied and the best solution found is taken as the starting solution of the next iteration.

An implementation of a Variable Depth Search Procedure for the JSP is reported by Dorndorf and Pesch (1993). They incorporate a Variable Depth Search procedure in a Genetic Algorithm. Starting from a solution assembled by the Genetic Algorithm, the procedure performs Variable Depth search iterations. Each iteration carries out a number of irrevocable $\mathcal{N}_1$ moves. The procedure stops if no further improvements can be gained and returns the local optimal solution obtained to the Genetic Algorithm.

Recently, Balas and Vazacopoulos (1994) have proposed a Variable Depth Search Procedure for the JSP under the name Guided Local Search (GLS). Starting from an initial solution obtained by a priority rule based schedule generation technique, GLS performs a neighborhood search guided by a search tree. A node of the search tree corresponds to an originator solution for which sibling nodes are generated by means of neighboring moves. Again, a move carried out remains fixed for all of its siblings. The depth of this tree is restricted by a logarithmic function of the number of operations involved. The width of the search tree is limited to a small number of siblings which are ranked according to their makespan achieved.

The GLS is incorporated in the Shifting Bottleneck algorithm (compare Sect. 2.3.2) leading to the SB-GLS algorithm. Here, the partial schedule already built by the Bottleneck procedure is re-optimized by GLS. The reader is referred to the original article for several variants of SB-GLS and a detailed description of the neighborhood definition used. Currently a variant of this approach is the most effective one for solving the JSP. A comprehensive survey and up to date results of recent Local Search approaches are given in Vaessens et al. (1995).

4. Evolutionary Algorithms

One way of searching in a large space is to pick solutions at random. This is an aimless approach unless the samples picked are used to guide further search. This is the basic principle of Evolutionary Algorithms (EA) which are introduced in this chapter. EA's maintain a whole family of solutions in parallel. The various solutions of this family can be seen as samples of the search space. They compete and cooperate through a number of iterations in order to gain improvements.

4.1 The Evolutionary Metaphor

EAs mimic the process of evolution as it was stated by Darwin (1809–1882) in the late 19'th century. The analogy to natural phenomena is best carried out by way of metaphor. Therefore we introduce the basic concept of EA's in terms of evolutionary genetics, see Smith (1989).

> "Due to Darwin, individuals with characteristics most favorable for survival and reproduction will not only have more offspring, but they will also pass their characteristics on to those offspring. This phenomenon is known as natural selection."

An individual's characteristics may be advantageously compared to the characteristics of other individuals of the species. These advantages are a relative measure called fitness. The fitness of an individual depends on how its characteristics match the environmental requirements. Since we assume the same global environment for all individuals, the species slowly evolves towards individuals of higher fitness by means of natural selection. In this way selection predicts the adaptation of individuals to their environment. The individual's fitness is determined by its acquired characteristics, called its phenotype. The phenotype itself is determined by the individual's genetic prerequisites, called its genotype. Only genotypical information is inherited to offspring. Hence we understand an evolutionary process of a species as a continuous change of genetic material over time. Since EA's are inspired by nature, the lingo used in the following is taken from biology.

4.1.1 Evolutionary Strategies

Some of the EA pioneers were Rechenberg (1973) and Schwefel (1975). They introduced Evolutionary Strategies (ES) for continuous optimization problems in engineering. A survey on ES is given in Bäck et al. (1991) and in Hoffmeister and Bäck (1990).

The goal is to optimize a function in a vector of continuous variables towards some criterion, e.g. the function's maximum. A solution to a problem is a vector of values within prescribed domain bounds. Such a solution is called individual. The objective function plays the role of the environment. Thus we can measure an individual's fitness by its objective value.

A population consists of a finite number of individuals. In the beginning the population is initialized with arbitrary arguments. The algorithm runs for a certain number of iterations which are called generations in the context of EA's. In each generation a number of offspring is generated by means of some mutation operator which alters the solutions of the individuals slightly. Next the fitness is obtained for the newly generated individuals. Now the population of the next generation is obtained by means of some selection operator. It selects preferably individuals with above average fitness to form the new population. Given the number of parents μ and the number of offspring λ with $\lambda \geq \mu$, we distinguish the (μ, λ) and the $(\mu + \lambda)$ strategy. The population size is fixed to μ over the number of generations. In the (μ, λ) strategy the new population is formed by the μ best offspring only, whereas in the $(\mu + \lambda)$ strategy the next population is selected from the parents and the offspring. The former strategy forces a further exploration of the search space whereas the latter strategy tends to preserve the solutions found so far.

We call an adaptation process due to mutation asexual reproduction, because no information interchange between individuals occurs. In the beginning strong mutations are needed in order to explore larger regions of the search space. From generation to generation the mutation step size is decreased in order to do refinements in later stages. Schwefel made the mutation step size itself to an object of evolution. ES require a mutation operator which respects the domain bounds of the real valued argument. The mutation operator must be "sizable" such that the degree of change can be continuously decreased over the generations. Such a mutation operator can be defined easily for continuous problems, but it can hardly be modified to fit the needs of combinatorics sufficiently well. Herdy (1990) presents an ES approach for the Traveling Salesman Problem (TSP), although his approach lacks generality in order to be applied to other combinatorial problems.

Evolutionary progress of a population is due to the progress of single individuals. The mutation step can be seen as taking samples from the search space while the selection step directs the search towards the most promising samples taken so far. Provided that an individual survives, it is subject to continuously refined mutations under increasing selection pressure within the population.

4.1.2 Genetic Algorithms

Genetic Algorithms (GA) were developed by Holland (1975) and his associates in the late sixties. A comprehensive introduction to GAs and their properties is given in Reeves (1993), the standard GA textbook was written by Goldberg (1989). Here again, continuous problems are the subject of optimization. Holland referred back to the basic research of Mendel (1822–1884) on genetic inheritance. Therefore he distinguishes between the genotype and the phenotype of an individual. GAs model sexual reproduction by forming offspring from genotypical information of two parental individuals.

In Hollands approach a system of continuous variables of a function to be optimized is coded in a binary vector, called a chromosome. A chromosome consists of a finite number of genes which can be thought of as values from the alphabet $\{0,1\}$. In the GA lingo we call positions within this vector loci and the possible values alleles. For fitness evaluation the chromosome is transformed into an argument of the function to be optimized, namely its phenotype. Then, the fitness is determined by means of the objective function.

New chromosomes are generated syntactically by so called genetic operators which do not use problem specific information. The backbone of genetic search is the crossover operator. It combines the genotypes of two parents in the hopes to produce an even more promising offspring. The logic of the crossover operator assumes that a successful solution can be assembled from highly adapted pieces of different chromosomes. About one half of the genotypical information of two mating individuals are recombined to form an offspring. In GAs the mutation operator plays a background role. A gene once lost by accident from the population will never appear again. Thus mutation slightly changes chromosomes in order to reintroduce lost genes. Again, mutation works without problem specific knowledge flipping a small number of alleles randomly.

```
algorithm GA is
        t := 0
        initialize P(t)
        evaluate individuals in P(t)
        while not terminate do
                t = t + 1
                select P(t) from P(t − 1)
                recombine individuals in P(t)
                evaluate individuals in P(t)
        end while
end algorithm
```

Fig. 4.1. Holland's reproductive plan.

Figure 4.1 gives a brief GA outline adopted from Holland (1975). Before we start the algorithm, a suitable problem coding has to be found such that solutions of the entire search space can be represented in a chromosome. In a first step we set the generation counter t to zero. Then the initial population $P(0)$ is filled with chromosomes, which consists of uniformly distributed binary values. We evaluate the fitness of all chromosomes in $P(0)$. The evaluation procedure decodes a chromosome into its phenotype and determines its fitness by means of the objective function value. Now we start a loop for a potentially infinite number of generations until some termination criterion is met. A simple termination criterion is a fixed number of generations. In each generation the counter t is incremented. A new population $P(t)$ is selected from $P(t-1)$ by some selection operator. Typically proportional selection, also called roulette wheel selection is used. The chance to place individuals in the new population in generation t is proportional to $f_i/\overline{f}_t$ where f_i is the fitness of the i'th individual and $\overline{f}_t$ is the average fitness in $P(t)$. Several other selection strategies are discussed in Goldberg (1989). The individuals in $P(t)$ are recombined by crossover and mutation. Finally the individuals in $P(t)$ are evaluated in order to obtain fitness values for the selection in the next generation.

4.1.3 Why Does Adaptation Work?

So far we have got a rough picture of how GAs work, but not much has been said about "why" they work. An introduction to this topic is given in Liepins and Hilliard (1989) and a more complete coverage is given in Goldberg (1989). In fact, this topic is more difficult to explain as it may appear at a first glance. We now neglect the progress of single individuals. In turn we view the evolution of the species, i.e. the frequency of certain gene combinations within the whole population. The gene variety of a population is often referred to as gene pool. The foundation of GA theory was laid by Holland (1975) introducing the schema theorem. A schema can be seen as a sample which matches a number of chromosomes by neglecting some allele values. Therefore the allele alphabet is extended by an asterisk as a "don't care" symbol.

```
chromosome  :  0  1  1  0  1  0
schema      :  *  1  *  0  *  *
```

An example of a schema is given above for a chromosome with six loci. The schema samples all chromosomes having a 1 at the second and a 0 at the fourth locus. Holland argued, that some schemata have a higher fitness contribution than other schemata. Chromosomes which include successful schemata result in highly fit offspring and therefore these schemata are inherited with a high probability. Since all schemata existing in a chromosome are tested in a single evaluation step, Holland calls the GA's schema processing feature intrinsic parallelism.

Schemata are disrupted by the crossover operator. The schema shown in the example above may be disrupted by a crossover operation cutting the chromosome at its third position. Schemata are classified by their order and their defining length. In the example we have a schema of order two (two alleles are specified) and a defining length of three (the distance between the first and last allele specified is three). It is unlikely that schemata of low order and small defining length are disrupted by a crossover operation. Hence the frequency of schemata of low order and small defining length, which show a fitness contribution of above average, increases drastically over time. These schemata called building blocks are regarded to be responsible for the GA's success. Building blocks may be combined with other successful schemata during the evolutionary adaptation process.

Over the GA's runtime the frequency of successful schemata in a population's gene pool is increased while inferior ones are discarded. Thus, the number of different schemata existing in a gene pool decreases continually throughout the environmental adaptation process. Although mutation introduces a small amount of genes, the population converges because of increasing selection pressure. In the context of GAs convergence denotes a declining gene diversity of a population resulting in very similar individuals.

The genetic operators should be chosen in a way that exploration of new solutions and exploitation of solutions found so far are well balanced. A GA tending to exploitation may converge to a relatively poor local optimum. This phenomenon is called premature convergence. In opposite, an excessive exploration prevents convergence by notoriously producing mediocre solutions. The crossover operator is of particular interest in this context. It should preserve building blocks and disrupt other schemata in order to test newly assembled chromosomes.

	one-point					two-point					uniform				
parent 1:	0	0	0	0	0	0	0	0	0	0	0	0	0	0	0
parent 2:	1	1	1	1	1	1	1	1	1	1	1	1	1	1	1
offspring:	0	0	0	1	1	0	1	1	0	0	1	0	1	0	1

Fig. 4.2. Three different crossover operators and their outcome are shown. The parts underlined in the mating chromosomes form the resulting offspring.

Holland suggested the one-point crossover operator in order to preserve as many building blocks as possible. The one-point crossover can be explained best by looking at a chromosome as a string. An offspring is assembled from nearly the half of the two parental strings split at one point randomly. Building blocks located at the begin or end of a chromosome are preserved at the expense of disrupting building blocks with a high probability which are located in the inner part of a chromosome.

A remedy has been proposed by introducing the two-point crossover, compare Fig. 4.2. Instead of viewing a chromosome as a string, it is looked at as a ring. A segment of one parent replaces a segment of the same size in the other parent. Now, all schemata are disrupted with the same probability. However, it has been pointed out by Syswerda (1989) that crossover operators using more than two crossing points are superior in some applications. Syswerda proposed the uniform crossover which uses a randomly picked number of cross points of the set $\{0, 1, \ldots, n - 1\}$ for chromosomes of length n. Since uniform crossover disrupts building blocks arbitrarily, the schema theorem cannot explain the success achieved by uniform crossover.

4.2 Adaptation in Epistatic Domains

The basic idea of GAs has been applied to combinatorial optimization during the eighties. Since most combinatorial problems cannot be coded naturally by strings of independent binary genes, a variety of non-standard codings were introduced. In the following we outline the differences between independent codings — which we have exclusively considered so far — and epistatic effects in non-standard codings: Changes of gene frequency at certain loci of the gene pool do not occur independently from changes at other loci. A host of combinatorial problems, e.g. the JSP, are epistatic as noted by Davis (1985a), Davis (1985b). Epistasis is well-known in biology, Smith (1989) mentions two impacts of epistasis in evolutionary genetics.

1. If two loci are linked, changes in frequency at one locus may cause changes at the other.
2. The fitness contribution of a gene at one locus may depend on what alleles are present at other loci.

From both statements obstacles arise concerning the genetic representation of a combinatorial problem. In case of linked loci, the crossover operator must change the allele of one locus with respect to changes of alleles at linked loci. Otherwise, invalid offspring (i.e. infeasible solutions) may be produced. Furthermore, a large number of linked loci leads to de-correlated fitness contribution of building blocks. Thus, the fitness contributions of schemata become less predictable when inherited to offspring. Both effects are discussed in the following with examples of two well-known combinatorial problems.

4.2.1 Crossover Procedures

Since we do not find a natural binary representation for most combinatorial problems, we encode a solution into a genotype of higher cardinality. Typically the cardinality of the allele alphabet corresponds to the length of the chromosomes such that each allele value occurs exactly once. We describe design principles of codings and operators for two combinatorial problems.

The Traveling Salesman Problem (TSP). The symmetrical TSP is the most frequently cited example for the application of GAs to combinatorial problems. A salesman has to visit each of a number of cities exactly once. He is interested in an overall tour of minimal length. Hence the objective can be mathematically formulated: Find a minimal Hamiltonian cycle among all involved cities. Consider a problem with four cities A, B, C, D which already define the allele alphabet for the chromosomal coding. Since each city has to be visited once, the coding uses a chromosome of length four. Any feasible chromosome is a permutation of the set $\{A, B, C, D\}$. The decoding procedure interprets alleles of two adjacent loci as an edge of the Hamiltonian cycle. E.g. the chromosome '$ACDB$' is interpreted as $(A, C), (C, D), (D, B), (B, A)$ in the decoding step. The tour length is calculated by summing up the distances between cities which are edge-weights in the corresponding undirected graph. The achieved tour length determines the fitness of an individual.

For the coding proposed above a standard crossover risks to assemble infeasible offspring. Consider two parents $p_1 = $ '$CADB$' and $p_2 = $ '$ABCD$'. Now form an offspring from the first two loci of p_1 and from the last two loci of p_2. This one-point crossover results in the infeasible tour '$CACD$' visiting city C twice while avoiding city B. Several non-standard crossover operators have been developed for the TSP in the last decade. It is obvious that not the absolute order (or position) of cities but the relative order of cities within a permutation is of importance for phenotypical characteristics. For example, the chromosomes '$ABCD$' and '$BCDA$' are equivalent in terms of their relative ordering since both represent the same edges.

One of the first attempts to preserve the order of two parental substrings in the offspring was given by Goldberg and Lingle (1985). They suggested that in case of non-standard codings a non-standard crossover operator is desired in order to preserve building blocks. Their approach resulted in the partially mapped crossover (PMX). Another approach named order crossover (OX) is due to Davis. Although both operators work similar, PMX tends to respect the absolute order of cities whereas OX tends to respect the relative order of cities. It was shown by Oliver et al. (1987) that OX works superior to PMX for the TSP.

parent 1	:	C	A	D	B
parent 2	:	A	B	C	D
offspring	:	A	C	D	B

Fig. 4.3. Order crossover (OX) applied to a four city TSP.

In Fig. 4.3, we choose a substring in parent 1. Then, we delete the elements in parent 2 which occur in the chosen substring. Finally, we combine the remaining part of parent 2 with the substring of parent 1. Up to now several more sophisticated crossover operators have been developed. The currently best one has been suggested by Whitley et al. (1989) under the name edge recombination operator (EX). Again, the ordering is emphasized: What is important is not that a particular city occurs in a particular position, but rather that the genetic operators preserve and exploit critical links that contribute to the minimization of the overall tour. In accordance with other researchers Whitley reports that for pure ordering problems two-point crossover can preserve characteristics much better than uniform crossover.

The Quadratic Assignment Problem (QAP). Let us consider a QAP example stated by Elshafei (1977). A fixed number of sites (locations) in a hospital are provided where magazines (units) have to be placed. Furthermore flows of medicaments occur in different intensities between the magazines. The goal is to assign the magazines to sites in such a way that the sum of 'flow intensity × distance' is minimized for all magazines involved. Mathematically, the QAP can be stated as follows.

$$\min_{\pi \in P(n)} \sum_{i=1}^{n} \sum_{j=1}^{n} a_{ij} b_{\pi_i \pi_j} \tag{4.1}$$

Generally speaking, a number of n units has to be assigned to n locations. Here $A = (a_{ij})$ denotes a quadratic matrix of flow intensity from unit i to unit j and $B = (b_{rs})$ denotes the distance matrix between two locations r and s. A solution to the QAP can be uniquely expressed by a permutation $\pi \in P(n)$ of size n. Notice that the distance indices r and s are obtained from the permutation by π_i and π_j. A coverage of interesting properties of the QAP and a comparison of standard heuristics is given in Taillard (1994).

We have seen that a permutation of size n utilizes a natural coding for the QAP. The size of the allele alphabet must be equal to n, representing the units which are assigned to locations. Each allele value must occur exactly at one locus. Note that for the TSP an identical coding has been proposed. But the local interactions of genes appear radically different for the QAP. For assignment problems the position of genes is of particular importance whereas the relative ordering is meaningless for phenotypical characteristics. Again we need a non-standard crossover operator in order to guarantee valid offspring. For the QAP an operator is needed which preserves the absolute ordering of genes. A uniform crossover is suggested by Fleurent and Ferland (1994).

1. If an allele is assigned to the same locus in both parents, it remains at the same locus in the offspring.
2. Unassigned loci are scanned from left to right. At each locus we pick an allele at random from one of the parents corresponding loci.
3. The remaining alleles are assigned randomly to so far unassigned loci.

parent 1	:	A	B	C	D
parent 2	:	C	B	D	A
offspring	:	A	B	D	C

Fig. 4.4. Example of a uniform crossover for a QAP consisting of four loci.

In Fig. 4.4, we place B at the second locus since it occurs at this position in both parents. Next, we traverse the chromosome from left to right. For each unassigned locus we choose a parental allele at random. In the example A is taken from parent 1 and D is taken from parent 2. At the last locus both parental alleles A and D have already been placed in the offspring. Therefore we place the remaining allele C at the last locus in a third step. Notice that it does not occur at the fourth locus in one of the parents. This phenomenon is called implicit mutation because new genetic information is introduced.

Implications. We have used the same coding structure for two different combinatorial problems. Chromosomes are decoded in a way that building blocks appear different in the TSP and the QAP context. Therefore we have introduced two crossover operators which preserve building blocks appropriate to the underlying problem. However, both crossover techniques work syntactically correct in the context of both problems. But as noted by Kargupta et al. (1992), the success of a genetic algorithm depends on how well the crossover operator respects the semantic properties of the underlying problem coding.

Kargupta et al. construct two artificial problems, one for which the absolute order is of importance and another for which the relative ordering of genes is particularly important. For both problems they use PMX which tends to preserve the absolute ordering in comparison to a relative ordering crossover similar to OX. They show, that a GA only works satisfactorily if the appropriate crossover is used. Their work gives an additional hint on the relevance of schema disruption within genetic reproduction.

We can state that it is not sufficient to produce just feasible chromosomes by some crossover technique. A single gene does not represent meaningful phenotypical characteristics in epistatic problems. Meaningful characteristics are encoded within blocks of dependent genes. Since we intend to inherit these building blocks we have to preserve them while crossover is active.

In order to avoid the production of invalid offspring three remedies next to non-standard operators are reported in literature.

- Penalize the fitness value of infeasible genotypes. The penalized genotypes will then be discarded from the population by means of selection with a high probability.
- Repair infeasible genotypes in the decoding step. Infeasible genotypes are transformed into similar feasible ones. The repair procedure guesses the crossover intention and repairs the chromosome adequately.
- Do not use genotypes at all. Genetic operators work directly on the phenotypical representation of the problem. Crossover ensures offspring feasibility by having direct access to the problem data.

A fitness penalty seems adequate if only a few infeasible solutions are generated within each generation. But for the class of combinatorial order problems, including the TSP and the QAP, most offspring resulting from standard crossover are invalid. Repairing chromosomes in the decoding step is a serious alternative to fitness penalties. A feasible offspring obtained from a repair procedure does not necessarily resemble the offspring actually intended by crossover. We hardly can repair infeasible solutions adequately in later steps, because the crosspoints are no longer visible in the decoding step.

The third remedy, phenotypical crossover, appears highly problem dependent and lacks comparability with other crossover approaches. Thus, the design of new non-standard crossover techniques is the most frequently used approach in applying genetic algorithms to combinatorial problems.

4.2.2 Fitness Contribution

We conjecture that the accumulation of building blocks in the gene pool of a population is responsible for the increasing fitness of individuals over the generations. In order to accumulate building blocks in the gene pool, a combination of these blocks in the chromosomes must be provided. Thus, we identify an individual's ability to combine building blocks adequately as a hallmark of successful adaptation.

The ability of combining building blocks highly depends on the degree of epistasis in the underlying coding structure. For independent codings (i.e. non-epistatic codings) arbitrary building blocks can be combined with one another. Here, the individual's fitness is determined by the overall fitness contributions of the various schemata represented in the chromosome. But in codings with a high degree of epistasis, the combination of two promising building blocks may, in extreme cases, result in a disastrous fitness contribution of the newly assembled individual.

What we can expect from artificial adaptation depends on the optimization problem under consideration. In order to give a qualitative impression of epistasis, we outline its effects by examples of the TSP and the QAP.

The Traveling Salesman Problem. Let us consider an allele representing a city at a certain locus of a permutation chromosome. We can figure out the degree of epistasis by examining the smallest number of genes involved in a meaningful fitness contribution. As stated earlier in this chapter, two adjacent genes determine an edge connecting two cities. The fitness contribution of two adjacent cities is calculated by the distance between both cities. Thus, a fitness contribution of a single city depends on the left and right cities in the chromosome. Both distances are taken into account with $1/2$ of their length, because edges are not directed in the symmetric TSP.

The fact that crossover may introduce new edges at the crosspoints, even if the relative ordering of cities is preserved almost entirely, makes the TSP hard to solve for a GA. But the introduction of these implicit mutations cannot be avoided in all cases. Hence, even a small degree of epistasis may lead to a large deviation of the tour length.

The Quadratic Assignment Problem. Let us consider a single gene representing a unit at a certain location of the QAP. Here, the degree of epistasis depends on the density of the flow matrix. Let us assume an extremely dense flow matrix such that flows occur from each unit to all other units. In this case each gene is linked to all other genes of the chromosome. In case of such a large degree of epistasis the QAP is also known to be very hard to solve for any kind of heuristic search.

Implications. Generally, a high degree of epistasis will result in a small number of outstanding building blocks. In other words, most schemata are indifferent concerning their fitness contribution. Selection pressure cannot increase the average fitness beyond some mediocre optimization quality. New genetic information is continually introduced by implicit mutations. The search process continues tediously combining different schemata without making further progress. The adaptation process has lost its direction of search.

Even if we assume a few outstanding building blocks for a problem, the GA will hardly maintain these schemata against the huge number of mediocre ones which are continuously sampled. Therefore selection pressure cannot increase. The GA is prevented from discovering promising schemata and driving out less promising ones from the gene pool. Only at the beginning of the adaptation process some obviously unfavorable schemata are discarded from the gene pool. However, after this stage, further progress is limited.

Various attempts have been made to overcome the obstacle of epistatic effects on fitness contribution.

- A severe selection scheme may reintroduce a direction of search. Therefore Baker (1985) suggests a ranking of the fitness values of a population. In this strategy the population is sorted according to the fitness values. Individuals are given a selection rate which is solely a function of their rank. Rank-based selection was also used by Whitley (1989). Generally speaking, ranking disassociates the fitness from the underlying objective value. This removes the need to determine the relative quality of individuals, as noted by Angeline and Pollack (1993) in a related context. Since we cannot rely on fitness proportions in epistatic domains, we confine individuals to the criterion of being better than others in order to be selected into the new population.
- The selection pressure can be artificially increased by rejecting unfavorable new individuals, compare Mühlenbein (1990). An offspring replaces its parent only if some prescribed acceptance criterion is met. Mühlenbein proposed a two stage selection for a parallel genetic algorithm where mate selection is restricted to relatively small demes. First, offspring replace their parents only in case of acceptance. Next, mates are chosen based on rank selection. The advantage of acceptance is twofold: Fitter individuals are preserved by the acceptance stage. Since unfavorable individuals are rejected, the selection pressure in the mate selection stage is increased.

- A so called culling scheme is used to remove unfavorable offspring from the next population, see Vaessens et al. (1992), Fleurent and Ferland (1994). Using Mühlenbein's acceptance, offspring are rejected by a direct comparison with their parents. In traditional GAs only an indirect relation between parents and their offspring exists. Therefore the average fitness of the population is used for the rejection of the least fit offspring. Given a fixed population size μ, in each generation $\mu + \lambda$ offspring are produced. The culling procedure removes the λ least fit offspring from the next population. Again, for the remaining fit individuals the selection pressure is artificially increased.
- The elitist strategy assures that the most fit individual(s) of the current population and the newly generated offspring are placed in the next population. Elitism was introduced by De Jong (1975) in order to obtain fast convergence. If a highly fit individual is continually involved in the mating process, the population moves towards this individual and is therefore forced to converge. The drawback of elitist models is obvious: Assume a good local optimum which is discovered by an elitist individual. Furthermore consider the global optimum in the search space "far away" from the local one discovered so far. Now the whole population will converge towards this local optimum which drastically decreases the chance to discover the global optimum. However, the elitist model introduces a direction of search whenever epistatic effects disorients genetic search.

Of course, what has been said about the elitist model is true for rank selection, acceptance and culling. Actually these mechanisms exclude large areas of the search space from being visited. Therefore these attempts were heavily criticized by GA theorists. However in practice, the GA is helped to maintain above average fit schemata against the majority of mediocre ones. A negative side-effect of these mechanisms is that schemata are discarded from the gene pool without having been tested sufficiently. The degree of epistasis is virtually reduced if individuals resemble each other because schemata are processed in a similar way only. Consider two linked loci such that the fitness contribution of the one locus depends on what allele is present at the other locus. Furthermore consider that the one locus carries the same allele in the entire gene pool. In this situation the epistatic effect concerning these two loci is eliminated and the search may proceed within the resulting subspace.

4.3 Genetic Hybrids

We have seen that non-standard codings require more sophisticated genetic operators than purely syntactical ones, which are used in traditional GAs. Whenever there is additional domain knowledge available, we may give up the "syntactical" view and turn to semantic genetic operators instead. The incorporation of problem specific heuristic knowledge into genetic operators is called hybridization. In the following we describe a model of plausibility for genetic hybrids taken from biology. Then we take a look on how heuristic knowledge can be incorporated into evolutionary search. Finally we discuss the incorporation of Local Search into an evolutionary framework.

4.3.1 Evolution versus Learning

Again, we stress evolutionary genetics in order to obtain an appropriate model of plausibility for genetic hybrids. The French biologist Lamarck (1744-1829) regarded individual learning to be responsible for the adaptation of a species to a given environment. During its lifetime an individual adapts to its environment by learning. Lamarck conjectured that these acquired characteristics are passed on to offspring. Later in the 19'th century Darwin rejected Lamarck's views and identified genotypical information to be responsible for the adaptation of species. In 1896 Baldwin (1861–1934) partially approved Lamarck's view by proposing that learning increases the individual fitness and therefore increases the probability to generate offspring, see Whitley et al. (1994).

Nowadays a societies culture is regarded to act as an intermediate system in order to transfer individual learning into the evolution of a population, see Smith (1987), Belew (1989). Although only genotypical information is biologically inherited, we emphasize that learned information is transmitted between generations.

Since a species could adapt to its environment much faster by passing on learned information to offspring than by a pure genotypical hereditary mechanism, we may ask why this phenomenon can hardly be found in nature? Smith (1989) gives a reasonable answer by distinguishing phenotypical changes of adaptive and non-adaptive origin. In nature, most phenotypical changes to an individual are non-adaptive resulting from injury, disease and old age; and hence worthless in order to be inherited. Since adaptive changes of a phenotype cannot be separated from non-adaptive ones, a transmittance of phenotypical changes to offspring would be unfavorable in most cases.

In the context of artificial adaptation learning is considered as a metaphor for individual improvement techniques (e.g. hill climbing). Here, we are able to control the phenotypical changes of individuals. Hence we may permit an individual to learn, but prevent the individual from inheriting unfavorable phenotypical changes.

Lamarckism is described by Schull (1990) as the adaptation by phenotypes whereas Darwinian evolution is regarded as the adaptation by the gene pool. Consequently Schull understands adaptation in the sense of Lamarck as a simple by-product of the achievements gained by individual learning. Herewith Schull formulates an extreme viewpoint in paying predominant attention to the individual hill climbing abilities. But we cannot rigidly neglect the effects of evolution, because the gene pool still provides the frame for individual learning. Hence we understand genetic hybridization as a continuous repetition of a two-stage learning process.

1. Genetic adaptation guides the search by maintaining the gene pool from which promising individuals are assembled. Genetic adaptation exploits favorable characteristics and therefore introduces a rough direction of search.
2. Individual learning produces fit individuals on the basis of the current gene pool. The individuals greedily explore promising points in the search space and return the characteristics acquired into the gene pool.

4.3.2 Hybridization Approaches

The first attempt to incorporate heuristic knowledge into a non-standard crossover was done by Grefenstette et al. (1985) for the TSP. In this approach the crossover operator plays an active role in the optimization process itself. The offspring is assembled by iteratively choosing those cities from both parents which increase the overall tour length by the least amount. This crossover operator requires access to the distance matrix of all cities involved. As noted by Suh and Van Gucht (1987), the operator attempts to glue together good (i.e. short) sub-paths of the parental tours. Crossover acts globally on the chromosome which is assembled by successively estimating the costs of the next city to be visited.

Suh and Van Gucht propose Local Search inside a TSP crossover. They apply the algorithm of Lin and Kernighan (1973) in order to fix a local optimum after the offspring is assembled in the mating step. A related approach is proposed by Mühlenbein (1991) who places the Lin and Kernighan algorithm in the decoding step of the fitness evaluation. The intention of using Local Search is to reduce the search space to the subset of local optimal solutions.

Provided that the decoding procedure does not alter the genotypical information, we obtain an identical offspring regardless whether the Local Search procedure is applied in the crossover or in the decoding procedure. Thus, the notion of heuristic crossover might be misleading if a Local Search procedure is placed inside the crossover, but does not actually control the assembly process on parental genes. For clarity, we distinguish heuristic re-optimization from heuristic crossover procedures. Both types of knowledge incorporation are discussed separately in the following.

Crossover: Heuristic knowledge is used to assemble highly fit offspring from parental solutions. The idea is to combine promising characteristics of both parents in an appropriate manner. The inherited genes are chosen by a problem specific heuristic. Typically, decision steps adopted from solution generation techniques (as described in Sect. 2.2 for the JSP) are used to assemble offspring. Futilely unfavorable offspring are avoided at the expense of excluding large areas of the search space from the search process. Local Search techniques (as described in Sect. 3.2) are less suitable, because they require an already assembled solution.

Evaluation: We can either use a solution generation technique in the decoding procedure or a Local Search technique which is applied after the decoding step is completed. The idea of the latter approach is to re-optimize individuals which are previously assembled by a syntactical crossover operation. Since the individual is modified by the re-optimizing heuristic, we typically write the transformed phenotype back to its genotype. This action of "writing back" is called updating or forcing, see e.g. Nakano and Yamada (1991). Heuristic decoding can be seen as a filter which discards or reinforces characteristics assembled by the crossover procedure. At the extreme we may view the adaptation of the gene pool solely as a result of the heuristic re-optimization procedure used.

It is noted by Davis (1991), that traditional GAs are never the best algorithms to use for any problem. By combining a GA with a problem specific heuristic we always expect better results compared to running the problem specific heuristic alone. For epistatic codings of combinatorial problems the benefit of using heuristic knowledge is twofold. First, the crossover procedure is helped to recombine individually successful parts of parental solutions into an offspring of similar or even better fitness. Second, the selection procedure is helped to prevail successful schemata against mediocre ones because building blocks are now evolved and expressed by both, artificial adaptation and heuristic knowledge.

4.3.3 Incorporating Local Search

In order to incorporate Local Search into a genetic algorithm we need a suitable problem coding, a decoding procedure as described in Sect. 4.2 and an efficient hill climbing procedure, compare Sect. 3.2. Additionally, an update procedure is required which transforms the re-optimized phenotype back into the genotype. Finally a fitness function is needed.

```
genotype g
function evaluate(g) is
    phenotype p

    p := decode(g)
    p := hillclimb(p)
    g := update(p)
    return fitness(p)
end function
```

Fig. 4.5. Evaluation function of a hybrid GA.

An illustration of a hybridized evaluation function is given in Fig. 4.5. First, the genotype g is decoded into the phenotype p. Next, a hill climbing procedure is applied to p. Then g is updated by the re-optimized p. Finally, p's fitness is returned.

Obviously, the schema theorem stated by Holland does not hold for genetic hybrids. Heuristic knowledge immediately discards several schemata from the gene pool. For other schemata a proliferation due to heuristic knowledge occurs. In both cases the schemata affected have not been tested sufficiently by the genetic adaptation process. Therefore Whitley (1993) raises the interesting issue of viewing genetic hybrids more as hill climbing and less as schema processing algorithms. This question is of particular importance when interactions between the evolution and individual hill climbing are considered.

The advantages of Local Search components inside an evolutionary framework are obvious. The search space is restricted to (learned) local optima. Characteristics of local optima are directly inherited to offspring. Whether a hybrid GA benefits from hill climbing highly depends on the problem under consideration. If near-optimal solutions tend to populate certain small areas of the search space, the hill climbing procedure can accelerate the proliferation of favorable solution characteristics in the population considerably.

Otherwise, individuals will hardly benefit from Local Search runs in previous generations. If cooperative effects based on gene exchanges are almost absent, evolution is restricted to a competition between individuals. In this sense we understand crossover to perturb parental genetic information regardless of building blocks. The hill climber explores new points in the search space on the basis of the perturbed chromosomes. Consequently, we may replace sexual reproduction by asexual reproduction due to mutation. A severe selection scheme can assure the survival of the best solution found so far.

This kind of adaptation process can be seen as a combinatorial counterpart to ES. A further simplification to the ES-like procedure described above has been made by Mühlenbein (1992) introducing the $(1+1, m, hc)$ algorithm. Following Schwefel's $\mu + \lambda$ notation, $1 + 1$ expresses that one parent produces one offspring in each generation. The probability of altering each bit of the binary chromosome by means of mutation is given by m. Finally hc denotes the hill climbing procedure used. A similar algorithm is proposed under the name random mutation hill climb (RMHC) by Mitchell and Holland (1994). Both algorithms iteratively alter a solution by means of mutation. Then a hill climber is applied to the mutated solution. If the objective value can be improved, the parent solution is replaced by its offspring. In fact, such algorithms show more similarities with Local Search techniques than with conventional EAs.

When thinking about genetic adaptation for the JSP light must be shed on two essential issues. First, do we find a genetic representation which configures the solution space in a way that the resulting search space is relatively easy to be searched? Second, do we find genetic operators for such a representation that inherit building blocks adequately to offspring? The following consideration for the JSP are based on the general discussions of this chapter.

5. Perspectives on Adaptive Scheduling

The interactions between the different components of a genetic adaptation process are difficult to understand and eventually even more difficult to control. Therefore we offer an outlook on the perspectives of evolutionary scheduling. In the first section different ways of configuring the solution space of a scheduling problem are discussed. Afterwards, the properties of a genetic representation, which configures the solution space in a promising way, are investigated. This investigation is inspired by the wish to understand the most important impacts of evolutionary scheduling.

5.1 Configuring the Solution Space

We now describe some general ideas of recently proposed search spaces for scheduling problems. Hereby we pay particular attention to their representation, to appropriate genetic operators and to the incorporation of problem specific knowledge. Finally we discuss the different search spaces and end up with a representation which is used from there on.

In literature we find numerous applications of evolutionary algorithms in production scheduling. Nissen (1994) lists 18 GA references on JSP related problems. The various approaches are not directly comparable because they cover problems including different constraints and objectives. Moreover, reports on computational results are rather scarce. Thus, a detailed comparison of all of these implementations cannot be covered in this thesis. Instead we classify the various approaches by their search spaces as proposed by Storer et al. (1992a). According to Storer et al. a deterministic heuristic h is a mapping of the problem instance p to a solution s. Therefore the couple (h, p) can be seen as an encoding of a solution $s = h(p)$. The common procedure of heuristic search is to modify a solution s iteratively. In contrast Storer et al. propose search spaces by either parameterizing the heuristic h or by modifying the problem p. The former attempt searches for a parameter vector for h, capable to generate a good solution s from p. The latter method modifies the problem p in a way that h generates a good solution s. Following Storer et al., we differentiate between a heuristic-, a problem-, and a solution search space.

5.1.1 Heuristic Search Space

The first GA application to scheduling has been proposed by Davis (1985b). Davis considered a simplified two product job shop with parallel machines and product dependent setup times. Unfortunately, this first approach suffered from the restricted production model and was therefore not continued by later research. Nevertheless Davis introduced the encoding/decoding principle for combinatorial problems. A genotype does not contain a complete solution but rather consists of encoded decision rules which are decoded into a feasible phenotype in the fitness evaluation. Thus, the genotype decoding by means of a schedule generation technique plays a central role in evolutionary scheduling.

A heuristic search for the JSP is proposed by Dorndorf and Pesch (1995). They use a schedule generation technique, described in Sect. 2.2, as the decoding procedure. Recall, that a schedule generation technique contains a reduction operator Ψ, which reduces the set of schedulable operations according to a prescribed criterion, e.g. the activeness of the resulting schedule. Furthermore a choice operator Φ is needed, which chooses an operation from the reduced set to be scheduled next. Dorndorf and Pesch engage the Giffler&Thompson (G&T) algorithm for Ψ, compare Sect. 2.2.2. The G&T algorithm reduces the set of schedulable operations in such a way that activeness of the resulting schedule is assured. If the reduced set resulting from Ψ contains more than one operation, one of them is selected by a priority rule Φ, compare Sect. 2.2.3. Within the GA each gene represents a priority rule from a given set of rules. While decoding a chromosome, the i-th rule is applied for scheduling the i-th operation. Therefore the length of a chromosome is equal to the number of operations involved. The idea is to produce chains of priority rules which fit the needs of a particular problem instance. The results obtained by the priority rule based GA are not really convincing, as reported by the authors.

Therefore Dorndorf and Pesch (1995) propose a second approach based on the Shifting Bottleneck (SB) algorithm, compare Sect. 2.3.2. Recall, that the SB algorithm optimizes the processing sequence of the bottleneck machine using the Branch&Bound (B&B) algorithm of Carlier (1982). In each stage of the SB algorithm the optimal sequence of the current bottleneck machine is added to the schedule. Dorndorf and Pesch do not rely on the bottleneck criterion, instead they make the order of inserting optimal single machine sequences into the partial schedule a subject of the GA. Thus, a chromosome of length m representing a permutation of all machines involved in the problem is a suitable coding. The SB algorithm acts as the decoding procedure by inserting the optimal machine sequences with respect to the order defined in the chromosome. The GA emerges orders of machine sequence insertions for the SB algorithm. Notice, that the search space is extremely small for this approach, whereas the decoding is computational expensive. Although this

approach comes up with good results (938 for the mt10 problem), it seems
to be limited to problem instances of moderate size.

For both representations sketched above a standard crossover guarantees
the generation of valid offspring, because genes representing priority rules are
independent of each other. A remaining question is whether we can identify
building blocks in chromosomes carrying priority rules? Storer et al. (1992b)
report that it is important to place priority rules of competing operations
close together in the chromosome. They regard the operations to be processed
on a single machine as competitors in the G&T algorithm. However, it may
be difficult to identify building blocks in a heuristic search space since a
permutation of priority rules is an indirect configuration of the solution space.

5.1.2 Problem Search Space

Instead of adopting the decoding procedure to the problem, the problem
instance itself can be adopted to the properties of the decoding procedure.
This novel and witty approach is proposed by Storer et al. (1992b).

Again, a variant of the G&T algorithm is used to produce active schedules. A deterministic scheduling algorithm is obtained by using the shortest
processing time rule (SPT) as operator Φ. In order to produce different solutions for a problem instance, the processing times of the operations are
slightly modified. A chromosome is defined as a vector of deviations δ of the
prescribed operation processing times p. First, the decoding procedure builds
up a solution which is based on the $p \pm \delta$ values. The obtained sequence of
operations for the modified problem is stored. Finally the fitness is determined for the stored sequence, now using the original processing times p.
The deviation vector indirectly defines a processing sequence of operations
by means of the deterministic decoding procedure.

Crossover combines parental δ values in order to obtain fitter offspring.
A modification of a δ value is only possible by a mutation which adds a
uniformly distributed random variable to a single δ. Storer et al. (1993) use
a high mutation rate of 15% for the described GA. This gives a hint on the
importance of mutations in their approach.

The problem space GA emerges operation sequences, which indirectly
result from modifications of the underlying problem. Although this configuration of the search space appears rather complex, a standard crossover can
be used. Since chromosomes consists of independent genes carrying δ values,
feasibility of the resulting solution is guaranteed in all cases. However, the
operation sequence of an active solution of the modified problem may not
correspond to an active solution of the original problem. Hence, the larger
the deviations of processing times grow, the less likely will the G&T algorithm fit the original data. Therefore optimal solutions of the original problem
may be excluded from search. In spite of the above considerations, the results
reported in Storer et al. (1993) are fairly good, e.g. 954 for the mt10 problem.

5.1.3 Solution Search Space

Now we turn to more traditional codings which directly encodes the solutions of a problem. In the following we differentiate between binary, symbolic and time dependent representations, all of them expressing precedence relations of operations. First a binary representation is described, next symbolic codings are discussed. Finally schedule representations are covered, which use the starting- or completion times of operations as genotypical information.

Binary Representation. A binary representation of the JSP is proposed by Nakano and Yamada (1991). Their coding consists of genes denoting precedence relations of operations which are processed on the same machine. A single gene determines whether operation v is sequenced prior to operation w ($v \prec w = 1$) or not ($v \prec w = 0$). Since each job is to be processed on each machine, we need a chromosome of length $m \cdot n$. In case that gene $v \prec w$ is specified, gene $w \prec v$ is redundant and therefore omitted. Hence, we end up with a chromosome length of $mn(n-1)/2$ bits.

An example of a schedule given in the acyclic graph representation is shown in Fig. 5.1. It corresponds to the machine selections previously presented in Fig. 2.3, merely the processing times are left out here. For the example all precedence relations (loci) and the specified binary alleles are given below.

$$
\begin{array}{ccccccccc}
1\prec6 & 2\prec4 & 3\prec5 & 1\prec8 & 2\prec7 & 3\prec9 & 6\prec8 & 4\prec7 & 5\prec9 \\
1 & 0 & 0 & 1 & 0 & 1 & 1 & 0 & 1
\end{array}
\tag{5.1}
$$

In terms of the graph representation, a gene determines the direction of a single (dashed) arc. Operation 1 is sequenced prior to operation 6 expressed by the allele 1 at the locus $1\prec6$. Next, operation 2 is sequenced after 4 expressed by a 0 etc. The chromosome 100101101 represents a unique solution.

This binary coding allows Nakano and Yamada to use a standard binary crossover. Unfortunately, the crossover produces infeasible solutions in many cases. Therefore a newly assembled chromosome has to pass a two stage repair mechanism in order to be decoded properly.

1. A local harmonization algorithm provides a legal machine sequence for each machine involved.
2. A global harmonization algorithm removes inconsistencies between the various machine sequences.

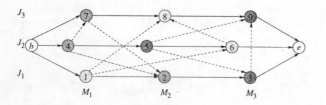

Fig. 5.1. The acyclic graph representation adopted from Fig. 2.3.

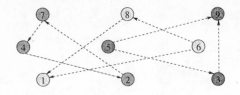

Fig. 5.2. Infeasible sequence $(2, 7, 4)$ resulting from binary crossover.

Let us consider the chromosome 000011101 which might result from a crossover. Decoding it according to (5.1) we obtain the machine sequences shown in Fig. 5.2. Here, the sequence $(2, 7, 4)$ contains a cycle. Therefore a local harmonizer may reverse arc $(4, 2)$. The algorithm achieves an arc constellation between operations of the same machine such that

$$\forall v \in O_i : \text{indegree}(v) + \text{outdegree}(v) = |O_i| - 1, \tag{5.2}$$

$$\forall v, w \in O_i, v \neq w : \text{indegree}(v) \neq \text{indegree}(w). \tag{5.3}$$

Set O_i consists of all operations to be processed on machine M_i. Now, (5.2) ensures that each of two operations are connected on every machine, which is a sufficient condition for the existence of a Hamiltonian path among the operations on every machine. According to (5.3) indegree(v) is injective on O_i, which is a necessary condition for the existence of a Hamiltonian path in the acyclic subgraph of a single machine.

Now the machine sequences obtained from the local harmonizer are introduced into the graph $\mathcal{D}$ which consists of technological constraints only, compare Sect. 2.1.2 and Fig. 2.8. This again may result in an infeasible solution as shown by the cycle emphasized in Fig. 5.3. Again, a machine sequence has to be modified in order to obtain a feasible schedule. This is the role of the global harmonizer which is part of the schedule builder. Each time the schedule builder runs into a cycle, the global harmonizer is called. Here, the arcs $(2, 7)$ and $(2, 4)$ may be reversed in order to repair the solution. Since arc $(2, 4)$ has been reversed previously by the local harmonizer, the reversal of only one arc in the chromosome results in a feasible schedule. Actually, the harmonization algorithm does not guarantee a minimum of arc reversals in order to obtain the feasible symbolic solution.

Together, the original chromosome 000011101 representing an infeasible solution may be changed to the chromosome 000001101. This modified chromosome is regarded as symbolic representation of the feasible solution shown in Fig. 5.4.

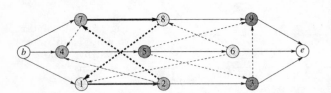

Fig. 5.3. The infeasible solution resulting from local harmonization.

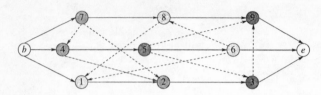

Fig. 5.4. The symbolic solution resulting from global harmonization.

Each chromosome evaluation requires the complex repair procedure described above. Obviously, this is a high price to pay for the advantage of using a binary representation. Moreover, the harmonization algorithm introduces a high degree of schema disruption due to the repair of the genotype. Therefore Nakano and Yamada update the original genotype by its repaired version in order to force the GA to learn valid building blocks. They show, that this kind of forcing improves the GA significantly. Hence, it appears promising to look for a genotype space which covers symbolic representations more directly.

Symbolic Representation. The basic idea for a symbolic representation has been formulated by Syswerda (1991). He states that a schedule consists of a number of potentially temporal overlapping tasks (operations).

> "This view allows us to consider scheduling as an ordering or combinatorial problem. What fundamentally must be done is to place a list of tasks in a particular order. ... To circumvent the problem of illegal orderings, we use a deterministic schedule builder that takes a particular task sequence and builds a legal schedule from it. ... What emerges is a legal schedule for the given ordered list of tasks."

In accordance to Syswerda we aim to consider permutations of operations as genotypes. The relative operation orders given in a permutation chromosome determine a precedence relation among the operations involved. This interpretation of genotypes is very close to the coding presented for the TSP in Sect. 4.2.1. For the TSP a Hamiltonian cycle among all cities determines a solution. For the scheduling problems considered in this thesis Hamiltonian paths among the operations of each machine determine a solution.

Flow shop problems (FSP) constitute a subclass of job shop problems. For FSP's, all jobs have an identical processing order (i.e. line processing). Bierwirth (1993) proposes a symbolic coding for the FSP which handles machine sequencing like an asymmetric TSP. An overall schedule is encoded by concatenating all machine sequences. The FSP shown in Fig. 5.5 is e.g. encoded by the permutation 741|825|369. For this approach a TSP crossover can

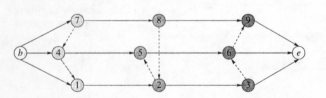

Fig. 5.5. A solution to a 3×3 FSP represented by 3 Hamiltonian paths.

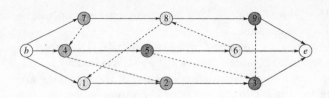

Fig. 5.6. Solution to a 3×3 JSP represented by 3 Hamiltonian paths.

be used which is applied to each substring of the chromosome separately. The decoding procedure establishes Hamiltonian paths for each machine sequence by scanning the operations within each substring from left to right.

Extending the coding of the FSP to the general JSP requires the consideration of interdependencies between different machine sequences, i.e. machine sequences cannot be handled separately anymore. Figure 5.6 shows a constellation of three Hamiltonian paths which constitute a feasible JSP solution. A valid chromosome for this example is the permutation 745681239. Again, the string is interpreted by scanning it from left to right. This leads to a temporal order, because an operation is only schedulable if all its predecessors have been scheduled before. Thus, valid permutations are restricted to possible topological sortings of the acyclic graph. Now consider the permutation 754681239 which may result from a crossover operation. The permutation differs from the one above in a swap of operation 4 and 5, and therefore does not constitute a valid topological sorting.

This obstacle of assembling infeasible chromosomes can be circumvented by using a slightly modified coding proposed by Fang et al. (1993) and Bierwirth (1995) independently. Bierwirth introduces a coding under the name 'permutation with repetition'. Its structure as well as its decoding has been outlined in detail in Sect. 2.2.3. Recall, that we use job identifiers instead of just operations in order to define a topological sorting of operations. An example is given in Fig. 5.7 for the schedule of Fig. 5.6.

permutation of jobs	3	2	2	2	3	1	1	1	3
index of occurrence	1	1	2	3	2	1	2	3	3
referred operation	7	4	5	6	8	1	2	3	9

Fig. 5.7. Permutation with repetition representation.

The permutation of jobs shown in Fig. 5.7 is decoded in the following way: First, schedule an operation of job 3. Then schedule an operation of job 2 followed again by an operation of job 2 etc. Notice, that each job identifier calls a well defined operation because each job allows at most one operation to be scheduled next. The second line of Fig. 5.7 is not part of the chromosome. It denotes the index of occurrence of a job identifier in the permutation with repetition. Finally, the third line shows the operation which is referred to by the corresponding index of the current job identifier, e.g. the identifier of job 3 with index 2 refers to operation 8. As described earlier in Sect. 2.2.3, this coding covers all feasible solutions of a problem instance. Therefore it can

serve as a genetic JSP representation, as long as genetic operators preserve
the index structure of a permutation.

Bierwirth (1994) proposes a generalized order crossover (GOX), which is
adopted from the OX operator, compare Sect. 4.2.1. First, a substring is chosen from the donating chromosome. Next, all operations of the substring are
deleted with respect to their index in the receiving chromosome. Finally, the
donator's substring is implanted into the receiver at the position where the
first operation of the substring has occured (before deletion) in the receiver.

parent 1	3	2	2	2	3	1	1	1	3
parent 2	1	1	3	2	2	1	2	3	3
offspring	1	3	2	2	2	3	1	1	3

Fig. 5.8. Generalized order crossover (GOX).

In Fig. 5.8 the underlined substring is taken from parent 1. It consists
of two operations of job 2 (index 2 and 3), of one operation of job 3 (index
2) and of one operation of job 1 (index 1). These operations are deleted in
parent 2. Afterwards, the substring is implanted in parent 2 at the former
position of job 2 (index 2). The case of contradicting relative job orderings
in the parents is automatically solved by implicit mutations. In the example
of Fig. 5.8, the immediate predecessor of the first operation of job 3 in the
offspring is the first operation of job 1. This constellation does not occur in
both parents.

GOX guarantees to produce valid permutations with repetition while pre-
serving the relative order of operations within both parents as far as possible.
A chromosome represents a unique schedule, but the opposite does not hold.
In general, every schedule can be represented by more than one chromosome.
Thus, the symbolic representation contains some redundancy, although its
amount is considerably smaller than for the binary coding described earlier
in this section.

In order to improve the solution quality, Fang et al. (1993) as well as
Bierwirth (1995) engage a hybrid decoding procedure. Both approaches use
the G&T algorithm for schedule building. The G&T algorithm reduces the set
of schedulable operations to a subset of operations leading to an active schedule. The operation which occurs at the left most position in the chromosome
is selected from this subset. After scheduling this operation the corresponding
job identifier is deleted in the chromosome. Hence, operations are typically
scheduled from left to right. Whenever scheduling an operation would lead
to a non-active schedule, it is skipped and the next operation on the right is
attempted to be scheduled. This procedure leads to a further increase of redundancy in the representation, because now even more permutations lead to
the same schedule. After the schedule is built, its actual shape is transformed
back into its genotype.

To summarize, genetic inheritance of this symbolic representation aims to
preserve the relative orderings of operations. The crossover procedure sup-

ports the preservation of operation orders. The decoding performs operation sequencing with respect to the gene order in the chromosome. Fang et al. obtain a solution quality of 960 for the mt10 whereas Bierwirth achieves the quasi-optimal 936. Fang et al. use a uniform crossover whereas Bierwirth uses the GOX operator. Since Bierwirth achieves even better results with 10 000 genotype evaluations than Fang et al. with 150 000 evaluations, we expect GOX to be superior compared to uniform crossover for the JSP.

Schedule Representation. A schedule can either be represented by using the starting times or the completion times of operations as allele values. The coding consists of a chromosome of the length equal to the number of operations. Each operation has a fixed locus carrying either its starting- or completion time. Literature reports two related approaches.

Yamada and Nakano (1992) store the completion times of operations in the chromosome. They propose the G&T crossover which ensures the assembling of valid offspring. G&T crossover starts with an empty schedule and passes one stage for each operation. In each stage the G&T algorithm builds the conflict set of schedulable operations. Now, one parent is chosen at random. The earliest completed operation reported in the parental chromosome which is member of the conflict set is chosen to be scheduled next. By repeating this step for all operations, a uniform crossover is performed which results in an active schedule.

Dorndorf and Pesch (1993) propose a similar approach in which standard crossover mixes up the starting times of operations of two parental schedules. Obviously, resulting offspring represent infeasible solutions in most cases. Therefore Dorndorf and Pesch apply the G&T algorithm in the decoding procedure in order to obtain a feasible active schedule. In each stage of the G&T algorithm the operation from the conflict set is chosen, which possesses a minimal starting time in the chromosome.

Both approaches show apparent similarities. In fact, both algorithms are driven by random decisions within the crossover procedure. Yamada and Nakano could also use a uniform crossover resulting in an invalid chromosome and apply the G&T algorithm while decoding it. This strategy or applying G&T crossover leads to identical results. Seemingly, the G&T crossover appears as a heuristic crossover but it rather is a repair procedure. In both approaches the parental chromosomes are used for rearranging the order of operations in the offspring close to the order of operations in the parents. The GA emerges deviations of starting times which are taken as hints for operation sequences. Both approaches are able to solve the mt10 problem to optimality. Yamada and Nakano found the optimum 930 in four times of 600 runs. Dorndorf and Pesch engage an effective Variable Depth Search procedure (compare Sect. 3.3.4) as a base heuristic in addition to the G&T algorithm and obtain 930 too.

5.1.4 Which Representation Fits Best?

Since the GA is a stochastic algorithm, it produces different results in different runs. Hence, we may be either interested in the best result or in the mean result of a number of runs. For the latter criterion the measured variance is of particular interest. The results reported in literature are not sufficiently clear at this point in order to evaluate the various approaches. Just to give a qualitative impression of the various representations and hybridizations used, Tab. 5.1 lists the best makespan obtained for the famous mt problems.

Table 5.1. Best results obtained by the GA approaches described throughout this section for the two famous benchmarks mt10 and mt20.

mt10	mt20	representation	hybridization	reference
960	1249	priority rule	Giffler&Thompson	Dorndorf and Pesch (1995)
938	1178	mach. insertions	Branch&Bound	Dorndorf and Pesch (1995)
954	1180	processing time	Giffler&Thompson	Storer et al. (1993)
965	1215	binary	semi-active sched.	Nakano and Yamada (1991)
949	1189	permutation	active scheduling	Fang et al. (1993)
936	1183	permutation	active scheduling	Bierwirth (1995)
930	1184	completion time	Giffler&Thompson	Yamada and Nakano (1992)
930	1165	starting time	Var. Depth Search	Dorndorf and Pesch (1993)

In order to benefit from previous GA approaches, we discuss some general aspects concerning the hybridization, extensibility, representation, and recombination used in the approaches of this section.

- Most GA approaches are tested with small and moderate sized problems only. Therefore we can only guess how the algorithms scale up to larger problems. It can be assumed that the time complexity of the base heuristic to be of particular importance for the runtime demand of the GA. A powerful base heuristics may be computational prohibitive.
- The extensibility to related problems and objectives is of particular interest when comparing GA approaches. If e.g. a coding relies on a specific base heuristic, it may be difficult to adopt the approach to a related problem. A representation which confines itself to the essentials of a problem might be more easy to adopt. We regard the order of operations to be at least one important essential in genetic scheduling.
- The success of a GA strongly depends on how well the coding respects the properties of the underlying problem. Here, the most natural representation known should be chosen. Since all approaches finally represent sequences of operations, a symbolic representation may describe the ordering constraints of the problem in a most natural way.
- Solutions should be recombined such that already evolved fit schemata are inherited. Since we cannot identify building blocks in advance, we can only conjecture which kind of crossover operator performs best. Obviously,

hybridization distorts the crossover properties. Nevertheless, for ordering problems the order of genes should be respected by crossover.

We view a JSP as a combinatorial ordering problem. Consequently, a configuration of the search space by means of an order based representation seems appropriate. Therefore we assume a permutation of operations to be a natural coding for the JSP. We emphasize the simplicity of the decoding procedure required: In the most simple version, the decoding procedure straightforwardly schedules operations coded in the chromosome in a temporal order and finally results in a semi-active schedule. This decoding procedure allows us to run the GA without any heuristic knowledge involved. Therefore we can assess the intrinsic properties of the coding independently of the distortions caused by heuristic knowledge involved.

Some design principles of chromosomal representations are given by Radcliff (1991). He states that ideally each member of the space being searched should be represented by only one chromosome in the permutation space. As noted earlier, the symbolic representation comes along with a considerable degree of freedom concerning the order of operations.

1. Certain sequences of operations result in infeasible schedules. Therefore the decoding procedure solves these conflicts by altering machine sequences. Consequently, the order of conflicting operations in the chromosome carries no meaningful information.
2. Operations which are not connected in the graph representation are unrelated. They can be scheduled independently always resulting in the same schedule. Again, the relative order of such operations in the chromosome does not obey to some meaningful order.

In order to avoid 1.) we engage a permutation of job identifiers instead of using the permutation of operations directly. We circumvent 2.) by arranging the operations in the order of ascending starting times. By using the order of starting times the topological sorting of the acyclic graph is preserved and unrelated operations appear in the order of increasing time. All-together, this mixture of a symbolic- and a schedule representation allows a direct mapping of the chromosomal representation to a solution.

5.2 Properties of the Search Space

The definition of the problem representation implicitly lays down a proximity relation between the various solutions of the solution space. We have defined a JSP representation which is based on precedence relations between any of two operations. Thus, all solutions of the solution space are configured in a way that two solutions are neighbored if they differ in one precedence relation. The precedence relations specified for a solution are called characteristics in the following.

First, an overall picture of the search space is sketched in terms of the fitness landscape. Then, a distance metric is introduced for the search space permitting a configuration space analysis. Next, we suggest a measure for the genotypical diversity within a population. Finally, the smoothness of the fitness landscape is determined. In several experiments[1] we analyze the properties of the induced search space configuration in order to evaluate the perspectives of the chosen JSP representation for genetic adaptation.

5.2.1 Fitness Landscape

The notion of the fitness landscape was introduced by the biologist Sewall Wright in the early thirties of this century under the name adaptive landscape. His basic idea is to view a genotype space of a species as a landscape, where related genotypes occupy nearby locations. The fitness of all members of the genotype space is forming a surface called the fitness landscape. Since the fitness of genotypes within a proximity is closely related, the fitness landscape states a model of the genotype space consisting of peaks, valleys, ridges, plateaus etc. If the evolution of a species is successful, its individuals adapt to regions of higher fitness within the fitness landscape.

Concerning combinatorial optimization problems, the objective function and the search space configuration define the fitness landscape. Any solution is located through its genotypical coordinates and its objective function value, i.e. its fitness, in the landscape. Unfortunately, a complete enumeration of a problem's search space is necessary in order to depict the fitness landscape entirely. Even more intricate is the definition of a genotypical coordinate system which expresses the configuration space. In order to achieve a fitness landscape we need a problem representation, a metric defining a distance between instances of the representation, and a fitness function determining the objective value of solutions.

A fitness landscape may convey insight about general properties of the problem under consideration. Assume a rugged landscape consisting of many peaks either connected by ridges or separated by cliffs falling into steep valleys of low fitness. Such a landscape is regarded to be more difficult to search than one consisting of a few peaks connected by smooth valleys.

A simple fitness landscape is proposed by Cartwright and Mott (1991) for an FSP in order to give a clue for a suitable GA parameter setting. The ruggedness of a problem's landscape helps to determine the population size and the mutation rate. In this approach a genotype consists of a sequence of operations. The landscape is generated by altering a chromosome such that neighboring points in the landscape differ in one gene position. The landscapes generated for different problems may look completely different.

---

[1] We report the results for the famous mt10 problem, compare Chap. 8. The results presented for the mt10 have been verified by sample for various other benchmark problems.

The visualization of a fitness landscape may explain the observed GA performance, but a GA parameter tuning based on a visual impression of the landscape can hardly satisfy.

However, we have generated fitness landscapes in analogy to Cartwright and Mott for several JSPs. A plot for the mt10 problem is presented in Fig. 5.9. A randomly initialized genotype is altered 50 times in two directions, shown by the two horizontal coordinates. For instance, a neighbor of the permutation '1234' is given by the permutation '1423'. Notice, that the axis of ordinate is reversed such that a peak denotes a high fitness, i.e. a short makespan. This first impression of the JSP landscape appears not encouraging at all. Moreover, the landscapes generated for other problems look more or less the same.

- At a first glance the landscape appears rugged because there are numerous peaks all over the portion of the landscape. Despite the sample of the search space is tiny, we conjecture numerous local optima distributed all over the entire configuration space.
- At a second glance we recognize a correlated fitness for neighboring locations of the landscape, although the extension of correlating locations seems to be small.

Notice, that the landscape presented in Fig. 5.9 just reflects a reasonable operator working on a certain representation. Although a landscape may appear rugged, the corresponding problem is not necessarily difficult to solve because there may exist another configuration of the search space which leads

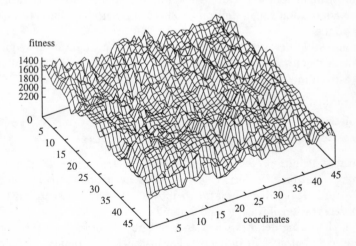

Fig. 5.9. Portion of the fitness landscape proposed by Cartwright and Mott (1991). The fitness is given for related chromosomes such that neighboring points differ in one position of a gene only.

to a much smoother landscape. To the contrary, it may be impossible to find a configuration of a problem's solution space resulting in a smooth landscape (although theoretically it exists). For sure such a problem is difficult to solve for any algorithm, adaptive ones included.

According to Jones (1995) a landscape should be defined by means of that operator which predominates the adaptation in order to reflect the actual opportunities of search. Consequently different representations and different operators lead to different landscapes. We partially approve this view, but we object that general properties of a problem exist. These properties makes for instance the JSP difficult to solve for any algorithm, regardless of the operator(s) performing the search. We have shown earlier in this chapter that the various ways of configuring the solution space can be essentially reduced to the specification of precedence relations among operations.

Therefore we propose a definition of the fitness landscape in terms of precedence relations among operations. In doing so, e.g. a peak denotes a solution which cannot be improved by altering a single precedence relation. We may walk on the landscape by means of the $\mathcal{N}_1$ Local Search operator, compare Definition 3.1.1, because it changes exactly one precedence relation in one step. In the remainder of this section we examine some properties of the JSP in terms of the fitness landscape.

5.2.2 Distance Metric

According to our first impression the fitness landscape of the JSP is multi-peaked, i.e. local optima are widely spread all over the landscape. In such cases near optimal solutions can have vastly dissimilar characteristics. Consequently, adaptation might fail on proliferating suitable characteristics in the gene pool.

A quantitative description of the search space configuration requires a metric which defines a computable distance d between any of two solutions x and y. Such a metric should obey the following conditions:

1. reflexivity, $d_{x,x} = 0$,
2. symmetry, $d_{x,y} = d_{y,x}$ and the
3. triangle inequality, $d_{x,y} + d_{y,z} \geq d_{x,z}$.

A suitable definition of a JSP search space metric, based on the acyclic graph representation of solutions, is achieved by a binary mapping of all disjunctive arcs (precedence relations) into a bit string. According to the binary representation of Nakano and Yamada (1991), described in Sect. 5.1.3, each bit of the string denotes whether a certain operation precedes another (bit=1) or not (bit=0). In doing so, for instance, the binary mapping of solutions of a rectangular $n \times m$ problem leads to a bit string of length $l = mn(n-1)/2$.

The well known Hamming distance serves as a JSP search space metric because it obviously fulfills the above conditions. The absolute Hamming distance $d_{x,y}$ between two bit strings x and y is determined by

$$d_{x,y} = \sum_{i=1}^{l} x_i \otimes y_i \tag{5.4}$$

where l denotes the length of the bit strings and $\otimes$ denotes the logical XOR operator. Furthermore $D_{x,y}$ denotes the normalized Hamming distance

$$D_{x,y} = \frac{d_{x,y}}{l}. \tag{5.5}$$

Identical bit strings have a normalized distance of $D = 0.0$ whereas maximally differing bit strings have a distance of $D = 1.0$. Consequently, we might expect a mean normalized Hamming distance of $D = 0.5$ for the elements of the search space. But actually our expectation fails. 1000 randomly generated solutions of the mt10 show a mean normalized distance of $D = 0.27$ only. The maximal observed distance is $D = 0.4$. The value of 1.0 appears to be a theoretical upper bound which may be approximated only under specific circumstances, e.g. under flow shop restrictions. The above observation is explained by the heterogeneity of technological job constraints involved in the mt10 problem instance.

For an example take a look at the symbolic representation of Fig. 5.4. Operation 6 is the last operation of its job. An operation sequence where operation 4 or 5 succeeds operation 6 is therefore permitted. Operation 1 is the first operation of its job and is processed on the same machine as operation 6. If operation 1 succeeds operation 6, then the job of operation 6 is entirely completed before processing of the job containing operation 1 can be started. Therefore it is unlikely that operation 6 precedes operation 1 in randomly generated operation sequences.

Since precedence relations of operations and not Hamiltonian paths are represented in the binary mapping, we achieve a lower mean distance as we might have expected. This result gives an additional hint at the high degree of redundancy of the binary representation. However, the binary mapping of precedence relations among operations allows us to obtain the distance between two solutions in an easy way.

5.2.3 Configuration Space Analysis

The following investigation of the JSP search space is based on the configuration space analysis as suggested by Kirkpatrick and Toulouse (1985) for the TSP. In the meantime this analysis is widely accepted, compare e.g. Mühlenbein (1990) or Inayoshi and Manderick (1994). Two solution pools $\mathcal{R}$ and $\mathcal{L}$, containing randomly generated solutions and local optimal solutions[2]

---

[2] Local optimal solutions are considered simply as good solutions, the property of a local optimum is of no meaning in this context.

respectively, are generated. For both pools the mean normalized Hamming distance of solutions to all other solutions of their pool are calculated. The distance values are plotted together with the fitness values in a two-dimensional distance/fitness diagram.

The resulting plot ideally shows two distinct clusters. The solutions of $\mathcal{R}$ show a low fitness and their distances are widely spread. The local optimal solutions of $\mathcal{L}$ come up with a far better fitness while their distances are considerably smaller. If we extrapolate the correlation of both clusters towards the region of near optimal fitness, then the following model of plausibility can be stated for genetic search.

1. The mean distances between solutions decrease while their mean fitness increase. Thus, the characteristics of near optimal solutions might at least partially be included in the genotypes of local optimal solutions.
2. Therefore the probability to obtain improved solutions by recombining relatively fit solutions is higher than that for randomly picked solutions.
3. A fitness based selection will guide genetic search into regions of higher fitness. It appears unlikely that selection excludes near optimal regions of the fitness landscape from being searched.

This model of plausibility clearly contradicts our impression of a JSP search space where local optima are widely spread, compare Fig. 5.9. In order to valuate the model for the JSP we perform a configuration space analysis for the mt10. We set up the pools $\mathcal{R}$ and $\mathcal{L}$ with 1 000 random solutions and 1 000 local optimal solutions respectively. The solutions of $\mathcal{L}$ are obtained using the Local Search neighborhood $\mathcal{N}_4$ (see Definition 3.1.4) and the steepest descending control strategy (see Tab. 3.3). This hill climbing procedure produces the best results of all hill climbers tested, compare Tab. 3.4. The mean fitness of $\mathcal{R}$ is 1730.8, whereas $\mathcal{L}$ shows a mean fitness of 1149.3. For each solution of a pool a mean distance value is calculated by the normalized Hamming distance to all other solutions of its pool.

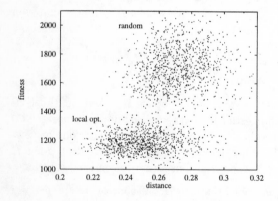

Fig. 5.10. Distance/fitness diagram for the mt10 problem.

The results obtained are presented in Fig. 5.10. It can be seen that Local Search improves the fitness significantly. The average distance in $\mathcal{L}$ is $D = 0.25$ which is slightly smaller than the value for $\mathcal{R}$, already calculated in the last section with $D = 0.27$. Nevertheless, the width of both clusters is hardly different. The fitness/distance diagram apparently shows a much too low correlation to explain how successful genetic search may work for the JSP. The only conclusion we may draw is that local optima typically share just a few characteristics. This confirms our conjecture that the fitness landscape of the JSP is multi-peaked.

Although multi-peaked landscapes are not well suited for genetic search, Kauffman (1993) has shown that recombination is worth its effort if two properties concerning the fitness landscape hold.

1. There is a Massif Central (in analogy to the Alps) where many near optimal solutions reside laying closer together than other local optima.
2. The better optima drain larger basins of attraction; that is, the better optima can be climbed to via adaptive walks from a greater volume of the search space than can mediocre local optima.

Since we know (at least) one global optimum of the mt10 problem we measure the distance between each solution of $\mathcal{L}$ and the global optimum. In doing so we figure out whether near optimal solutions share a considerable amount of solution characteristics with an optimal solution.

Figure 5.11 shows the normalized Hamming distances between solutions of $\mathcal{L}$ and the global optimum of the mt10 problem. By looking at the fitness in $\mathcal{L}$, a funnel-shaped distribution of points can be recognized. Near optimal solutions show a significantly shorter distance to the global optimum than solutions of average quality. We conclude that near optimal solutions lay close together, i.e. there is a Massif Central in the fitness landscape of the mt10. Solutions of mediocre fitness have a distance to the global optimum similar to random solutions of $\mathcal{R}$.

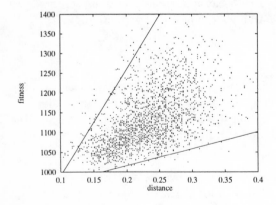

Fig. 5.11. Normalized Hamming distance between local optima and the global optimum vs. fitness for the mt10 problem.

Next, we attempt to estimate the basins of attraction of local optima. Starting from a random solution we count the $\mathcal{N}_4$ moves performed by the hill climber until a local optimum is reached. In doing so, we assume the number of performed moves to measure the basin of attraction of the local optimum obtained.

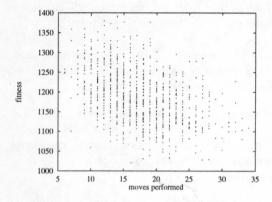

Fig. 5.12. Moves performed on random solutions by the local hill climbing procedure. The number of moves is shown according to the fitness achieved.

Figure 5.12 shows the results obtained in 1 000 runs. The number of performed moves obviously shows an influence on the fitness gained. It can be seen that a fitness better than 1050 requires at least 18 moves. As one would expect, a larger number of moves produces a solution of better fitness in average. Vice versa, if a large sequence of moves is necessary to reach a local optimum, we conjecture that this solution can be reached from many other points of the search space too. Therefore we conjecture that near optimal solutions drain larger basins than local optima of mediocre quality.

Summarizing, we have verified that a JSP may have a large number of local optima which hardly share solution characteristics. This results in a difficult to search multi-peaked fitness landscape. In spite of this observation, recombination may aid search because many near optimal solutions are closely related and drain comparably large basins of attraction.

5.2.4 Population Entropy

We now define a numerical measure for the genotypical diversity of a population. Therefore we define the entropy for the JSP in analogy to Grefenstette (1987) for the TSP and to Fleurent and Ferland (1994) for the QAP. The entropy of a population is achieved by counting solution characteristics in a population.

- For the TSP edges in a tour are considered as characteristics.
- For the QAP assignments of units to locations are characteristics.

We suggest a definition of the entropy which is based on the frequency of arcs in the Hamiltonian paths[3] of machines. The entropy E is calculated in three steps.

$$E_{ij} = \frac{-1}{\log(n-1)} \sum_{k=1}^{n} \left(\frac{\omega_{ijk}}{\mu} \right) \log \left(\frac{\omega_{ijk}}{\mu} \right) \qquad (5.6)$$

$$E_i = \frac{1}{n} \sum_{j=1}^{n} E_{ij} \qquad (5.7)$$

$$E = \frac{1}{m} \sum_{i=1}^{m} E_i \qquad (5.8)$$

In (5.6) we calculate the entropy E_{ij} for each single operation. Here, j calls the job identifier and i calls the destination machine of the operation. The frequency in the population of processing a job k immediately after job j on machine i is denoted by ω_{ijk}. Thus, the ratio $\frac{\omega_{ijk}}{\mu}$ gives the relative frequency of one Hamiltonian arc in a population of size μ. Multiplying this ratio by its logarithm leads to a negative value θ which is close to zero either if the referred arc hardly occurs in the population or if the arc is observed in almost every solution. Both cases indicate a partial similarity of the various solutions within a population. For job j we now we sum up the θ values for those arcs whose target belong to some other job k. The resulting sum is finally multiplied by $\frac{-1}{\log(n-1)}$ normalizing E_{ij} to the range $[0, 1]$. Equation (5.7) defines the entropy E_i of machine i as the average value of all E_{ij}. Finally the entropy E of a population is obtained in (5.8). A value of $E = 0.0$ indicates a population of identical solutions, i.e. exactly $m(n-1)$ arcs occur. A value of $E = 1.0$ can be reached if and only if all $mn(n-1)$ arcs occur with identical frequency in a population.

solution	TSP	QAP
random	1.00	0.99
local opt.	0.32	0.97

Table 5.2. Entropy within populations of random- and local opt. solutions for the TSP and the QAP.

Based on the work of Fleurent and Ferland, Taillard (1994) measures an entropy of approximately 1.0 for a large population of randomly generated QAP solutions. After running a hill climber on all solutions of the population, an entropy of 0.97 is measured. Hill climbing hardly reduces the diversity

[3] Recall Fig. 2.4 in order to clarify the difference between the representation by precedence relations of operations (given by S_i) and the representation by Hamiltonian paths (given by $\mathcal{H}_i$) for machine i. A machine selection S_i is defined by $n(n-1)/2$ disjunctive arcs, whereas the Hamiltonian selection $\mathcal{H}_i$ is defined by only $n-1$ of them. In the following the disjunctive arcs of a Hamiltonian selection are referred to as Hamiltonian arcs.

of the gene pool. Obviously, the local optima of a QAP are widely spread throughout the entire search space. For the TSP, Grefenstette initializes a GA with a population of local optimal solutions. Here, we observe an entropy of approximately 0.32 (taken from a plot) which is in accordance with the results of Mühlenbein (1990). He conjectures that the average difference between two arbitrary 2-opt tours is $1/3c$, where c denotes the number of cities. For the TSP the local optima are within a vicinity in the search space because approximately 2/3 of the edges are identical in arbitrary local optimal tours.

The results presented lack comparability, since the problems as well as the hill climbing techniques differ from each other. However, the result shown in Tab. 5.2 gives a hint on the usefulness of proliferating characteristics of local optima in the gene pool. This makes sense for the TSP, but for the QAP this approach seems to be less fruitful.

For the JSP we expect a high diversity for a randomly generated population (e.g. the solution pool $\mathcal{R}$) as well as for a population of local optima (e.g. the pool $\mathcal{L}$) by taking the results presented in Fig. 5.10 into account.

problem	solution	fitness	entropy
JSP	random	1730.8	0.848
	local opt.	1149.3	0.813
FSP	random	2371.6	0.998
	local opt.	1332.9	0.997

Table 5.3. Average fitness and entropy of 10 000 solutions for the JSP and FSP variant of mt10.

The upper line of Tab. 5.3 shows the mean fitness values and the entropy obtained for the solutions pools $\mathcal{R}$ and $\mathcal{L}$ of the mt10, compare Sect. 5.2.3. The entropy of a random population is $E \approx 0.85$, hence we assume that roughly 15% of Hamiltonian path constellations lead to infeasible solutions. Although hill climbing impressively improves the solution quality, the entropy is hardly reduced. That means, Local Search cannot substantially proliferate preferable arcs of high quality solutions.

In order to make these results more transparent, we construct an FSP variant of the mt10 problem such that the processing times for the operations are taken from the mt10 problem. The machine assignments of operations are modified from the original problem such that the h-th operation of job j has to be processed on machine h. For an FSP the machine sequences can be scheduled independently, thus we expect a uniformly distributed frequency of arcs in a random pool, see the lower line of Tab. 5.3. The entropy of $E \approx 1.0$ indicates that nearly all disjunctive arcs occur with identical frequency. Again hill climbing improves the solution quality, and again the population entropy is hardly changed, this time even less than for the JSP.

We are interested in the distribution of arcs among the four FSP and JSP pools. Therefore we determine the frequency of arcs within the 10 000 solutions of each pool. For the JSP as well as for the FSP a maximum of 900 arcs may theoretically occur. The frequency of arcs is determined for each

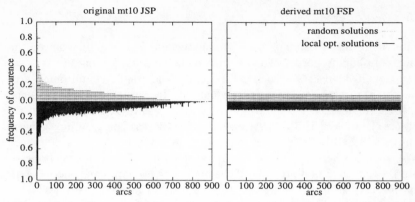

Fig. 5.13. Relative frequency of Hamiltonian arcs in random- and local optimal solutions. The arcs are sorted according to their frequency of occurrence.

pool separately and the arcs observed are sorted according to their relative frequency. A value of 1.0 for some arc means that it occurs in all solutions.

The results obtained are shown in Fig. 5.13. Since the FSP variant of the mt10 problem comes up with the expected frequencies, we start with the discussion of the FSP plot on the right side of the figure. The frequency of Hamiltonian arcs in random solutions is uniformly distributed, each arc occurs in roughly 10% of the solutions. The arc frequencies of local optimal solutions are displayed bottom up in black shading. The proliferation vs. dwindle of arcs is negligible. The left side of the figure shows the arc frequencies for the JSP. The most striking difference between the JSP and the FSP is the distribution of arc frequencies. Again the deviations of arc frequencies between random- and local optimal solutions are insignificant. It can be seen clearly that a few arcs occur in almost every random- as well as in every local optimal solution. Beside, other arcs do not occur at all; even not in 10 000 randomly generated solutions!

The explanation for this phenomenon has already given by example in Sect. 5.2.2. Consider again two operations to be processed on the same machine. A constellation which cannot appear for the FSP is, that one of them is the first operation of a job and the other one is the last operation of some other job. Although we can construct such a schedule by hand, where the latter is scheduled directly before the former operation, it is rather unlikely to generate it at random.

Be aware that the arc distribution presented follows the inherent properties of the underlying combinatorial optimization problem. Thus, they are not due to a genetic representation whatsoever it may be. In other combinatorial domains we face different situations. E.g. for the TSP Hamiltonian arcs and their genetic representation stand in a 1:1 relation. Moreover, it is shown that Local Search strongly decreases the population entropy, compare Tab. 5.2. Obviously, both aspects simplify genetic search considerably.

5.2.5 Fragile Arcs

The frequency distribution of Hamiltonian arcs has a strong influence on the schema sampling properties of a GA. In the following we differentiate between robust Hamiltonian arcs occurring frequently and fragile Hamiltonian arcs which occur rarely. We are concerned about the rare occurrence of some arcs, because we expect these fragile arcs to be destroyed easily by genetic operators. But, even if a robust arc has a low fitness contribution, genetic operators will hardly drive it out from the gene pool.

We now ask whether a fragile arc can be of eminent importance in order to obtain the optimum of a problem. If the answer is yes, how can genetic adaptation preserve such an arc against the majority of more robust ones? This question is of interest if we identify at least one Hamiltonian arc to be fragile and which is involved in an optimal solution. This question is subject to the following experiment. Brucker et al. (1994) have made an interesting observation concerning their B&B algorithm. It solves the notorious mt10 problem to optimality in about 20 minutes. But using a slightly different branching scheme, the B&B requires several hours to obtain the optimum. Brucker et al. have noticed that one arc connecting operations 57 and operation 22 on machine 1 is of particular importance.

solution	arc	frequency
random	(57, 22)	65
	(22, 57)	1174
	—	8761
local opt.	(57, 22)	57
	(22, 57)	1382
	—	8561

Table 5.4. For the mt10 problem the arc (57, 22) is of eminent importance for reaching the optimum. The table shows its observed frequency in 10 000 solutions.

We are interested in finding out if the mentioned arc is a fragile one and therefore we count its occurrence in the pools $\mathcal{R}$ and $\mathcal{L}$. Table 5.4 shows the results obtained. The frequency of the Hamiltonian arc (57, 22) is 65. The redirected Hamiltonian arc occurs with a frequency of 1174.

In the remaining 8761 solutions the operations 22 and 57 are not directly connected, i.e. the disjunctive edge is not expressed in the Hamiltonian path of machine 1. Thus, (57, 22) is an extremely fragile arc; its probability of occurrence in an arbitrary solution is 0.0065%. It is remarkable that this arc occurs within $\mathcal{L}$ even more rarely, although the deviation from 65 to 57 appears insignificant. But, the redirected arc (22, 57) occurs with 1382 significantly more often than in random solutions. Thus we state that hill climbing tends to destroy a substantial characteristic of optimality.

Now consider a population of 100 individuals. The probability that the mentioned arc is part of the initial solutions is 0.65%. If we assume the fragile arc to be part of the initial population at all, we conjecture genetic operators to destroy the arc very fast. Nevertheless, if a GA converges to optimality, we must admit that genetic adaptation is able to prevail a fragile arc because of its superior fitness contribution.

To sum up, the maintenance of solution characteristics by selection is distorted by problem inherent properties, tending to exhibit certain characteristics, over proportional. Genetic adaptation cannot rely on the maintenance of the gene pool by Local Search in order to reach the global optimum.

5.2.6 Correlation Length

The fact that local optima are widely spread all over the landscape does not necessarily imply a rugged landscape, i.e. the existence of cliffs falling into steep valleys and the like. Since a population can adapt to a smooth landscape more easily than to a rugged one, we next examine the smoothness of the mt10 landscape.

Therefore we produce random walks on the fitness landscape. A random walk of length l results in a sequence of fitness samples $y_t (1 \leq t \leq l)$, interpreted as a time series of l lags. The autocorrelation function for an interval of length h is estimated by

$$Q_h = \frac{\sum_{t=1}^{l-h}(y_t - \overline{y})(y_{t+h} - \overline{y})}{\sum_{t=1}^{l}(y_t - \overline{y})^2}.$$

Thereby we assume that the landscape is statistically isotropic (Q_h does not depend on one particular walk performed) and that the process described by the random walk is stationary, compare Weinberger (1990). The length h^* for which the process still shows correlation, is called the correlation length of the fitness landscape. In literature we find different definitions of the correlation length. The definition mainly depends on the operator used for generating the walk and the general properties of the problem, compare Weinberger (1990), Lipsitch (1991), Manderick et al. (1991). For our purpose the most appealing definition of the correlation length h^* is given by Manderick et al. (1991) with $Q_h = 1/2$.

Next we have to define an operator for generating a random walk. The landscape shown in Fig. 5.9 is generated by altering the position of one operation in the permutation. This operation changes the absolute order within a chromosome and is therefore called position based mutation (PBM) introduced by Syswerda (1991). A random walk based on PBM may change more than one precedence relation of operations at a time. In order to achieve a random walk which exchanges exactly one precedence relation from step to step, we engage the Local Search neighborhood $\mathcal{N}_1$, see Definition 3.1.1. Notice, that an $\mathcal{N}_1$ walk works directly on the graph representation by exchanging adjacent operations on the critical path. Therefore an $\mathcal{N}_1$ step results in a solution with a Hamming distance $d = 1$ to its originator solution. Thus we may use the number of steps h and the Hamming distance d interchangeably (neglecting that subsequent steps may reverse precedences relations already reversed before).

The properties of this neighborhood meet our needs almost perfectly, because an $\mathcal{N}_1$ walk performs the smallest possible step size that guarantees to alter the makespan. Since we assume the landscape to be isotropic, we start a random walk from an arbitrary picked solution. Then we iteratively walk to arbitrary $\mathcal{N}_1$ neighbors of the current solution.

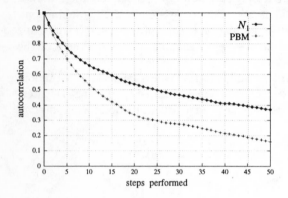

Fig. 5.14. Observed autocorrelations of the mt10 landscape for an $\mathcal{N}_1$ walk and a PBM walk.

For both operators defined we perform a walk of 10 000 steps. The results obtained are shown in Fig. 5.14 for $1 \leq h \leq 50$. The PBM walk shows a small correlation length of $h^* = 10$. The correlation length of the $\mathcal{N}_1$ walk is with $h^* = 25$ considerably larger. Since one $\mathcal{N}_1$ step changes exactly one precedence relation, we assume an offspring to correlate with its parent if less than 25 precedence relations are changed. Since solutions of the mt10 differ in maximal 450 precedence relations, we assume points in the landscape with a normalized Hamming distance of $D \approx 0.06$ to correlate with one another.

For different problem instances the correlation length may differ with respect to the problem size. The amount of change an operator produces (i.e. the absolute Hamming distance between the offspring solution and the originator solution) is fixed regardless of the size of the problem instance. In contradistinction, the normalized Hamming distance an operator produces becomes smaller with increasing problem size – and so does the deviation of the objective value. A small deviation of the objective value in turn results in a big correlation length. Therefore larger problem instances often show a bigger correlation length than smaller instances do.

Be aware that the correlation lengths for different combinatorial problems are not directly comparable because the operators used for producing the random walk are not comparable. Nevertheless, the correlation length gives us a rough impression of the objective value deviation we can expect when applying a slight modification to an existing solution. For the TSP Manderick et al. (1991) have observed correlation lengths between $h^* = 10$ and $h^* = 20$ for different mutation operators. Thus, we conjecture the landscapes of the TSP and the JSP to be of at least similar smoothness. Since the correlation length of $\mathcal{N}_1$ is considerably larger than the one of PBM, we conjecture the mt10 landscape to be smoother than shown in Fig. 5.9.

By all odds, a comparison of the TSP and the JSP landscapes points to an important characteristic of the JSP fitness landscape. For the TSP good local optima are concentrated at some region of the fitness landscape, compare Fig. 5.2. The way towards this massif from some lower region is relatively smooth and therefore easy to climb via an adaptive walk.

For the JSP, the local optima are widely spread all over the landscape by showing a smoothness of the landscape comparable to the one of the TSP. This observation suggests smooth proximities around the various local peaks. Therefore we conjecture that a (local) peak of the JSP landscape can be climbed easily from its vicinity – leading to local entrapments in most cases.

5.3 Summary of Perspectives

In this chapter we have discussed several configurations of the JSP search space. Then we have chosen a representation which configures the solution search space by precedence relations among operations. Finally we have examined the properties of this configuration exemplary for the famous mt10.

- Based on the distance metric we have analyzed the configuration space. Various local optima are spread over the entire search space, hence we deal with a multi-peaked fitness landscape. Multi-peaked landscapes are generally difficult to search for adaptive search techniques, because the search process is easily trapped in local optima.
- Next we have evaluated the correlation between the fitness of solutions and their distances to the optimum. We have found that better local optima share a bit more characteristics with the optimal solution than mediocre ones do. In terms of the fitness landscape we find a "Massif Central". Moreover, this "Massif Central" can be climbed from a greater volume of points in the landscape than regions of lower fitness. This observations hold promise that genetic adaptation may succeed.
- By determining the frequency distribution of characteristics in a randomly generated gene pool we have seen that the genes are not uniformly distributed (as one could have expected). Instead, we must differentiate between robust and fragile solution characteristics. Thus we state that, regardless of their fitness, some portions of the landscape seem inhospitable

and can be searched by particularly adapted individuals only. Other regions of the landscape are much more easy to be searched and therefore will attract the majority of the population. This fact may heavily distort the properties of genetic adaptation.

– Finally we have calculated the distance, for which a fitness correlation between solutions exists. This can be viewed as determining the smoothness of the fitness landscape. We state that a fitness correlation exists for relatively large distances. This fact is sufficient for a proper population flow on the fitness landscape. Therefore we expect adaptation to gain significant improvements.

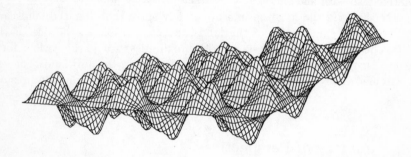

Fig. 5.15. An idealized JSP landscape as it may appear for genetic adaptation.

Figure 5.15 gives an impression of the fitness landscape as it might appear for genetic adaptation. The landscape is multi-peaked but smooth within its localities. The properties of climbing a peak from its proximity of lower fitness are sufficient because a peak differs significantly from its surrounding. To the contrary, recombining individuals located on different peaks results in a jump beyond the correlation length of the landscape and will therefore fail in most cases. Nevertheless, there is a Massif Central where good local optima reside. Since some regions of the landscape are less viable than others, at least for the famous mt10 problem we seem to have lost the battle for optimality before it even started.

6. Population Flow in Adaptive Scheduling

Thus far we got an impression of the JSP fitness landscape. Evolutionary Search aims to guide a population to regions of higher fitness in the landscape from generation to generation. The adaptation process due to reproduction and selection can be regarded as a population flow on the fitness landscape. The control of the population flow is subject of the following considerations.

Figure 6.1 shows an ideal population flow. Snapshots of the population are made in four distinct generations showing the fitness (x-axis) and the Hamming distance to the optimal solution (y-axis). The corner in the front of the plot refers to the optimal solution. The z-axis gives the frequency of individuals occupying a certain cluster in the landscape. The initial population is widely spread among regions of low fitness. Then adaptation draws the population towards regions of higher fitness and finally the population converges nearby the optimum.

The success of the population flow mainly depends on the ability to reproduce the individuals in a convenient way. For these aspects of heredity the notion 'inheritance management' is used hereafter. The inheritance management covers the genetic representation, the way of initializing a population and the genetic operators as well as their probabilities of being applied. Up to now we have merely defined a suitable representation for the JSP.

Provided that the inheritance management is completely described, the population flow is furthermore controlled by the 'population management'. The population management covers the population size, the termination criterion, the selection scheme and the fitness evaluation procedure, including an optional hybridization method. Their shaping has to be chosen carefully in a way that the population control interacts properly with the inheritance management. The components of the population management balance the degree of exploration vs. exploitation of the adaptation process.

This chapter starts with a discussion of a simple GA template. Next, asexual and sexual reproduction operators are discussed and evaluated separately. Then, an appropriate population management for the chosen inheritance management is discussed. Finally, results of adaptive scheduling are presented for a genuine GA and a hybrid GA.

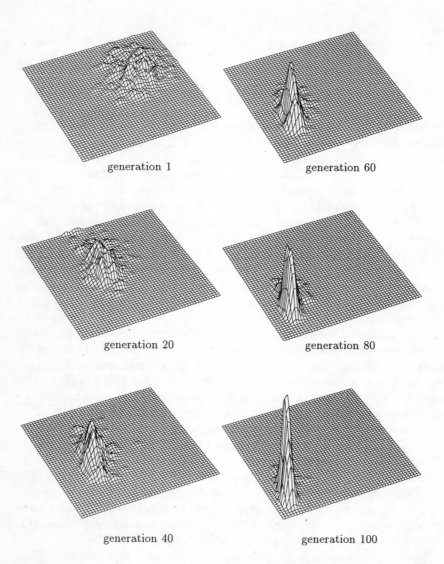

generation 1

generation 60

generation 20

generation 80

generation 40

generation 100

Fig. 6.1. Population flow on the mt10 landscape. The horizontal extensions give the fitness and the Hamming distance to the optimal solution. The height of the peaks correspond to the frequency of individuals occupying a certain cluster. The corner in the front refers to the global optimum of the problem.

6.1 Genetic Algorithm Template

In the following we discuss a GA template adopted from the rough outline of Holland's reproductive plan (compare Fig. 4.1). Although various other ways of modeling the population management have been proposed, e.g. by Whitley (1989) and Mühlenbein and Schlierkamp-Voosen (1994), we follow Goldberg (1989) in the outline of the algorithmic template.

algorithm GA **is**
   initialize P randomly
   while not terminate **do**
     $F := \text{evaluate}(P)$
     $P' := \emptyset$
     while $|P'| \leq |P|$ **do**
       $i = \text{select}_F(P)$
       if $\text{rand}_{\text{unif}} < \rho_c$ **then**
         $j := \text{select}_F(P)$
         $k := \text{crossover}(i, j)$
       else
         $k := i$
       end if
       if $\text{rand}_{\text{unif}} < \rho_m$ **then**
         $k := \text{mutate}(k)$
       end if
       $P' := P' \cup \{k\}$
     end while
     $P := P'$
   end while
end algorithm

Fig. 6.2. Simple Genetic Algorithm template.

Figure 6.2 shows the algorithmic template. In the beginning the population P is initialized with randomly generated individuals. A generation-loop is performed as long as the termination criterion does not hold. In each generation the fitness F of individuals in P is evaluated. A temporary population P' is initialized empty and afterwards filled on the basis of P in the inner population-loop of the algorithm. When P' is full, it replaces P in the next generation. Using the temporary population P', a so called generation gap is introduced. Offspring are placed in P' and therefore cannot be selected for reproduction in the current generation. This feature guarantees an identical selection environment for all individuals of a population.

Inside the population-loop an individual i is selected from P based on F, such that preferably individuals of above average fitness are selected. Then, crossover is applied with the rate ρ_c. If crossover is performed, a mate j is selected for i. Crossover recombines i and j producing the offspring k. If crossover is not performed, i is just copied to k. Now k may be mutated with the rate ρ_m before it is added to P'.

6.2 Inheritance Management

Once introduced the GA template, we may now formulate its components. Figure 5.11 shows that near optimal solutions share a considerable amount of characteristics. Thus it seems worthwhile to spend effort on sexual reproduction. In this section we examine whether crossover is capable to preserve exploitable problem structure over the generations. In this case it seems worthwhile to spend effort on sexual recombination. In case that parental characteristics cannot be preserved adequately, preference should be given to an asexual reproduction scheme.

6.2.1 Mutation Operators

Due to the GA paradigm, a mutation merely reintroduces genes lost by accident into the gene pool. In order to spread offspring genes throughout the population, mutated individuals must survive by means of selection in forthcoming generations. Therefore mutated offspring should come up with a similar fitness compared to their parents.

We conjecture that a slight genotypical modification leads to a slight deviation of the fitness. Concerning the JSP a slightly modified chromosome does not necessarily lead to a modified schedule. And even if a modified schedule is produced, its makespan (i.e. its fitness) may not differ from the one obtained for the parental schedule, if the modification does not affect the critical path, compare Sect. 2.1.3.

For scheduling problems Syswerda (1991) notes, that the relative ordering of genes as well as the position of genes in the permutation chromosome is meaningful: The relative order of genes determines that an operation is scheduled before some other operation. The absolute order determines that if for instance an operation occurs at the back part of the chromosome, this operation is unlikely to be scheduled early on its machine. Therefore we propose three mutation operators which differ in respecting the gene order of the permutation chromosome.

OBM The order based mutation picks two loci in the chromosome at random and exchanges their alleles.
PBM The position based mutation deletes a randomly picked locus and puts its allele to a newly inserted locus at an arbitrary position.
SBM The swap based mutation picks one locus at random and exchanges the alleles with an adjacent locus.

Since the outcome of these mutation operators is uncertain to some extent, we examine the fitness deviation effect of OBM, PBM and SBM with respect to the actual schedule modifications. The altering of a schedule is measured by the Hamming distance d (i.e. the number of differing precedence relations among operations) between the parent and its offspring.

In order to measure the fitness deviation between parents and their offspring, Manderick et al. (1991) introduce the correlation coefficient for unary operators. Mühlenbein and Schlierkamp-Voosen (1994) suggest a similar investigation. We generate l parents and apply a single mutation to each of them. The fitness values of parents and offspring are denoted as x_t and $y_t (1 \leq t \leq l)$ respectively. The correlation coefficient $R_{x,y}$ of the operator is calculated by

$$
\begin{aligned}
Cov_{x,y} &= \frac{1}{l} \sum_{t=1}^{l} (x_t - \overline{x})(y_t - \overline{y}) \\
\sigma_x &= \frac{1}{l} \sum_{t=1}^{l} \sqrt{(x_t - \overline{x})^2} \\
R_{x,y} &= \frac{Cov_{x,y}}{\sigma_x \sigma_y}.
\end{aligned}
\tag{6.1}
$$

We perform the experiment for the mt10 by generating 10 000 solutions at random. Their fitness is determined, each of them is mutated once and then the fitness of the offspring is evaluated again.

mutation	d	R
SBM	0.37	0.99
PBM	4.14	0.91
OBM	10.28	0.82

Table 6.1. Fitness correlation vs. mean Hamming distance of three mutation operators applied to random solutions of the mt10.

The correlation coefficients of the proposed mutation operators are shown in Tab. 6.1 together with the mean observed Hamming distance. The correlation $R = 0.99$ for SBM indicates a very slight fitness deviation. Since SBM changes adjacent operations in the permutation, at most one precedence relation of operations is changed in one mutation. Hence, the distance $d = 0.37$ expresses that only 37% of the mutations actually have altered a solution. Thus, SBM mutations cannot substantially affect the adaptation process.

Comparing the mutation operators PBM and OBM, PBM is clearly superior to OBM in producing a slight fitness deviation. PBM changes approximately 4 precedence relations in one mutation and therefore we observe $R = 0.91$. In contradiction, OBM alters roughly 10 precedence relations in one mutation and therefore it shows an unacceptable $R = 0.82$. Obviously, changing the position of one operation in the chromosome produces a slighter fitness deviation than exchanging the positions of two operations.

Together, PBM may perform considerable long jumps in the landscape, but it does not jump beyond the correlation length of the landscape. Therefore we use PBM in the following, but we keep in mind that even PBM can produce considerable long jumps within the fitness landscape.

6.2.2 Crossover Operators

We have seen from the experiment presented in Fig. 5.11 that sexual reproduction may succeed in spite of a rugged fitness landscape. But still the question remains if crossover can preserve favorable characteristics adequately?

Epistasis revisited. In Sect. 4.2 we have emphasized the obstacles arising from epistasis. Thereby we have differentiated between epistatic effects of linked loci and fitness contribution effects of epistasis. We have discussed the permutation representation and suitable crossover operators for the TSP and the QAP. We now extend these considerations to the JSP in order to work out the obstacles arising for the design of a suitable crossover operator.

- Since we use a permutation representation for the JSP, we have to deal with epistatic effects of linked loci. Crossover cannot combine solutions without partially destroying the parental information because it has to respect the permutation property. Our representation of the JSP obeys to the same restrictions pronounced for the TSP and the QAP.
- As shown by the JSP entropy in Tab. 5.3 roughly 15% of arc constellations are avoided because they lead to infeasible solutions. Since a chromosome cannot be decoded into a unique feasible solution, the epistatic effect due to linked loci is even larger than for the TSP and the QAP.
- Crossover has to respect the semantical properties of the underlying problem. For the TSP the relative order of genes is important whereas the absolute order is meaningless. For the QAP things are the other way round. Turning to the JSP we have to respect both, the relative order and the absolute order of genes, compare Sect. 6.2.1.
- In Sect. 4.2.2 we have examined the fitness contribution effects of epistasis. Thereby we have determined the number of linked genes which directly influence the fitness contribution of a single gene. For the TSP we have seen that the fitness contribution of each city depends on two other cities whereas for the QAP the fitness contribution of one unit may depend on the location of all other units in extreme cases. For the JSP the fitness contribution of a single operation depends on the predecessors and successors of both, its job and its machine. Hence at most four other operations directly influence the fitness contribution of a single operation.

To sum up, the assembling of an offspring from parental characteristics is more or less distorted by epistatic effects. On the genotypical level the combination of genes may cause implicit mutations. While decoding the genotype, the effect of crossover may be lost in order to avoid infeasible phenotypes. Finally the fitness is derived from the phenotype where the fitness contribution of a single characteristic depends on the occurrence of other characteristics. Since we cannot valuate the various epistatic effects in advance, three different crossover operators are defined and tested in the following.

Definition of Operators. The GOX crossover has been previously presented in Fig. 5.8. This operator performs syntactically correct for the permutation with repetition representation. Derived from GOX, which tends to respect the relative order of operations, we propose the generalized position crossover (GPX), which tends to respect the absolute order of operations.

1. parent	3	2	2	2	3	1	1	1	3
2. parent	1̸	1	3	2	2̸	1	1̸	3̸	3
GOX offspring	1	3	2	2	2	3	1	1	3
GPX offspring	1	3	2	2	3	1	2	1	3

Fig. 6.3. Generalized position crossover (GPX) in comparison to GOX.

Examples of GOX and GPX operations are given in Fig. 6.3. Recall that GOX implants a donator's substring at the position where the first operation of the substring has occured (before deletion) in the receiver. Hereby the first operation of the donator's substring is placed at its corresponding position in the receiver at the expense of neglecting the positions of the remainder operations in the substring. Therefore GOX performs well only if chromosomes of similar characteristics are crossed. GPX implants a substring in the receiver at that position where it occurs in the donator. The absolute order within the donator's substring is respected by neglecting the relative order of operations. GPX is assumed to outperform GOX when crossing less similar chromosomes.

The donator's substring is implanted without modifications whereas the receiving chromosome is strongly disrupted. In order to inherit the same amount of characteristics from both parents, the length of the donating substring should be smaller than the receiving string after deletion. We follow Gorges-Schleuter (1989) in varying the length of the donating substring uniformly in the range between 1/3 and 1/2 of the chromosome length.

Additionally we propose a uniform crossover (GUX) which purely respects the absolute order of operations. The offspring chromosome is initialized empty. A parent is chosen at random and the operation at the first position of the parental chromosome is appended to the offspring. Then this operation is deleted from both parents. This step is repeated until both parent strings are empty and the offspring contains all operations involved.

Summing up, all operators proposed recombine offspring by about the same amount of information of the two parents. Hereby, GOX tends to inherit the relative order of operations, GUX inherits just positions of operations, and GPX inherits the absolute order of operations respecting the relative ordering to some extent.

Operator evaluation. In order to valuate the above defined operators, we carry out some experiments in the following. We first concentrate on the properties of inheriting characteristics in terms of precedence relations among operations. Later, crossover effects on the fitness are taken into account.

The normalized Hamming distance D is used as a measure of the genotypical difference between parents and their offspring. In order to take the distortions caused by decoding into consideration, we evaluate the difference between genotypes as shown in Fig. 6.4. First the genotypes are decoded into the phenotypes of acyclic graphs. Next, a binary mapping of precedence relations is done for the phenotypes to determine their Hamming distance. In this way the Hamming distance reflects the characteristics of phenotypes instead of just considering genotypical information.

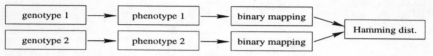

Fig. 6.4. Scheme for the Hamming distance calculation.

Now suppose a crossover operation of two arbitrary parents resulting in one offspring. Ideally the offspring inherits one half of the genotypical information from each parent. In the following experiment the normalized Hamming distance $D_{p1,p2}$ between two randomly generated parents $p1$ and $p2$ is measured. Then crossover is performed and the distance of the offspring o to the first parent $D_{o,p1}$ and to the second parent $D_{o,p2}$ is calculated.

operator	$D_{p1,p2}$	$D_{o,p1}$	$D_{o,p2}$	$D_{o,p1}+D_{o,p2}$
GUX	0.273	0.137	0.136	0.273
GPX	0.273	0.141	0.139	0.280
GOX	0.273	0.150	0.152	0.302

Table 6.2. Genotypical preservation of crossover.

Table 6.2 shows the results achieved for 1 000 crossover operations carried out on the mt10 problem. The mean normalized Hamming distance between two arbitrary solutions is 0.273. For the crossover operators considered we observe $D_{o,p1} \approx D_{o,p2}$. This proofs all operators to inherit the same portion of parental information to the offspring. For the GUX operator $D_{o,p1} + D_{o,p2} = D_{p1,p2}$ holds, thus we regard GUX to inherit parental characteristics almost perfectly. For the remaining operators we observe a sum which is larger than the distance between both parents, i.e. GPX and even worse GOX introduce implicit mutations.

Thus far we have examined the recombination of arbitrary solutions. Next, we are going to find out whether the similarity of parents is of importance for the success of recombination or if parents can be recombined regardless of their differences. Furthermore we investigate whether the values of Tab. 6.2 correspond to the fitness deviations of offspring. The experiment is performed as follows.

1. We generate pairs of parents p_1, p_2 such that the normalized Hamming distance of a pair falls into one of the 11 clustering intervals $[D_h, D_{h+1}]$ with $D_1 = 0.000, D_2 = 0.025, \ldots D_{11} = 0.275$. Therefore we generate p_1 randomly, then copy p_1 to p_2 and finally mutate p_2 iteratively until it falls into the desired cluster. In this experiment each cluster contains 1 000 parental pairs.

2. In order to determine the genotypical correlation between parents and offspring, we measure the normalized Hamming distance $D_{p2,p1}$ for a parental pair, denoted as $x_t (1 \le t \le 1\,000)$. Then we produce offspring by applying crossover to each of the 1 000 pairs. The sum of the distances $D_{o,p1}$ and $D_{o,p2}$ denotes y_t for pair t. For each cluster the correlation coefficient $R_{x,y}$ is calculated by (6.1).

3. We have seen in Sect. 4.2.1 that a purely syntactical view on crossover operators cannot satisfy. Therefore, additionally to the distance correlation we obtain the fitness correlation. Given the mean fitness x_t of parental solutions we apply crossover to achieve the fitness y_t of their offspring. Analogous to 2.) we calculate the fitness correlation coefficients for each cluster separately.

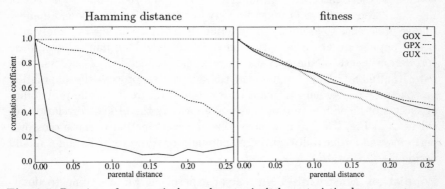

Fig. 6.5. Preserve of genotypical vs. phenotypical characteristics by crossover.

The experimental results are presented in Fig. 6.5. Let us start with a description of the distance correlation for GOX, GPX and GUX on the left side of the figure. Concerning GUX, the distance correlation coefficient is 1.0 in all clusters. This means that exactly half of the genetic information of both parents is inherited to offspring. The result is in accordance to the data of Tab. 6.2. GPX performs quite well as long as parents do not differ too much. The correlation coefficient decreases continuously with an increasing parental distance. In contrast, GOX offspring do hardly correlate with their parents.

The correlation of the fitness is shown on the right side of Fig. 6.5. Here we face a completely different situation. In clusters of $D < 0.075$ all operators perform more or less similar. For larger distances the fitness coefficient of

GUX decreases faster than the correlation coefficients of GOX and GPX. The difference between GPX and GOX is insignificant. It is amazing that GOX shows a strong fitness correlation while hardly correlating in terms of the Hamming distance. The dependencies of inherited genetic information appears to be more complex than we might have expected.

We have proofed the Hamming distance between offspring and parents to be of almost no importance. Furthermore, we have seen that the fitness correlation decreases for less similar parents regardless of the recombination operator used. This fact can be explained by observations reported earlier in Sect. 5.2. We have seen that numerous local optima are spread all over the search space. Since the correlation length of the landscape is approximately 0.06 we have conjectured that many good solutions do not correlate with one another. Although the definition of the correlation length appears somewhat vague, we can approve this conjecture from Fig. 6.5 implying that solutions of larger distances cannot be recombined effectively.

Recall, that the mean distance between randomly generated solutions is about 0.27. Calculating the fitness correlation coefficients based on randomly generated parents as proposed by Manderick et al. (1991) we obtain $R = 0.23$ for GUX, $R = 0.41$ for GOX and $R = 0.42$ for GPX. These values can be verified at the right border (argument 0.27) of the right hand side plot of Fig. 6.5. These coefficients suggest a very low correlation and therefore imply to give preference to asexual reproduction. In a GA we have a randomly generated population at initialization only. There, even long jumps beyond the correlation length of the operator have a high probability of success, compare Kauffman (1993). Later on in the adaptation process the population has partially converged by means of selection pressure. Now the probability of success of recombination increases as shown by the fitness correlation coefficients in Fig. 6.5. We now favor sexual recombination because crossover performs well for partially converged populations. However, we cannot finally decide if GOX or GPX works best.

Population Mastermind. In a final experiment we are going to determine the crossover operator of our choice. We setup a GA as sketched in Fig. 6.2. The experiment has much in common with the well known game "Mastermind". One player chooses a permutation of colored pins which is kept obscured for the second player. The second player attempts to find out the chosen permutation in a minimal number of trials. After each attempt the first player reveals the number of pins at the right position but conceals which pins are the ones scored. The GA considered in the following can be thought of as playing "Population Mastermind".

The normalized Hamming distance to the optimal solution is taken as the measure of fitness and consequently, the objective is to find a solution of distance $D = 0.0$. In doing so, the fitness determines how many precedence relations are set correctly. This fitness measure switches off the epistatic effects on the makespan from consideration. Instead, it isolates epistatic effects caused by linked loci in the representation.

We will give preference to that operator which gains near optimal solutions by exploiting favorable characteristics while exploring large regions of the search space at the same time. In order to measure the degree of exploration we introduce the online performance. This measure is calculated by summing up the so far obtained fitness of all individuals in all generations and dividing the sum by the number of evaluations performed. Thereby, a high online performance denotes a high degree of exploration.

The experiment is performed for GUX, GPX and GOX solving the mt10 problem. We use a population size of 100 individuals and a termination criterion of 350 generations. In each generation the fitness of the best individual, the average fitness of all individuals and the online performance are recorded. The results are averaged on the 10 runs performed.

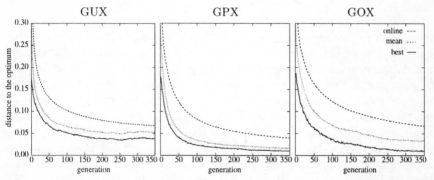

Fig. 6.6. Average curves of 10 runs each for the mt10 problem performed with GUX, GPX and GOX. The fitness is the Hamming distance to the optimum.

The results achieved are shown in Fig. 6.6. What immediately strikes is that the GUX based GA is not able to find a near optimal solution. GUX adapts too fast to regions of high fitness at the expense of neglecting a thorough exploration of the search space. In later phases of adaptation process the average fitness does not converge asymptotically to the currently best fitness gained, i.e. GUX does not recombine even resembling individuals adequately.

The GPX based GA shows a similar dynamic in the early phase of adaptation, but different to GUX, GPX gains further improvements in later phases. Again, the tendency to exploit characteristics is much higher than the tendency to explore various regions of the search space. In spite of the fast convergence observed, GPX continuously improves the solution quality. Notice, that the fitness measure provides a comparably smooth fitness landscape which is dominated by a single peak. A high degree of exploration is not necessary in such a landscape, but will be desired when the makespan is used as the fitness criterion.

The GOX based GA shows an unexpected dynamic. Although GOX improves considerably slower than GPX, in the end the same level of quality is reached. Even after 350 generations the average fitness is much higher than the fitness of the best individual of the population. Compared to GPX and GUX, GOX maintains the population diversity shown by the high online performance. GOX is able to preserve characteristics of near optimal solutions and to explore far away regions of the search space at the same time.

To sum up, we assume GPX as well as GOX to inherit building blocks which are constituted by absolute and relative order dependencies of operations. In spite of the low distance correlation of GOX, the property to inherit building blocks are sufficient. For a less rugged fitness landscape GPX would be an appropriate operator too, but for the JSP the GOX operator is the crossover of our choice.

6.2.3 Crossover- and Mutation Rate

The crossover rate ρ_c determines the probability of applying crossover to selected individuals. Analogous, the mutation rate ρ_m determines the probability of altering chromosomes by means of mutation. It can be inferred from Fig. 6.2 that an individual can enter the population of the next generation by applying neither crossover nor mutation. Together, both rates determine the likelihood for selected individuals to pass the reproduction without being modified. The more individuals are just copied to the next generation, the more adaptation tends to exploit characteristics in the gene pool.

Literature suggests a crossover rate $\rho_c = 0.6$ which has been proofed to work well for our purpose too. The mutation rate should be chosen with respect to the rate of implicit mutations caused by the crossover. Since GOX introduces a considerable amount of implicit mutations, a relatively low mutation rate is sufficient in order to maintain the population diversity. The mutation rate can either be given as the probability of affecting a certain individual or as the probability of affecting a certain gene of the gene pool. Since the crossover rate is given in terms of individuals affected, we determine the mutation rate in the same scale with $\rho_m = 0.03$.

6.3 Population Management

We now turn to the discussion of an appropriate population management. Concerning the population management we endeavor to use a widely accepted standard setting because of the following reasons. First, it keeps our implementation comparable to previous research. Second, we regard the population management to be of subordinate importance compared to the inheritance management. Third, we do not assume that conclusions for a general problem class can be drawn from a population management tuned to the requirements of a certain problem instance under consideration.

6.3.1 Population Size

This parameter is regarded to be crucial for GA performance. If the population size μ is too small, the schema processing feature is virtually disabled and the GA converges prematurely. In order to obtain a certain level of near-optimal quality in a prescribed runtime, either a large population size can be used or the algorithm can be run several times engaging a considerably smaller population size. The question arises, whether an optimal population size exists which maximizes the probability of reaching the goal?

A larger population is likely to produce a better solution, but there seems to be a saturation of the tendency, as noted by Nakano et al. (1994). According to them the probability to reach a certain solution quality with the population size μ follows an exponential dependency, asymptotically converging to 1 if μ tends to infinity. Nakano et al. have tested their theoretical work with the G&T GA formerly presented in Sect. 5.1.3. They show that an optimal population size exists for a problem instance, but no conclusion about optimal population sizes in general can be drawn.

For our purpose it is sufficient to state that there is a saturation of the tendency concerning the number of individuals involved. The decoding procedure for the JSP is computational expensive and therefore we should always take a close look at the tradeoff between an enlargement of the population size and the (marginal) improvements expected thereby.

6.3.2 Selection Scheme

Selection proliferates building blocks in the gene pool. Therefore building blocks must be identified by their fitness contribution, compare Sect. 4.2.2. We see the main obstacle for applying GAs to the JSP successfully in the fitness contribution of building blocks.

Recall from Sect. 2.1.3, that the fitness of a solution is determined by the length of the critical path in the acyclic graph. If an operation is touched by the critical path, its precedence relations to neighboring operations are potentially unfavorable. Favorable precedence relations of (a few) operations are regarded to form building blocks. The decoding of such building blocks does not improve the fitness of a solution as long as the critical path does not touch operations involved in the building block. Actually, the critical path potentially avoids operations within building blocks. Instead, the fitness of a solution is determined by unfavorable precedence relations among operations.

Therefore selection cannot prevail building blocks adequately but will merely drive out unfavorable characteristics from the gene pool. In terms of the fitness landscape, the population will flow towards regions of higher fitness just because regions of lower fitness are avoided. Based upon these considerations we conjecture a weak selection scheme to result in a tedious recombination of individuals without gaining substantial improvements. A severe selection scheme, which persistently drives out unfavorable characteristics, seems to be more adequate for the JSP.

In Sect. 4.2.2 we have discussed several selection schemes, in particular ranking and proportional selection. In our opinion there is no reason to believe that a sophisticated selection scheme performs better for the JSP.

Therefore we use the well known proportional selection in the following. Since the objective values of near optimal solutions differ within a small range only, we scale the fitness f within a population to the range $[0, f_{max} - f_{min}]$. In doing so, we achieve a more severe selection scheme compared to selection based upon the original fitness values. As a side effect, the worst individual is discarded from being selected.

6.3.3 Termination Criterion

At least three termination criterions are proposed in literature. The most simple one is a static number of generations. A more intricate one is a number of generations in which no improvement is gained. More flexible termination criterions are based on diversity tests of the population. For instance, this can be done by calculating the population entropy, compare Sect.5.2.4. The GA terminates when the population entropy drops below a given threshold. We reject flexible termination criterions because of the following reasons.

- In some GA runs the progress of adaptation suddenly stops for a number of generations at a mediocre level of quality before further substantial improvements are gained. In other runs for the same problem we observe a continuously increasing fitness.
- For some problems the gene pool diversity decreases drastically right at the beginning of the adaptation. Nevertheless, substantial improvements are gained. For other problems the gene pool diversity remains high for a large number of generations, although little improvements are found.

In order to achieve comparable runtimes in several runs for the same problem, we use a static number of generations as the termination criterion.

6.3.4 Local Search Hybridization

Hybrid GAs have been shown to outperform genuine GAs whenever an efficient base heuristic is available, compare e.g. Davis (1991). Hybrid GAs do not only produce superior results, moreover they achieve these results with smaller populations and in less generations. In spite of the comparably small number of fitness evaluations, hybrid GAs are not necessarily faster than genuine GAs because hybridization typically requires a considerable amount of runtime. However, the degree of hybridization directly influences the setting of the population management.

The base heuristic may gain a fitness improvement of the genotype obtained from reproduction. For the JSP, the G&T algorithm is typically incorporated in the decoding procedure in order to restrict the search space to the subset of active schedules. Alternatively, we may apply a Local Search procedure after decoding in order to reduce the search space to local optimal solutions.

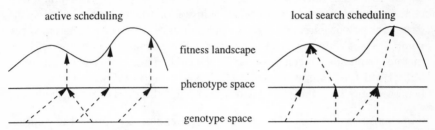

Fig. 6.7. Scheme of hybrid fitness evaluation.

Figure 6.7 illustrates the difference between active scheduling and Local Search based scheduling in analogy to the model of layers presented by Schull (1990). The bottom line represents a simplified (one dimensional) genotype space. The line in the middle represents the phenotype space which does not necessarily show the same dimensionality than the genotype space. The decoding maps genotypes to corresponding phenotypes. The fitness of a phenotype appears as a point in the fitness landscape.

The effect of the G&T algorithm is shown on the left side of Fig. 6.7. It distorts the mapping of a permutation chromosome (genotype) to its corresponding acyclic graph (phenotypes) by altering the scheduling order of operations while decoding. Then, the makespan (fitness) is determined directly for the phenotype. Local Search based scheduling is shown on the right side of the figure. Here, the semi-active decoding just avoids cyclic graphs (infeasible phenotypes). The mapping of genotypes to phenotypes is therefore more direct compared to G&T based decoding. After a phenotype is assembled, hill climbing transforms the phenotype to a local optimal solution.

Instead of assuring activeness of schedules (like many other GA approaches, compare Tab. 5.1), we incorporate local hill climbing after semi-active decoding, compare Fig. 4.5. Based upon our examination of several hill climbing procedures in Sect. 3.2.3 we engage the $\mathcal{N}_3$ neighborhood in combination with the steepest descendent control $\mathcal{C}_{st}$. This procedure has been proofed to work efficiently, i.e. to produce good results in a short runtime. The incorporation of this relatively weak local search procedure into a GA has certain advantages shown by example for the mt10.

– The proposed hill climber obtains a better average solution quality than the G&T algorithm (1213 compared to 1265) when running alone. Beside, the best objective value achieved by the hill climber in 1 000 runs (1008) is

far better than to the one obtained by the G&T algorithm (1088). Thus, hill climbing is superior to the G&T algorithm in terms of effectiveness.
- The entropy of a population of local optimal solutions is 0.816 whereas the a population of active solutions shows an entropy of 0.845. Since the entropy of randomly generated solutions is 0.848 (compare Tab. 5.3), we regard active schedules to have almost no exploitable problem structure in common. To the contrary, local optimal solutions share a certain amount of characteristics, required to obtain a solution of a near optimal makespan.
- The population learns favorable characteristics over time. Therefore the computational amount of hill climbing will continuously decrease with an increasing number of generations. To the contrary, active scheduling shows almost constant computational costs. Thus, using Local Search as the base heuristic may be even faster than active scheduling in later generations.

To sum up, we expect Local Search hybridization to improve the solution quality while decreasing the number of evaluations needed. The effect of hybridization will be investigated in the next section.

6.4 Applying Adaptive Scheduling

Yet everything is prepared well in order to apply GAs to the JSP. In order to get an impression of the GA performance, we carry out the following experiment. A GA is parameterized as follows: GOX is applied with a crossover rate of 60%. PBM mutations are carried out at a rate of 3%. A proportional selection scheme based on the scaled fitness is used. The population size is set to 100 individuals. Now, two GAs run for a total of 1 000 iterations solving the mt10 problem. The genuine GA runs 100 generations whereas the hybrid GA runs 50 generations only.

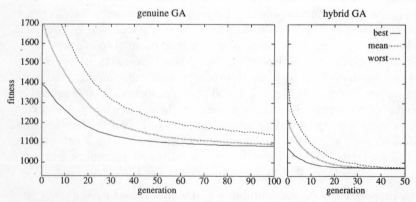

Fig. 6.8. Adaptation curves for a genuine and a hybrid GA averaged over 1 000 runs solving the mt10 problem.

The adaptation of both GAs is shown in Fig. 6.8. in terms of the best, mean and worst fitness of the current generation. The results are averaged over 1 000 runs carried out. The adaptation of the genuine GA, shown on the left hand side, achieves substantial improvements in the early phase of the adaptation process. After 50 generations further progress is limited until the population converges entirely in generation 100 with a fitness of approximately 1080. This result is far better than the average makespan obtained by the best hill climber (1149) using the intricate $\mathcal{N}_4$ neighborhood, compare Sect. 3.2.3. Notice, that the genuine GA works without any problem specific knowledge involved whereas the $\mathcal{N}_4/\mathcal{C}_{st}$ hill climber depends highly on the problem and objective under consideration.

The adaptation process of the hybrid GA, shown on the right hand side of Fig. 6.8, converges faster. After about 40 generations it has converged entirely with a fitness of approximately 960. The hybrid GA starts at a fitness which is roughly met by the genuine GA after 100 generations.

Table 6.3. Results obtained for a genuine GA and for a hybrid GA from 1 000 runs solving the mt10 problem.

GA	pop.	gen.	best	mean	err.	dev.	time[a]	eval[b]
genuine	100	100	1001	1082.5	16.3	3.6	12.0	1.20
hybrid	100	50	930	960.4	3.2	1.2	17.5	3.50

[a] Runtime in seconds.
[b] Evaluation time in milliseconds.

Table 6.3 shows the experimental results in more detail. The hybrid GA is able to solve the mt10 to the optimum 930 (best) and gains a far better mean fitness (mean) compared to the genuine GA. The mean relative error (err.) is computed by

$$err = 100 \cdot \frac{f_{mean} - f_{known}}{f_{known}} \tag{6.2}$$

where 'known' is the optimal makespan of 930 for this problem instance. The relative error of 16.3 for the genuine version can be significantly reduced to 3.2 by the hybrid GA. The standard deviation of the fitness from the mean fitness in percent (dev.) is 3.6 and 1.2 respectively. Notice the relatively short runtimes of 12.0 and 17.5 seconds for both versions. Because of hill climbing the runtime of the hybrid GA increases about 30% using 50% less generations.

The evaluation time in milliseconds (msec) is computed by dividing the total runtime of the GA by the number of evaluations performed. The CPU time needed for selection, reproduction and evaluation within the hybrid GA is 3.5 msec. Since a single evaluation requires 1.2 msec. for the genuine GA, the additional CPU time needed for hill climbing is roughly 2.3 msec.

Now recall from Tab. 3.6, that a single run of the $\mathcal{N}_3/\mathcal{C}_{st}$ hill climber requires 16.8 msec in average. Because of $\rho_c = 0.6$ used, roughly 40% of the individuals pass the reproduction without modification and evaluation.

Subtracting 40% of 16.8 msec. leads to approximately 10 msec. CPU time for a single hill climb. Actually, the hybrid GA spends only 2.3 msec. for hill climbing in average. This amazing difference is explained by the observation, that the population flows towards regions of favorable characteristics in the fitness landscape, compare Fig. 6.1. Therefore in later stages of adaptation the number of moves performed by the hill climber decreases strongly.

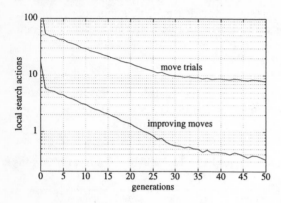

Fig. 6.9. The hill climbing improvements vs. the move trials performed given for a single individual over time. Mean of 100 runs solving mt10.

Figure 6.9 confirms the above explanation. Recall from Sect. 3.2 that the basic outline of the steepest descending control. In order to gain one successful move, all promising move candidates along the critical path are evaluated (actually they are estimated). After a successful move the critical path changes unpredictably and the procedure is repeated until no improving move can be gained. Figure 6.9 shows the number of move trials and improving moves performed by individuals in generation 0 up to generation 50. A randomly generated individual requires a considerable amount of moves in order to become a local optimum. Over the generations the amount of moves decreases continuously. After about 25 generations only one improving move can be performed for a recombined offspring in average.

Up to generation 30 move trials and improving moves decrease at a proportional rate. From then on, typically local optimal solutions are assembled by crossover. Local optimal solutions cannot be improved by hill climbing moves. Therefore the number of move candidates (along the critical path) remain constant at approximately 10 trials whereas the improving moves further decrease with an increasing number of generations. At this point of time the computational amount needed for hill climbing is almost negligible.

Figure 6.10 presents the distribution of makespan frequencies obtained by the hybrid GA. Although the mean fitness of 960 seems to be fairly good, the observed deviations in 1 000 runs appear quite high. Actually the optimum 930 is found two times only. Although the majority of results is better than 980, we observe even some worse results above 1000 units.

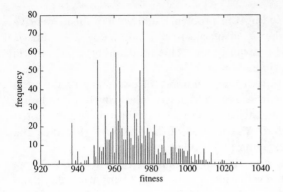

Fig. 6.10. Distribution of results obtained by the hybrid GA in 1 000 runs solving the mt10 problem.

Thus far we have just considered the famous mt10 problem. In order to valuate the hybrid GA (called GA1 in the following), one single result will hardly satisfy. Therefore we present the results obtained for a well known test suite of particularly hard, but medium sized problems. The suite consists of the mt10, the mt20 and another 10 tough problems collected by Applegate and Cook (1991), all-together listed in Tab. 8.3.

We use the set of parameters described above without further parameters tuning. Since most of the problems are considerably larger than the mt10, we merely enhance the number of generations to 100, i.e. in each run 10 000 evaluations are carried out. The GA1 runs for a total of 50 iterations on each of the 12 benchmark problems.

prob.	n	m	known	mean	err.	dev.
mt10	10	10	930	959.1	3.1	1.2
mt20	20	5	1165	1181.9	1.5	0.4
abz7	20	15	665	687.9	3.1	1.1
abz8	20	15	670	699.6	4.4	0.8
abz9	20	15	686	716.2	3.6	0.7
la21	15	10	1046	1070.0	2.3	0.9
la24	15	10	935	955.9	2.2	0.9
la25	15	10	977	990.0	1.3	0.5
la27	20	10	1235	1265.7	2.5	0.2
la29	20	10	1153	1212.1	4.8	1.4
la38	15	15	1196	1235.2	3.3	1.2
la40	15	15	1222	1258.0	2.9	0.8

Table 6.4. GA1 results obtained for the mt10, mt20 and another 10 tough problems, see Tab. 8.3.

Table 6.4 shows the results obtained. Beside the problem name the size ($n{\times}m$) and the best known makespan is referred. The last three columns list the computational results. First, the mean fitness is given. The relative error is calculated as shown in (6.2). Finally the standard deviation in percent is calculated for the mean fitness obtained. The mean makespan obtained differ roughly 30 units from the best known makespan which is proofed to be optimal for all instances except la29. The average of the mean relative error over all problems is 2.9, including the problem la29 with a mean relative error of 4.8. The standard deviation of the results obtained in 50 runs is with an average value of 0.84 pleasantly low. This proofs hybridized genetic adaptation to be a robust optimization strategy.

Larger problems may require a larger number of evaluations than used in these computations. Therefore we could have enlarged the population size in order to reduce the mean fitness and the deviation. But as noted by Nakano et al. (1994), there is a saturation of the tendency regarding the improvements obtained by engaging larger population sizes.

Furthermore we could have used a larger number of generations in order to increase the number of evaluations carried out. Comparing the mean makespan obtained for the mt10 problem in Tab. 6.3 and Tab. 6.4 we observe an improvement of only 1 unit in makespan, although the number of generations performed is doubled from 50 to 100.

This observation is not amazing by considering that the population has already converged at generation 40 in case of the mt10, compare Fig. 6.8. Thus, a considerably higher mutation rate is needed in order to delay convergence. Consequently, an even more severe selection scheme is required in order to keep up selection pressure. Actually such a strategy results in a direction-less search at a near-optimal level of solution quality. Furthermore, we do not expect mutations to explore a so far unexplored region of the search space. Although slightly better results may be gained, the runtime amount needed in order to find these improved solutions may be enormous. Hence, we confine the GA1 to 10 000 evaluations in order to keep the algorithm fast.

To sum up, the hybrid approach presented is capable of finding near optimal solutions considerably fast. Nevertheless it appears doubtful whether further substantial improvements can be gained by a more sophisticated parameter setting in the underlying GA template.

7. Adaptation of Structured Populations

So far, we have presupposed a complete dispersion of individuals over a large (potentially infinite) population. This model assumes, that an individual can recombine with any other individual of the population. It is referred to as random mating in the following. Already in the early thirties Sewall Wright recognized, that random mating is susceptible to local optima in the fitness landscape. Selection reduces the variation in the population by favoring genotypes located at peaks of the landscape. Once occupying those peaks, selection prevents the population to escape from there.

We agree with Schull (1990) in arguing that individuals, but not populations, can be expected to accept short term losses in order to achieve long term gains. Therefore only single individuals may discover a location "far away" of similar or even better quality in the landscape. A typically "slow" move of the population in the direction of such a newly discovered point in the landscape is called genetic drift. Genetic drift causes a significant change of gene frequencies in the gene pool triggered by a small fraction of superior, newly introduced genes.

The predominance of mediocre genes, resulting from the majority of individuals occupying a small portion of the landscape, prevent newly introduced genes from being preserved in the gene pool. This phenomenon is reinforced by epistatic effects of the genetic representation. In this case, individuals cannot recombine adequately and the offspring of highly fit parents are excluded from selection because of their typically low fitness.

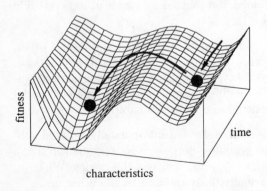

Fig. 7.1. The population got stuck in a local optimum of a minimization problem. How can this population surmount the hillside in order to gain the fitness improvement?

Figure 7.1 illustrates the situation of a population trapped in a local optimum for a minimization problem. Even if a single individual improves its fitness significantly by performing a long jump from the valley on the right over the hilltop, it will be almost impossible to draw the entire population towards the newly discovered location. Since evolution (i.e. changes of the gene frequency in a population's gene pool) is taking place in small moves within the fitness landscape, the population will hardly surmount the hillside.

Wright suggested that the problem of getting stuck in local optima would be less acute when a population is divided in "local" sub-populations. Therefore spatially divided populations are subject of the following considerations.

7.1 Finite and Structured Populations

Random mating is an abstraction for biological populations, where individuals are more likely to mate with their neighbors. The mating of individuals is therefore restricted to local recombination among neighbors forming a sub-population. In a first step we view the various sub-populations as finite populations of small size. The assumption of finite populations has significant consequences for the population flow on the fitness landscape, which partially contradict to each other.

– The individuals within a finite population perform an exploring search in the fitness landscape because sampling error in small populations increases the importance of mutation and genetic drift compared to selection. Hence selection pressure may not sufficiently hold the population at regions of high fitness in the landscape.
– Evolution in finite populations is very fast compared to evolution in large (theoretically infinite) populations. Therefore inbreeding occurs early in the adaptation process. But, promising gene constellations will persist and spread rapidly in the finite population once they arise.
– The various sub-populations will adapt to different regions of high fitness in the landscape in parallel. Premature convergence as observed for random mating populations is avoided, but inbreeding may lead to genetically incompatible sub-populations.

In fact, sub-populations are not completely isolated from each other. Instead a diluted gene flow occurs between the various sub-populations. Smith (1989) names three different ways of modeling the phenomenon of limited dispersal in a population. These different models reflect different spatial density distributions of individuals in a population's habitat.

– In the island model the population is divided into partially isolated sub-populations, called demes. The gene flow between demes occurs through a small fraction of the individuals migrating between the demes. When an individual does migrate, it is equally likely to move to any other deme.

– The stepping-stone model introduces a distance between the demes. The migrants always move to a deme in their proximity. Apart from this proximity relation of demes, this model is identical to the island model. The island- and the stepping stone model are referred to as migration models.
– In the continuous model there are no demes, but dispersal distances are short, such that mating individuals were also born in the proximity of one another. The model depicts a spatially uniform distribution of individuals. Here, diffusion of genes occurs due to overlapping spatial neighborhoods. Therefore this model is also referred to as diffusion model.

Each of the three models lead to a structure of the overall population. The local mating scheme quickly reduces the genotypical diversity in the various sub-populations. On the other hand a high population diversity is maintained for the overall population. Thereby a limited number of genes are continuously exchanged between the sub-populations. Whenever individuals can be recombined successfully, new highly fit genes are spread out rapidly within their sub-population.

In the presence of epistasis, genetically incompatible sub-populations evolve and the overall population cannot converge entirely. We doubt the usefulness of the migration models in the presence of epistasis. Migrating individuals cannot recombine successfully in most cases and their offspring will be excluded from being selected. Therefore we concentrate on the continuous model hereafter.

7.1.1 Structured Population GAs

Literature reports various attempts of modeling structured populations GAs (SP-GAs). A comprehensive survey of structured population approaches and local mating strategies is given in Gorges-Schleuter (1992).

The first approach of a continuous population model within a GA is due to Mühlenbein et al. (1988). This research has lead to the famous ASPARAGOS approach of Gorges-Schleuter (1989). This approach is motivated by the excellent suitability of SP-GAs for a (parallel) transputer hardware. Here, the population is mapped to a connected grid of processors, such that each individual resides on one processor. Since a central control of the algorithm is not needed when using a structured population, a considerable speed-up of the parallel implementation can be observed. Due to this fact SP-GAs are often referred to as 'massively parallel GAs', compare Spiessens and Manderick (1991). Meanwhile, the interest in transputer hardware is declining, despite parallel implementations of SP-GAs are still a topic of research, compare e.g. Stender (1993).

Figure 7.2 shows a population mapped onto a torodial connected grid. A torus has the advantage of introducing a spatial distance between individuals by avoiding border locations. In the exemplary illustration each individual has four neighbors located to its east, north, west and south. This spatial

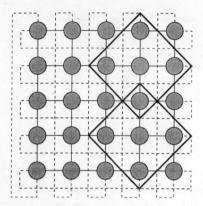

Fig. 7.2. A structured population on a torodial grid avoids border locations. The overlapping sub-populations consist of five individuals each.

structure can be seen as an artificial habitat in which mating is restricted to overlapping neighborhoods. A population structure as well as a suitable definition of the local mating scheme has to be chosen in a way such that a sufficient gene flow through the population and a sufficient spatial distance between the individuals is "well balanced".

Whenever hybridization is incorporated into a GA, smaller population sizes are needed. A torodial population structure comes up with a maximal distance between the individuals of $\beta = \lfloor \sqrt{(\mu/2)} \rfloor$ for the population size μ. This means, that it will take at least β generations to spread a newly introduced gene throughout the entire population. In populations of small size, this distance might not be sufficient in order to separate the individuals adequately from each other. Therefore Gorges-Schleuter (1989) proposes a ladder-structured population in order to provide larger β for a given μ than the β achieved by a torodial structure. A ladder shows a considerable larger $\beta = \lfloor \mu/4 \rfloor + 1$. At the extreme a ring provides a maximal $\beta = \lfloor \mu/2 \rfloor$.

Both, the mating scheme and the population structure determine the degree of dispersal within a population. Davidor (1991) suggests a torodial structure with a neighborhood size of eight by also including the individuals in the north-east, north-west, south-east and south-west. Additionally to this eight-individual neighborhood Collins and Jefferson (1991) simulate a more realistic mating process. They let an individual perform a random walk of a few steps on the torodial grid in order to find an appropriate mate. Both approaches increase the dispersal within the population which in turn requires larger population sizes in order to provide sufficient spatial distances between the various neighborhoods of the habitat.

There may exist an optimal mating scheme/population structure for a fixed population size and a problem under consideration. However, an optimal population structure appears to be highly problem dependent because the gene flow through the habitat strongly depends on the individuals ability to recombine themselves successfully.

7.1.2 Incorporating the Diffusion Model

In order to compare the performance of an SP-GA with the GA1 presented in Chap. 6, we use the same inheritance management (representation, crossover and mutation) as given in Sect. 6.2. Here, we skip evaluation of a genuine SP-GA variant and turn to a hybridized SP-GA directly. This approach is referred to as GA2 in the following.

We confine ourselves to the basic torodial population structure shown in Fig. 7.2. Thereby each individual has four neighbors and locally mates within this sub-population. Therefore the selection scheme of the GA1 is replaced by a local mating scheme. Obviously, the sub-population size of five individuals is too small in order to rely on selection holding the sub-population at regions of high fitness in the search space. Instead, we set the crossover rate $\rho_c = 1.0$ and select a partner for each mating individual from its neighborhood. The selection is based on the scaled fitness values, compare Sect. 6.3.2. Recall, that the fitness scaling excludes the worst individual from being selected. This results in a very severe selection scheme by taking just 3 of 4 neighboring individuals into account. After being recombined an individual is mutated with probability $\rho_m = 0.03$.

Experiments have shown, that even this severe selection scheme does not suffice in holding the population at a level of high fitness. Therefore we follow Gorges-Schleuter (1989) by introducing the acceptance criterion ξ which controls the replacement of a parent by its offspring, compare Sect. 4.2.2. We use a flexible acceptance criterion based on the fitness f and the lower bound LB of the problem instance as proposed by Taillard (1993b). The mating individual p is replaced by its offspring o only if $f_o < f_p + (f_p - LB) \cdot \xi$ holds. Otherwise the offspring is discarded and the affected parent enters the next generation unchanged. We found by experiment that $\xi = 0.10$ works well for our purpose. The acceptance criterion leads to a continuously decreasing rate of accepted individuals[1] with an increasing mean fitness of the population.

As previously done in Chap. 6 for the GA1 we test the GA2 with several benchmarks. Again 50 runs are carried out with the population size and the number of generations both set to 100.

The results obtained for the GA2 are shown in Tab. 7.1. By comparing the results with the ones for the GA1 shown in Tab. 6.4, we recognize significant improvements of the average results obtained for the 12 benchmarks. This is expressed by a mean relative error averaged over the problems of 2.4 compared to 2.9 for the GA1. The standard deviation of the makespan from the mean makespan in percent is significantly reduced as well. The GA2 shows an average over all problems of 0.73 compared to 0.84 for the GA1. However, we notice a runtime increase of $\approx 40\%$, because the crossover rate is increased

---

[1] For the mt10 we calculate an $LB = 796$. By applying the acceptance criterion we allow 93 makespan units deterioration for a random solution of quality 1730. The optimal solution 930 may be replaced by an inferior solution differing in at most 13 units.

prob.	size	known	mean	err.	dev.
mt10	10×10	930	950.7	2.2	0.9
mt20	20×05	1165	1181.1	1.4	0.5
abz7	20×15	665	687.0	3.0	0.8
abz8	20×15	670	698.0	4.2	0.6
abz9	20×15	686	714.4	3.4	0.7
la21	15×10	1046	1061.1	1.4	0.6
la24	15×10	935	945.3	1.1	1.1
la25	15×10	977	988.5	1.2	0.4
la27	20×10	1235	1264.0	2.4	0.4
la29	20×10	1153	1202.2	3.9	1.0
la38	15×15	1196	1225.7	2.5	0.9
la40	15×15	1222	1247.4	2.1	0.8

Table 7.1. GA2 results obtained for the mt10, mt20 and another 10 tough problems listed in Tab. 8.3. For each problem 50 runs are performed.

from $\rho_c = 0.6$ for the GA1 to $\rho_c = 1.0$ for the GA2. The management of the structured population itself is of negligible influence on the runtime.

7.1.3 Population Flow in the Diffusion Model

The advantage of the GA2 is best outlined by describing a typical run. Figure 7.3 on pp. 118–119 documents three distinct generations, namely 25, 75 and 150. The run is carried out with a population size of $\mu = 2\,500$ residing on a 50×50 torus, referred to as the population's habitat in the following. In order to visualize the individuals adequately, the torus is cut resulting in a two dimensional grid. We have chosen the extremely large population size of 2 500 in order to achieve a visual impression of the population flow. We discuss four different measures which are shown by means of the following filters:

Fitness obtained. The plots a)–c) show the fitness obtained in the range [930,1050]. Thereby a dark gray shade indicates a high fitness whereas light shades indicate individuals or low fitness. Larger makespans than 1050, which merely are observed in plot a), are mapped to white shade. Most individuals have obtained a fitness < 1050 even in generation 25 as can be seen in plot a). Furthermore we identify several spots indicating neighboring individuals of similar fitness. In generation 75, shown in plot b), some spots have enlarged to areas by driving out other spots of inferior fitness. This process has resulted in a substantial improvement of the mean fitness of the population. Three large areas in the habitat have evolved to a near-optimal fitness independently (indicated by dark shade).

Finally, plot c) shows the habitat in generation 150 consisting of a few large areas of similar fitness. In the upper right corner of the habitat an optimal fitness of 930 has been achieved. Because of the predominant dark shade we can clearly identify mutated individuals of inferior fitness as light gray spots. In this phase of the evolution further enlargement of the fitness areas stops. Actually, we obtain a similar picture as in plot c) for generation 300 (not shown).

Distance to the optimum. The plots d)–f) show the normalized Hamming distance D to the optimal solution as defined in (5.5). The mean normalized Hamming distance of an initial population is $D = 0.27$ and the maximally observed distance is $D \approx 0.4$, compare Sect. 5.2.3. Notice, that the actual values are mapped to six distinct shades representing the range [0.0,0.4]. We conjecture resembling genotypes of neighboring individuals to have a similar distance to the optimal solution. Actually there is no proof, since the distance metric does not obey the condition of transitivity.

Plot d) of generation 25 clearly shows various regions of similar distance which loosely correspond to the fitness spots observed in plot a). Even in this early stage we identify two regions of near-optimal distance indicated by black shade. In generation 75 the smaller region has been driven out, but the larger region has persisted by gradually extending its size. Amazingly, the region of near-optimal distance (black) shows an inferior fitness in plot b).

Plot f) of generation 150 closely corresponds to the shaping of the areas of similar fitness shown in plot c). The region of the small distance to the optimum of plot e) has been strongly enlarged in the meantime. Plot c) shows that its individuals already have found the optimal fitness of 930. Although another region on the left of plot f) has evolved independently to a very small distance to the optimum, its corresponding fitness is still not optimal.

In a randomly mating population the black area in plot e) would have been quickly driven out by selecting putative superior individuals indicated by dark shade in plot b). In structured populations such regions of putative inferior individuals may persist, what Davidor (1991) calls the niche phenomenon. The individuals are given a longer time to evolve their prerequisites in order to improve their fitness before they are taken over by other individuals of superior fitness. Davidor et al. (1993) verify the niche phenomenon exemplary for the JSP. The results of the G&T GA of Yamada and Nakano (1992), compare Sect. 5.1.3, can be improved considerably by engaging structured populations.

Neighborhood entropy. The plots g)–i) document the entropy E as given in (5.8). Recall, that E denotes the gene diversity within a population, compare Sect. 5.2.4. Here, E is measured for a sub-population consisting of the individual considered and its four-individual neighborhood. E tends to 1.0 for very large populations only. By considering a sub-population of five individuals the maximally observed entropy is $E = 0.5$. The E values are therefore clustered to six distinct shades representing the range [0.0,0.5].

Plot g) shows the entropy within the various neighborhoods in generation 25. As formerly conjectured from plot d), already in this early phase of adaptation small regions of almost identical genotypes have been formed. Here, spots of black shade indicate neighborhoods consisting of almost identical individuals. In generation 75 the overall picture has changed drastically. Regions of similar genotypes have been enlarged, enclosed by relatively thin but long areas of neighborhoods with a higher genotypical variation.

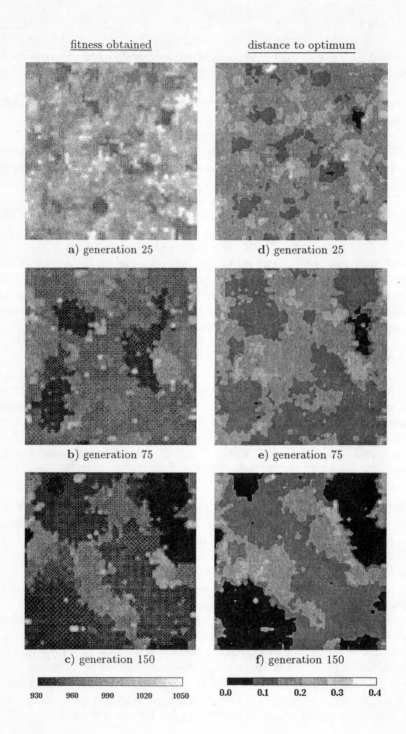

fitness obtained   distance to optimum

a) generation 25   d) generation 25

b) generation 75   e) generation 75

c) generation 150   f) generation 150

930   960   990   1020   1050   0.0   0.1   0.2   0.3   0.4

neighborhood entropy   hill climbing moves

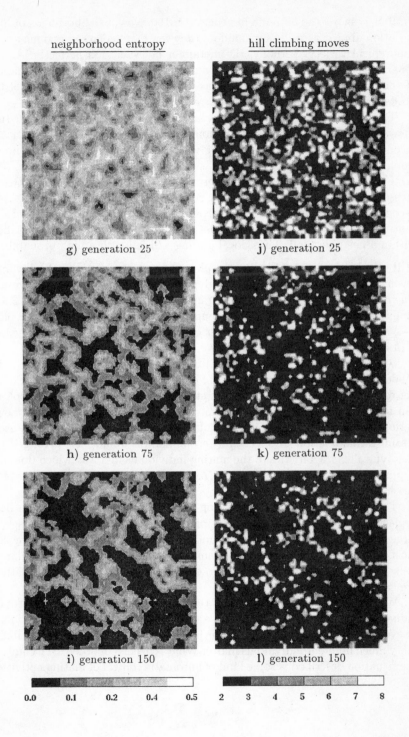

g) generation 25   j) generation 25

h) generation 75   k) generation 75

i) generation 150   l) generation 150

0.0   0.1   0.2   0.4   0.5   2   3   4   5   6   7   8

Plot i) shows the extreme in generation 150. Now, neighborhoods of high variation appear as walls surrounding the even more enlarged regions of low genotypical variety. Actually, the metaphor of "wall" fits perfectly: A wall separates two different regions of low variation. In order to achieve the shaping of the areas observed in c) and f), we merely add half of the width of the border walls to the sizes of the black regions in i).

The overall picture of plot i) has hardly changed in generation 300 (not shown). Therefore we conjecture regions separated by walls to be genetically incompatible. Otherwise local mating within the overlapping neighborhoods would have continued to enlarge and shrink areas of similar genotypes.

The above conjecture can be verified by considering the properties of crossover, compare Sect. 6.2.2. The right plot of Fig. 6.5 on p. 99 shows a continuously decreasing fitness correlation for increasing genotypical distances of the parents. The walls in plot i) indicate high genotypical distances within a neighborhood. Thus, local mating will fail with a high probability.

Hill climbing moves. Finally, the plots j)–l) give the number of hill climbing moves performed after the decoding of a newly recombined individual. The number of moves is given in the range $[2,8]$ neglecting the values < 2 and mapping the values > 8 to 8. By comparing the overall picture of the plots j)–l) we observe a decreasing number of moves performed. This observation is in accordance with Fig. 6.9 for a random mating population.

By taking a first glance on plot l) it surprises that only black and white shades are left. This indicates that hill climbing either performs a large number of steps or it performs almost no steps at all. By taking a closer look we can identify at least some of the walls of plot i). A high number of moves performed in a later phase of the adaptation process indicates an unsuccessful recombination. A successful recombination would have arranged the genotypical characteristics of the mating individuals in a way which does not require local hill climbing anymore. Again, this gives a hint to genotypical incompatibilities due to epistasis.

Thus far we have concentrated on the white spots in plot l). We have neglected that most of the habitat is of black shade. Since we have observed large regions of similarity for c), f) and i), it is not surprising anymore that most individuals recombine (successfully) with genetically very similar or even identical neighbors. In the lingo of evolutionary genetics such matings are called inbreeding.

We state that in later phases of the adaptation process mating of individuals becomes futile either because of inbreeding (resembling individuals or even identical individuals mate) or because of genotypical incompatibility (very much different individuals mate). What is needed in order to circumvent the situation described is some kind of automatic control of mating activities.

7.2 Inheritance of Attitudes

In structured populations derived from the diffusion model mating is restricted to a small number of nearby individuals. Hence global premature convergence is postponed at the expense of inbreeding in the neighborhood. In the following we describe a model of behavioral inheritance previously presented by Mattfeld et al. (1994) in order to control inbreeding.

The control model makes use of the fact that crossover reduces the genotypical variation within a population whereas mutation increases this variation. In an early phase of the adaptation process we expect crossover to explore promising regions of the search space efficiently by means of stochastic sampling. In this phase mutations would merely lead to early entrapments in local regions of the search space. Nevertheless, in later phases of adaptation we expect mutations to maintain the gene pool diversity.

In our approach the degree of crossover vs. mutation is auto-adaptive over the GA's runtime. Instead of a global control mechanism we give preference to a local control scheme.

7.2.1 Metaphor of Learned Behavior

In a randomly mating GA the gene pool diversity changes constantly at a slow pace and evolution from generation to generation works well. The genotypical environment is the same for all individuals of the population. Whenever localities are introduced, evolution within the sub-populations is too fast to maintain similar mating conditions for all neighborhoods.

Instead, each individual faces its own specific environmental conditions given by the genotypical diversity of its neighborhood. Hence, it is most desirable that individuals change their behavior as a function of changes of their environment in a useful way. We propose a model in which inherited behavior controls the way of reproduction for an individual. Thereby we borrow the basic ideas from the (psychologist) school of Behaviorism.

This school became important in the early days of the twentieth century. Staats (1975) gives a comprehensive survey and emphasizes that complex functional behavior of an individual is learned and that environmental events can affect the individuals behavior. Thorndike (1874–1949) laid the foundations in 1898 with his "law of effect": One effect of successful behavior is to increase the probability that it will be used again in similar circumstances. Rewards granted in case of success lead to patterns of behavior, called habits.

In 1947 Doob extended the formal learning theory to the consideration of attitudes. He suggested that attitudes are anticipatory responses which can mediate behavior. An attitude can be seen as a disposition to react favorably or unfavorably to a class of environmental stimuli. Staats notes that in social interactions attitudes are formed by social rewards which stimulate reinforcement on certain behavior.

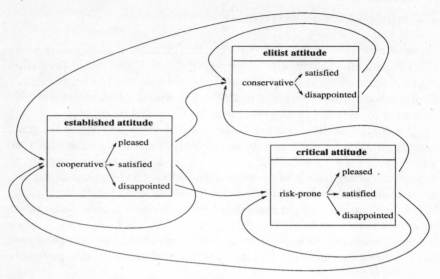

Fig. 7.4. Scheme of attitude transitions.

As shown in Fig. 7.4 we classify individual behavior by three general cases. The initial attitude of individuals is an established one, i.e. they all act cooperatively within their environment. Secondly, the elitist attitude follows a conservative attitude. The last attitude is a more critical one, which tends to act risk-prone. The actual behavior carried out is rewarded in terms of social interaction. Again we classify three simple responses which are defined by reinforcements. An individual can be pleased, satisfied or disappointed.

The success of the actual behavior carried out may change its attitude and therefore changes its habit in a similar situation within the near future. The individual will react differently and may receive a different reinforcement on the same environmental situation.

In most cases a cooperative individual will be satisfied and therefore does not change its attitude. If pleased by the success of its habit, next time it will tend to act conservative trying to keep its previous performance level. With this elitist attitude an individual can only be satisfied or disappointed by the success of its habit. In case of disappointment it will change back to the established attitude.

Failing on cooperative behavior brings up a critical attitude of the individual towards its neighborhood environment. It will then tend towards a more risk-prone behavior. The critical attitude is kept so long as a disappointing response is still received. If the individual is satisfied by the result of its behavior, it may change to the established attitude again. In rare cases a risk-prone individual will receive a pleasing response. Then it changes towards the elitist attitude directly.

Don't expect Fig. 7.4 to be a blueprint of the complete transition structure of the attitude changes. In fact the response on a certain behavior gives only a rough idea of which attitude may be suitable for the next trial. In general, attitudes are changed only after a number of identical reinforcements. Strong reinforcements can lead to immediate attitude changes, while, in general, weak and moderate reinforcements lead to memory adjustments only.

7.2.2 Model of Attitude Inheritance

In order to implement attitude inheritance we transform our metaphor into a local mating scheme. The established attitude corresponds to cooperation with one of the neighbors by crossover. The critical attitude corresponds to a mutation. The conservative behavior tries to save the state reached so far. Here, the he individual performs no active operation (i.e. is sleeping) in order to avoid replacement by offspring.

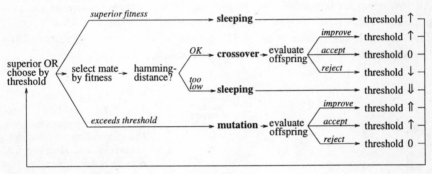

Fig. 7.5. Control model of local recombination.

In Fig. 7.5, an individual first compares its fitness with the fitness in its neighborhood. If the fitness is superior to all neighbors, the conservative behavior will cause the individual to sleep. If several best individuals exist in one neighborhood none of them will be superior. For this reason incorporating attitude inheritance does not introduce an elitist strategy.

An inferior individual determines its attitude. Therefore its actual behavior is drawn probabilistically from an interval [0,1]. Initially a threshold is set to 1.0 enforcing crossover. Decreasing the threshold increases the probability of mutation. In case of crossover, the Hamming distance to the selected mate is evaluated. If mates differ in less than 1% of their genes it seems not worthwhile to try a crossover. Again, the individual sleeps, but now because of a different reason. If crossover or mutation is carried out, the fitness of the offspring is evaluated. Either an offspring dominates both parents (improve), or the acceptance rule decides whether to replace the individual by its offspring (accept) or not (reject).

Summing up all distinct operations we count eight responses which are tied to reinforcements of the threshold. We modify the threshold by rules of plausibility. In Fig. 7.5 the symbols "⇑⇓↓↑" express the degree of changes of the threshold. This rule set attempts to adjust the behavior of each single individual towards the environment of its neighborhood. In our implementation the setting ⇑ = +0.15, ⇓ = −0.15, ↑ = +0.05, ↓ = −0.05 performed well. This setting reacts adaptively on the occurrence of inbreeding with a strong decrease of the threshold. It favors risky behavior by mutations in later generations. In turn, a succeeding mutation increases the threshold and leads to crossover again.

The implementation of inherited attitudes into the GA2 is referred to as GA3 in the following. Apart from the local mating strategy all other parameters are taken from the GA2 without modifications.

7.2.3 Operation Frequencies

An investigation is carried out performing 50 GA3 runs for the mt10. The population size is set to 196 individuals residing on a 14×14 torodial grid. The termination criterion is set to 150 generations. The results presented are the average obtained from the 50 runs performed.

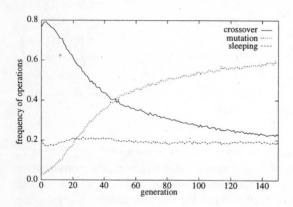

Fig. 7.6. Relative frequency of operations over the generations. Crossover, mutation and sleeping frequencies are given in the range [0,1].

Figure 7.6 shows the relative frequencies of reproduction operations performed in the GA3. In the beginning crossover dominates mutation as well as sleeping. While the crossover frequency decreases, the mutation frequency increases. Sleeping occurs at an almost constant rate of $\approx 20\%$. In the following we evaluate each of the three operation frequencies separately.

Figure 7.7 shows the frequency of sleeping due to one of two distinct reasons. Sleeping is either performed due to a superior fitness of an individual in its sub-population or due to a small Hamming distance in case of a crossover attempt. In the initial phase of adaptation sleeping caused by a very small Hamming distance between mating individuals rarely occurs. Here, sleeping

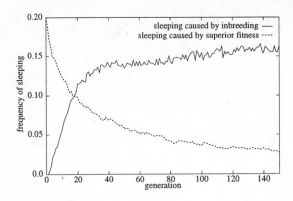

Fig. 7.7. Two distinct reasons for sleeping are shown separately. The sum of the two cases corresponds to the sleeping curve shown in Fig. 7.6.

caused by a superior fitness is almost solely responsible for the overall sleeping rate. Over time sleeping caused by a superior fitness decreases whereas sleeping caused by inbreeding increases. Notice, that together the GA3 saves about 20% of the evaluations needed in comparison to the GA2.

Both curves of Fig. 7.7 give an approximation of the size and number of the areas of low genotypical variation in the habitat, compare Fig. 7.3 for the GA2. Recall, that sleeping caused by superior fitness occurs only if an individual is superior to all its neighbors. Over time the areas of low genotypical variation enlarge and consequently sleeping caused by superior fitness is observed less often. To the contrary, with enlarging areas of low genotypical variation mates recognize a too small distance in case of a crossover attempt more often. As previously seen for the GA2 in Fig. 7.3, area enlargements stop in later generations. We conjecture a similar behavior for the GA3, because there seems to be a saturation for both curves shown in Fig. 7.7.

We now turn to a detailed evaluation of the crossover outcome which forms three of eight responses for reinforcements of the attitude inheritance model shown in Fig. 7.5. Therefore we classify crossover outcome of Fig. 7.6 into three cases: A crossover may lead to an offspring whose fitness dominates both parents (improve). Furthermore, the fitness of the offspring either satisfies the acceptance criterion or not. In the former case the offspring replaces its parent (accept) whereas in the latter case the offspring is rejected and the parent is left untouched (reject).

Figure 7.8 shows that the outcome of most crossover operations do not satisfy the acceptance criterion. The GA3 tends to apply crossover if mating individuals differ significantly from each other in terms of their Hamming distance. This leads to crossover at the borders of the areas of low genotypical variation, compare Fig. 7.3. Crossover is performed in an attempt to produce successful long jumps within the domain of the fitness landscape, compare Sect. 5.2.6. Of course, long jumps fail with a high probability; nevertheless such trials are needed in order to discover so far unexplored regions of the fitness landscape.

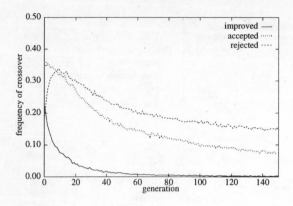

Fig. 7.8. Classification of crossover outcomes for the GA3. The outcomes are distinguished by the three crossover responses considered in Fig. 7.5.

In the initial phase of the adaptation the curve of improving crossover and the curve of rejected crossover show an interesting time development. In the first generation both cases occur with a frequency of each ≈ 20% of all operations performed. The improving crossover curve rapidly declines and converges asymptotically towards zero. The rejected crossover curve increases strongly up to generation 10 and decreases continuously from then on.

This strong increase of the rejected crossover curve in the very beginning of the adaptation might be surprising, but can be explained by the properties of crossover. The initial population is generated at random resulting in individuals which differ maximally from each other. The majority of recombinations fail in generating offspring of similar fitness compared with their parents. At the same time a minority of recombinations succeed in producing offspring of improved fitness. Within the first few generations these superior offspring are selected for mating with a high probability and introduce a rough direction of search. From then on genetic adaptation works well in generating offspring of similar fitness compared to their parents.

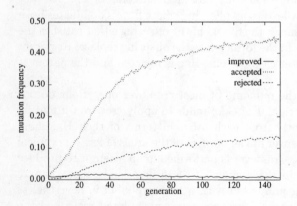

Fig. 7.9. Classification of mutation outcomes for the GA3. The outcomes are distinguished by the three mutation responses considered in Fig. 7.5.

In Figure 7.9 the majority of mutation attempts are accepted. The rejection rate increases over time, but the rate of mutated offspring satisfying the acceptance criterion increases even stronger. The rate of improving mutations is very low although is does not drop to zero as observed for crossover.

In conclusion, mutations are a serious alternative to crossover when applied to areas of low genotypical variation in the habitat. But notice, that just a very high mutation rate fails. The auto-adaptive control by means of inherited attitudes performs mutations where needed and relies on crossover in other cases.

7.2.4 Inbreeding Coefficients

Thus far we have regarded inbreeding to be a generally negative factor for genetic adaptation. This view is exposed as an oversimplification when taking convergence into account. The convergence of a population is achieved by the reduction of the gene pool diversity. If a population does not converge, we observe a low selection pressure which leads to a poor GA performance. Obviously, convergence comes along with increasing inbreeding rates. Thus, inbreeding is closely linked to one of the basic concepts of genetic adaptation.

In accordance with Smith (1989) we differentiate between inbreeding by descendent (IBD) and inbreeding by kinship (IBK) in the following.

- The genes of two mating individuals may be copies of the same gene in an earlier member of the line, during the last t generations. If so, they are said to be identical by descendent.
- The genes of two mating individuals may be identical because the gene was common in the population from which the line was derived. If so, genes are said to be identical by kinship.

Apparently there is something arbitrary in the definition of IBD. Genotypical identity always indicates some common ancestry. In random mating populations we differentiate between IBD and IBK by choosing a past generation count t. Individuals with identical genes, which have mated in the last t generations, are said to be IBD and IBK otherwise.

In the diffusion model we measure IBD for the mating individuals within small sub-populations. The chance that their ancestors have already mated in previous generations is very high. To the contrary, individuals of different sub-populations cannot be IBD by definition. Therefore IBK is measured by selecting individuals at random from the overall population. In doing so, IBK indicates the degree of convergence in the overall population whereas IBD indicates the degree of inbreeding in the sub-populations.

For a measure of inbreeding we follow Collins and Jefferson (1991). The normalized Hamming distance D between two individuals determines the inbreeding coefficient $\mathcal{F}$.

$$\mathcal{F} = (\overline{D}_0 - \overline{D}_t)/\overline{D}_0 \tag{7.1}$$

The expected rate of genotypical diversity is given by the mean Hamming distance $\overline{D}_0$ of the population in generation 0, whereas the observed rate of genotypical diversity is given by $\overline{D}_t$ in generation t. $\overline{D}_t$ is measured in the IBD case by taking the average Hamming distance between all mating couples in generation t. IBK is measured by picking the same number of couples from the overall population at random.

To compare the inbreeding coefficients of GA2 and GA3 we perform 50 runs each with a population size of $\mu = 196$ and a termination criterion of 150 generations. For both GAs we record $\mathcal{F}_{\text{IBD}}$ and $\mathcal{F}_{\text{IBK}}$ separately.

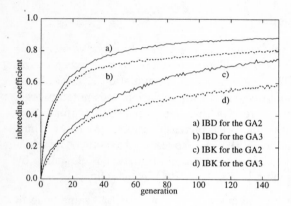

Fig. 7.10. Inbreeding coefficients $\mathcal{F}$ for the GA2 vs. the GA3. The inbreeding by descendent (IBD) as well as the inbreeding by kinship (IBK) are shown.

a) IBD for the GA2
b) IBD for the GA3
c) IBK for the GA2
d) IBK for the GA3

Figure 7.10 shows the mean inbreeding coefficients recorded. Independently of the type of algorithm run (GA2 or GA3) we observe a significantly higher $\mathcal{F}_{\text{IBD}}$ compared to the corresponding $\mathcal{F}_{\text{IBK}}$. This phenomenon is in accordance with the considerations made in the beginning of this chapter and with the observations from Fig 7.3. The spatial neighborhood structure of the population leads to a fast convergence within the various sub-populations whereas for the entire population a genotypical variation is kept over the generations. Even after 150 generations the population hasn't fully converged; instead it has evolved to large areas of genetically incompatible individuals.

Curve a) in Fig. 7.10 shows the $\mathcal{F}_{\text{IBD}}$ for GA2. We observe a strong increase of inbreeding right at the beginning of the genetic adaptation. Later on the increase of $\mathcal{F}_{\text{IBD}}$ becomes smaller. After 150 generations $\mathcal{F}_{\text{IBD}}$ has raised to ≈ 0.87. The $\mathcal{F}_{\text{IBK}}$ for GA2 is given in curve c). In generation 150 we observe a value of ≈ 0.75. The inbreeding coefficients of GA3 are generally smaller compared to the GA2 coefficients. The $\mathcal{F}_{\text{IBD}}$ of GA3 is shown in curve b) which increases up to ≈ 0.80 in generation 150. The corresponding $\mathcal{F}_{\text{IBK}}$ shown in d) increases only slowly up to ≈ 0.60 in the last generation.

Up to 15 generations GA2 and GA3 perform almost identical. Then, inbreeding firstly occurs within the sub-populations and the attitude inheritance mechanism starts to work by favoring mutation. This leads to a slower increase of b) compared with a) and in a similar way a slower increase of

d) in comparison to c). Surprisingly, the difference between c) and d) becomes larger from generation t to generation $t + 1$. GA2 tends to converge in later generations whereas GA3 shows a larger genotypical variation within the population in later stages. This observation indicates that GA3 keeps on searching in different regions of the search space even in later generations.

This phenomenon is described best by comparing the outcome of adaptation within the habitat in generation 150 of two distinct GA runs. Therefore we compare the GA2 run previously shown in Fig. 7.3 with a GA3 run performed with an identical parameter setting.

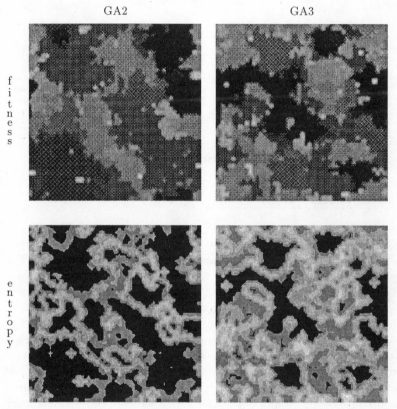

GA2   GA3

f
i
t
n
e
s
s

e
n
t
r
o
p
y

Fig. 7.11. The fitness obtained and the neighborhood entropy for a GA2 and a GA3 run with a population size of 2 500 in generation 150. The GA2 plots are taken from Fig. 7.3. For the legend the reader is referred to pp. 118–119.

Figure 7.11 shows the fitness obtained and the neighborhood entropy within the habitat in generation 150. Both algorithms have obtained a similar solution quality. In contradiction to GA2, which shows a few large areas of similar fitness, the habitat of GA3 population consists of numerous areas of considerably smaller size. This situation is reflected by the entropy of the

considerably smaller size. This situation is reflected by the entropy of the neighborhoods. Here, only relatively small areas of low gene variety (black) can be observed. Thus we conjecture, that GA3 explores the search space more thoroughly than done by GA2.

We expect the more differentiated search of GA3 to produce a further improvement of computational results. In order to verify our expectation we run GA3 on the same benchmark problems as previously done for GA1 (compare Tab. 6.4) and for GA2 (compare Tab. 7.1). Again, 50 runs are performed for each problem instance. As before, a population size of 100 individuals and a fixed number of 100 generations is used.

prob.	size	known	mean	err.	dev.
mt10	10×10	930	943.7	1.5	0.9
mt20	20×05	1165	1180.3	1.3	0.4
abz7	20×15	665	682.9	2.4	0.7
abz8	20×15	670	696.2	3.9	0.6
abz9	20×15	686	712.5	3.1	0.7
la21	15×10	1046	1059.4	1.3	0.6
la24	15×10	935	945.3	1.1	0.9
la25	15×10	977	986.6	1.0	0.3
la27	20×10	1235	1261.6	2.2	0.4
la29	20×10	1153	1199.8	3.7	0.9
la38	15×15	1196	1222.5	2.2	1.0
la40	15×15	1222	1243.6	1.8	0.7

Table 7.2. GA3 results obtained for the mt10, mt20 and another 10 tough problems listed in Tab. 8.3.

Table 7.2 shows the results obtained. The mean relative error averaged over the 12 benchmarks is reduced from 2.4 for GA2 to 2.1 for GA3. The standard deviation of the mean results obtained is reduced from 0.73 for GA2 to 0.67 for GA3. Keep in mind that GA3 saves about 20% of the fitness evaluations. This means, that GA3 effectively carries out roughly 8000 of 10000 possible evaluations in a single run.

GA3 outperforms GA2 in obtaining a shorter makespan in the average for most problem instances. This is particularly remarkably when we consider that already GA2 produces (almost) satisfying results. A further increase of the solution quality is even more difficult to obtain. In conclusion, GA3 does not only produce better results but it also achieves these results at a smaller computational cost compared to GA2.

8. A Computational Study

In this chapter we give a survey on the GA approaches considered so far. We continue with a detailed computational study of the most powerful algorithm on 162 benchmark problems. Finally we discuss the suitability of the algorithm for either very large or very difficult JSP instances.

8.1 Survey of the GA-Approaches

Throughout this thesis we have considered three different GAs. The GA1 follows the mainstream of previous GA research. The GA2 introduces spatial distances between the individuals by means of structured populations. The GA3 enhances the structured population model by allowing the individuals to react to their specific environment. In the following we describe the parameter settings of the approaches and give a summary of the results achieved.

8.1.1 Overview of Parameters

Care has been taken to keep the three different approaches comparable. Therefore the same representation, genetic operators and heuristic decoding procedure are used within all of our approaches. Furthermore an identical population size of 100 and a fixed number of generations of 100 (resulting in at most 10 000 evaluations) are used always. Obviously, GA parameters show strong interdependencies. Thus, by modifying one parameter other parameters may have to be adjusted to the new configuration. E.g. the introduction of a structured population into a GA requires the appliance of an acceptance criterion (which can be left ouf from being considered for a global mating GA). Whenever there is a tradeoff between the comparability of the approaches and their efficiency, preference is given to the more efficient alternative.

Table 8.1 lists the parameter setting of the three approaches considered. We choose a representation which reflects the essentials of scheduling problems. A schedule representation by precedence relations among operations can cope with a wide array of additional constraints (e.g. release times and due dates) and objectives (e.g. minimization of job tardiness or maximization of machine work load). The algorithm can therefore easily be adopted to requirements of real world production scheduling.

Table 8.1. Summary of the settings of GA parameters used for the GA1, the GA2 and the GA3.

parameter	description	GA1	GA2	GA3
representation	A permutation with repetition (PwR) of job identifiers expresses the precedence relations among operations.	PwR	PwR	PwR
decoding	A semi-active schedule is built and then re-optimized by a hill climber using the $\mathcal{N}_3$ Local Search neighborhood and the $\mathcal{C}_{st}$ control strategy.	yes	yes	yes
fitness eval.	The fitness f_i is evaluated for individual i by computing the makespan C_{max} for a decoded schedule.	C_{max}	C_{max}	C_{max}
crossover op.	Crossover tries to preserve the relative order of operations in the recombined permutations.	GOX	GOX	GOX
mutation op.	A mutations alters the absolute order of operations in the permutation by modifying the position of one operation in the permutation arbitrarily.	PBM	PBM	PBM
crossover-rate	The probability ρ_c for an individual to perform crossover.	0.60	1.00	$-^{b}$
mutation-rate	The probability ρ_m for an individual to perform a mutation (independent of ρ_c).	0.03	0.03	$-^{b}$
population size	A fixed number of individuals μ form the GA population.	100	100	100
pop. structure	The individuals reside on a torodial grid resulting in a limited dispersal of the population.	$-^{a}$	10×10	10×10
# of offspring	The number of offspring λ is equal to the population size μ, thus each individual produces exactly one offspring.	100	100	100
# of neighbors	The number of individuals on which selection is based and from which a mating partner is chosen.	100	4	4
selection scheme	Proportional selection based on the scaled fitness $f_i - f_{min}$ is used, where f_i denotes the fitness of individual i and f_{min} gives the minimal fitness within the neighborhood.	yes	yes	yes
acceptance crit.	An offspring o replaces its parent p if $f_o < f_p + (f_p - LB) \cdot \xi$ holds. LB denotes the lower bound of the problem instance and ξ is the acceptance criterion.	–	0.10	0.10
termination crit.	A fixed number of generations is used.	100	100	100

[a] global population
[b] auto-adaptive

On the other hand we have seen that a genuine GA produces poor re-sults, hence we borrow a Local Search based re-optimization procedure in order to improve the solution quality. This procedure clearly depends on the objective under consideration and it is questionable whether such an efficient re-optimization procedure exists for other objectives than for the reduction of makespan.

The reproduction operators are chosen to work on a genotypical level independently of additional constraints involved or a certain objective pur-sued. By respecting the order of genes we follow previous GA research in combinatorial optimization. Although the crossover as well as the mutation operator appear simple, they have shown to preserve parental characteristics quite well.

We use a relatively small population size and generation number in order to achieve a reasonable runtime. The same reason dictates to produce only a single offspring for each parent (i.e. two offspring for each couple). Thus, selection is based on a relatively small number of individuals. Therefore a severe selection scheme based on scaled fitness values is necessary to increase the selection pressure over time. For GA2 and GA3 the extremely small neighborhood additionally requires an acceptance criterion in order to achieve a sufficient selection pressure.

8.1.2 Comparison of Results

We have seen that GA1 gets easily trapped in local optima. This phenomenon is partially circumvented by introducing structured populations in GA2. Structured populations come along with a considerable degree of inbreeding causing an inefficient search. The phenomenon of local inbreeding is reduced by introducing the model of attitude inheritance which leads to GA3.

relative error			std. deviation			
GA1	GA2	GA3	GA1	GA2	GA3	
2.9	2.4	2.1	0.84	0.73	0.67	

Table 8.2. Comparison of the approaches of this thesis.

A summary of the relative error and the standard deviation of the makespan obtained for the three approaches is given in Tab. 8.2. The values presented are the average results of the 12 benchmarks considered in Tab. 6.4, 7.1 and 7.2. GA2 clearly outperforms GA1 and in , GA3 outperforms GA2. This rank holds for the relative error as well as for the deviation of results obtained from various runs.

In the following section we let GA3 operate on very large and difficult benchmark problems in order to assess its suitability for such problems.

8.2 Benchmark Study

The JSP has been widely studied within the last 30 years. In order to compare the various solution techniques proposed, several suites of benchmark problems have been provided for public use by different authors.

First we give a short description of the benchmark suites[1]. Then, some properties of the benchmark instances are discussed. Finally, we document an extensive computational study on 162 instances for the GA3.

8.2.1 Available Benchmark Suites

Up to our knowledge, all available JSP benchmarks are listed in the tables of this section. The various suites are presented below.

- The most widely distributed suite of benchmark problems is the three problem test set due to Fisher and Thompson (1963). The 10×10 problem is of particular interest since almost any JSP algorithm proposed so far has been applied to this problem. Although it has been stated back in 1963, after 26 years of research the makespan of 930 has been proofed to be minimal by Carlier and Pinson (1989). The problems are listed in Tab. 8.5. They are prefixed with mt or ft in literature.
- Five instances prefixed with abz were generated by Adams et al. (1988). Problem 5 and 6 are quite easy to solve, but the problems number 7, 8 and 9 of size 20 × 15 are most difficult to solve, see Tab. 8.6.
- For some unknown reason Yamada and Nakano (1992) have not tested the G&T GA with commonly available benchmarks. Instead they have generated four 20 × 20 instances on their own prefixed with yam. Although this suite is hardly known in literature, we have included the problems into the investigation. Table 8.7 lists the instances.
- Another suite (prefixed with orb) is due to Applegate and Cook (1991). It consists of ten 10 × 10 problem instances. Only the first 5 problems are considered in literature, because the latter 5 instances are quite easy to solve. Table 8.8 lists the instances.
- A further test set was generated by Storer et al. (1992a). It consists of 20 problem instances prefixed with swv of sizes between 10×20 and 50×10. This benchmark suite is not that widely accepted by the research community. Of the 50 × 10 problems 5 are regarded to be easy while the other 5 are hard to solve. The instances are listed in Tab. 8.9.
- A large suite has been proposed by Lawrence (1984). It consists of 40 problem instances of varying size in the range of 10×5 to 30×10. Although most of the instances are quite easy to solve, some larger instances remain a computational challenge. The instances prefixed with la are listed in Tab. 8.10.

---

[1] All instances considered in this section can be obtained via Internet from mscmga.ms.ic.ac.uk. The procedure for obtaining OR test problems is described in Beasley (1990).

Since different names are used in literature, the alternate name is given in parenthesis.

– A large set of 80 problem instances is proposed by Taillard (1993b). They are of particular interest because of their large size up to 100×20. Furthermore Taillard developed a problem generation procedure and made it available for public use. The instances are prefixed with ta, see Tab. 8.11 and Tab. 8.12.

Table 8.3 lists 13 benchmark instances which serve as a test-bed for the three different GA approaches considered throughout this thesis. Beside two famous problems of Fisher and Thompson other difficult problems due to Adams, Balas and Zawack as well as Lawrence are selected. Among these, for abz7, abz8, abz9 and la29 optimality could still not be proofed.

name	size	table
mt10	10×10	8.5
mt20	20×05	8.5
abz7	20×15	8.6
abz8	20×15	8.6
abz9	20×15	8.6
la21	15×10	8.10
la24	15×10	8.10
la25	15×10	8.10
la27	20×10	8.10
la29	20×10	8.10
la38	15×15	8.10
la40	15×15	8.10

Table 8.3. The collection of benchmarks used throughout this thesis. It consists of the two famous instances due to Fisher and Thompson (1963) and ten other tough job shop problems selected by Applegate and Cook (1991). This collection of problem instances provides medium sized problems which are generally hard to solve.

Different to most authors Taillard (1993b) describes the procedure for generating rectangular problem instances. Processing times for the operations are uniformly distributed in the range [1,99]. Operations are assigned to machines in a uniform distribution. Hard problems were identified by a large deviation between the lower bound and an upper bound obtained by a Tabu Search algorithms also due to Taillard (1993a). Other distributions (e.g. normal distribution) for processing times and machine assignments were tested, but Taillard found the resulting problem instances easy to solve in general (personal communication 1994).

An interesting observation has been noted by Storer et al. (1992a). They found most problems with uniformly distributed job/machine assignments easy to solve. Storer et al. follow Fisher and Thompson (1963) in generating precedence relations of each job. Recall that each job has to pass all machines. Fisher and Thompson divide the set of machines into two sub-sets of the same size. Now challenging problems are generated by letting each job pass all machines of the first set before the machines of the second set are passed. This technique has been used also for the hard swv11 – swv15 instances whereas the easy swv16 – swv20 instances in Tab. 8.9 were generated with uniformly distributed precedence relations for each job.

A striking observation due to Taillard is that large problems are easy to solve if $n \geq m * 6$. For these cases it could be observed that the lower bound does always determine the makespan. Even for 100×20 instances the lower bound was reached by Taillard's Tabu Search approach for 97 of 100 problems generated. Quadratic problem instances remain more difficult even in case of medium size. Taillard's observations are in accordance with the results presented in the remainder of this section. Given a fixed number of operations involved, quadratic instances are generally more difficult to solve than their rectangular counterparts.

8.2.2 Computational Results

In the tables in the remainder of this section the name and size of the problem instances are given in column 1 and 2. All problems considered are of rectangular size, where $n \times m$ denotes n jobs and m machines involved. In column 3 a lower bound LB is given for instances which could not proofed to be solved to optimality. The lower bounds have been received from Vaessens at Eindhoven University (personal communication 1995), who engaged the 'edge-finder' algorithm due to Applegate and Cook (1991) to improve the bounds. Column 4 shows the best known makespan found so far. Column 5 gives a reference on the approach which first found the best known makespan. The abbreviations used are given in Tab. 8.4.

Table 8.4. Abbreviations of references.

abbr.	algorithm	reference
LLR	Branch & Bound	Lageweg et al. (1977)
La	Branch & Bound	Lageweg 1984 (unpublished)
ABZ	Shifting Bottleneck	Adams et al. (1988)
AC	Shuffle Algorithm	Applegate and Cook (1991)
ALLU	Simulated Annealing	Aarts et al. (1994)
BV	Guided Local Search	Balas and Vazacopoulos (1994)
CP1	Branch & Bound	Carlier and Pinson (1989)
CP2	Branch & Bound	Carlier and Pinson (1990)
CP3	Branch & Bound	Carlier and Pinson (1994)
We	Tabu Search	Wennink 1995 (pers. comm.)
LAL	Simulated Annealing	Van Laarhoven et al. (1992)
MSS	Simulated Annealing	Matsuo et al. (1988)
NS	Tabu Search	Nowicki and Smutnicki (1995)
SWV	Genetic Algorithm	Storer et al. (1992a)
Ta1	Tabu Search	Taillard (1993b)
Ta2	Tabu Search	Taillard (1993a)
VA	Shuffle Algorithm	Vaessens 1995 (pers. comm.)
VAL	Shuffle Algorithm	Vaessens et al. (1995)
YN	Simulated Annealing	Yamada and Nakano (1995)

The columns 6–10 lists the results obtained by the GA3 as described in Sect. 7.2.2. A summary of the GA parameters is given in Tab. 8.1. The GA3 is written in the C++ language by massively use of the LEDA-library, compare Mehlhorn and Näher (1989). All runs are performed on a SUN 10/41 workstation running the Solaris™ operating system. The algorithm is run for a total of 30 iterations for each problem considered.

Column 6 gives the best makespan found in the 30 runs carried out. Column 7 lists the mean result obtained in these runs. Column 8 lists the relative error calculated by 100(mean − known)/known. Column 9 gives the standard deviation of the makespan from the mean makespan obtained in percent. The last column no. 10 lists the average runtime needed in seconds.

Table 8.5. Benchmarks proposed by Fisher and Thompson.

name	size	LB	known	by	best	mean	err.	dev.	sec.
	problem description				GA3 results				
mt06	6×6		55	LLR	55	55.0	0.0	0.0	6
mt10	10×10		930	La	930	943.7	1.5	0.7	40
mt20	20×5		1165	CP1	1165	1180.3	1.3	0.4	47

Table 8.6. Benchmarks proposed by Adams, Balas and Zawack.

name	size	LB	known	by	best	mean	err.	dev.	sec.
	problem description				GA3 results				
abz5	10×10		1234	AC	1234	1239.7	0.5	0.2	24
abz6	10×10		943	ABZ	934	947.2	0.4	0.1	20
abz7	20×15	655	665	Ta2	668	682.9	2.4	0.7	170
abz8	20×15	638	670	ALLU	684	696.2	3.9	0.6	182
abz9	20×15	656	686	YN	702	712.6	3.1	0.7	187

Table 8.7. Benchmarks proposed by Nakano and Yamada.

name	size	LB	known	by	best	mean	err.	dev.	sec.
	problem description				GA3 results				
yam1	20×20	826	888	We	904	911.9	2.7	0.5	279
yam2	20×20	861	912	BV	928	940.5	3.1	0.6	263
yam3	20×20	827	898	We	907	918.8	2.3	0.8	278
yam4	20×20	918	977	We	992	1012.0	3.6	1.0	319

Table 8.8. Benchmarks proposed by Applegate and Cook.

problem description					GA3 results				
name	size	LB	known	by	best	mean	err.	dev.	sec.
orb1	10×10		1059	AC	1064	1087.3	2.7	1.0	35
orb2	10×10		888	AC	888	892.1	0.5	0.4	35
orb3	10×10		1005	AC	1005	1035.0	3.0	1.2	42
orb4	10×10		1005	AC	1005	1017.2	1.2	0.6	38
orb5	10×10		887	AC	887	890.5	0.4	0.3	41
orb6	10×10		1010	AC	1010	1026.1	1.6	0.5	33
orb7	10×10		397	AC	397	399.9	0.7	0.7	28
orb8	10×10		899	AC	899	914.8	1.8	1.1	43
orb9	10×10		934	AC	934	946.2	1.3	0.5	31
orb10	10×10		944	AC	944	944.4	0.0	0.2	33

Table 8.9. Benchmarks proposed by Storer, Wu and Vaccari.

problem description					GA3 results				
name	size	LB	known	by	best	mean	err.	dev.	sec.
swv01	20×10	1392	1418	BV	1501	1556.4	9.8	1.6	135
swv02	20×10	1475	1491	Va	1551	1593.7	6.9	1.3	138
swv03	20×10	1328	1398	Va	1478	1531.7	9.6	1.5	146
swv04	20×10	1369	1497	Va	1566	1601.6	7.0	1.2	148
swv05	20×10	1450	1452	Va	1535	1582.8	9.0	1.4	147
swv06	20×15	1591	1718	BV	1807	1874.8	9.1	1.5	260
swv07	20×15	1446	1652	BV	1758	1795.2	8.7	1.0	261
swv08	20×15	1638	1798	BV	1913	1962.3	9.1	1.2	260
swv09	20×15	1600	1710	BV	1803	1846.5	8.0	1.2	268
swv10	20×15	1631	1794	BV	1891	1933.8	7.8	1.1	259
swv11	50×10	2983	3047	BV	3624	3793.8	24.5	1.6	643
swv12	50×10	2972	3045	BV	3653	3774.3	24.0	1.8	674
swv13	50×10	3104	3173	BV	3628	3804.4	19.9	1.9	658
swv14	50×10		2968	BV	3467	3621.6	22.0	2.1	742
swv15	50×10	2885	3022	BV	3513	3698.7	22.4	2.1	642
swv16	50×10		2924	SWV	2924	2924.0	0.0	0.0	266
swv17	50×10		2794	SWV	2794	2794.0	0.0	0.0	355
swv18	50×10		2852	SWV	2852	2852.0	0.0	0.0	274
swv19	50×10		2843	SWV	2843	2843.0	0.0	0.0	453
swv20	50×10		2823	SWV	2823	2823.0	0.0	0.0	281

Table 8.10. Benchmarks proposed by Lawrence.

name	size	LB	known	by	best	mean	err.	dev.	sec.
\multicolumn{5}{problem description}					GA3 results				

name	size	LB	known	by	best	mean	err.	dev.	sec.
la01 (F1)	10×5		666	ABZ	666	666.0	0.0	0.0	13
la02 (F2)	10×5		655	LAL	655	655.0	0.0	0.0	16
la03 (F3)	10×5		597	MSS	597	597.0	0.0	0.0	16
la04 (F4)	10×5		590	LAL	590	590.0	0.0	0.0	13
la05 (F5)	10×5		593	ABZ	593	593.0	0.0	0.0	12
la06 (G1)	15×5		926	ABZ	926	926.0	0.0	0.0	19
la07 (G2)	15×5		890	ABZ	890	890.0	0.0	0.0	23
la08 (G3)	15×5		863	ABZ	863	863.0	0.0	0.0	21
la09 (G4)	15×5		951	ABZ	951	951.0	0.0	0.0	19
la10 (G5)	15×5		958	LAL	958	958.0	0.0	0.0	17
la11 (H1)	20×5		1222	ABZ	1222	1222.0	0.0	0.0	27
la12 (H2)	20×5		1039	ABZ	1039	1039.0	0.0	0.0	27
la13 (H3)	20×5		1150	ABZ	1150	1150.0	0.0	0.0	26
la14 (H4)	20×5		1292	ABZ	1292	1292.0	0.0	0.0	24
la15 (H5)	20×5		1207	ABZ	1207	1207.0	0.0	0.0	32
la16 (A1)	10×10		945	CP2	945	950.3	0.6	1.1	22
la17 (A2)	10×10		784	MSS	784	784.8	0.1	0.1	22
la18 (A3)	10×10		848	MSS	848	848.0	0.0	0.0	25
la19 (A4)	10×10		842	MSS	842	844.6	0.3	0.4	29
la20 (A5)	10×10		902	LAL	902	906.7	0.5	0.1	31
la21 (B1)	15×10		1046	VAL	1047	1059.4	1.3	0.6	65
la22 (B2)	15×10		927	MSS	927	934.2	0.8	0.4	57
la23 (B3)	15×10		1032	ABZ	1032	1032.0	0.0	0.0	55
la24 (B4)	15×10		935	AC	938	945.3	1.1	0.9	56
la25 (B5)	15×10		977	AC	977	986.6	1.0	0.3	52
la26 (C1)	20×10		1218	LAL	1218	1218.0	0.0	0.0	105
la27 (C2)	20×10		1235	CP3	1236	1261.6	2.2	0.4	108
la28 (C3)	20×10		1216	MSS	1216	1229.0	1.1	0.7	101
la29 (C4)	20×10	1130	1153	VA	1180	1199.9	3.7	0.9	104
la30 (C5)	20×10		1355	ABZ	1355	1355.0	0.0	0.0	98
la31 (D1)	30×10		1784	ABZ	1784	1784.0	0.0	0.0	140
la32 (D2)	30×10		1850	ABZ	1850	1850.0	0.0	0.0	174
la33 (D3)	30×10		1719	ABZ	1719	1719.0	0.0	0.0	150
la34 (D4)	30×10		1721	ABZ	1721	1721.0	0.0	0.0	169
la35 (D5)	30×10		1888	ABZ	1888	1888.0	0.0	0.0	153
la36 (I1)	15×15		1268	CP2	1269	1291.6	1.9	0.5	79
la37 (I2)	15×15		1397	AC	1402	1431.0	2.4	0.7	95
la38 (I3)	15×15		1196	NS	1201	1222.5	2.2	1.0	92
la39 (I4)	15×15		1233	AC	1240	1248.6	1.3	0.4	89
la40 (I5)	15×15		1222	AC	1228	1243.7	1.8	0.7	99

Table 8.11. Benchmarks proposed by Taillard (part 1).

| | problem description | | | | | GA3 results | | | |
name	size	LB	known	by	best	mean	err.	dev.	sec.
ta01	15×15		1231	Ta1	1247	1255.6	2.0	0.4	92
ta02	15×15		1244	NS	1247	1269.4	2.0	0.6	99
ta03	15×15	1206	1218	BV	1221	1236.5	1.5	0.9	101
ta04	15×15	1170	1175	We	1181	1191.6	1.4	1.1	108
ta05	15×15	1210	1228	We	1233	1243.4	1.3	0.8	104
ta06	15×15	1210	1240	We	1247	1257.8	1.4	0.5	101
ta07	15×15	1223	1228	Ta1	1228	1250.2	1.8	0.6	90
ta08	15×15	1187	1217	BV	1217	1241.1	2.0	0.7	98
ta09	15×15	1247	1274	BV	1296	1318.3	3.5	0.9	107
ta10	15×15		1241	BV	1255	1282.6	3.4	0.6	90
ta11	20×15	1321	1373	Va	1411	1428.8	4.1	0.7	193
ta12	20×15	1321	1367	BV	1389	1415.5	3.5	0.7	175
ta13	20×15	1271	1350	BV	1368	1396.0	3.4	1.1	197
ta14	20×15		1345	NS	1360	1370.7	1.9	0.4	166
ta15	20×15	1293	1353	BV	1391	1417.0	4.7	0.9	191
ta16	20×15	1300	1371	Ta1	1381	1412.0	3.0	0.9	185
ta17	20×15	1458	1478	BV	1496	1522.1	3.0	1.0	158
ta18	20×15	1369	1409	BV	1459	1477.6	4.9	0.7	203
ta19	20×15	1276	1343	Va	1382	1425.7	6.2	1.5	174
ta20	20×15	1316	1353	We	1381	1396.4	3.2	0.5	192
ta21	20×20	1539	1658	We	1723	1748.7	5.5	0.7	288
ta22	20×20	1511	1618	BV	1626	1649.7	2.0	0.8	281
ta23	20×20	1472	1563	We	1613	1623.5	3.9	0.5	276
ta24	20×20	1594	1659	BV	1689	1719.4	3.6	0.8	257
ta25	20×20	1496	1598	Ta1	1635	1658.5	3.8	0.7	249
ta26	20×20	1539	1655	We	1700	1718.1	3.8	0.6	289
ta27	20×20	1616	1697	We	1751	1772.0	4.4	0.8	291
ta28	20×20	1591	1615	BV	1651	1676.4	3.8	0.9	267
ta29	20×20	1514	1629	NS	1631	1651.5	1.4	0.5	280
ta30	20×20	1468	1612	BV	1627	1653.2	2.6	1.1	277
ta31	30×15	1764	1766	NS	1813	1839.8	4.2	0.9	386
ta32	30×15	1774	1810	BV	1894	1922.5	6.2	0.8	377
ta33	30×15	1778	1796	BV	1896	1919.0	6.8	0.6	367
ta34	30×15	1828	1836	BV	1930	1949.3	6.2	0.7	341
ta35	30×15		2007	Ta1	2019	2044.5	1.9	0.7	341
ta36	30×15	1819	1826	BV	1889	1914.8	4.9	0.8	381
ta37	30×15	1771	1787	BV	1846	1876.0	5.0	1.0	381
ta38	30×15	1673	1681	BV	1760	1786.0	6.2	0.8	367
ta39	30×15	1795	1806	BV	1871	1906.3	5.6	0.9	351
ta40	30×15	1631	1695	BV	1763	1804.4	6.5	0.8	392

Table 8.12. Benchmarks proposed by Taillard (part 2).

name	size	LB	known	by	best	mean	err.	dev.	sec.
	problem description				GA3 results				
ta41	30×20	1859	2026	BV	2156	2199.5	8.6	0.8	611
ta42	30×20	1867	1974	BV	2088	2125.3	7.7	0.9	623
ta43	30×20	1809	1886	BV	1990	2027.1	7.5	0.9	617
ta44	30×20	1927	2021	BV	2138	2174.4	7.6	1.0	611
ta45	30×20	1997	2027	BV	2106	2132.6	5.2	0.8	629
ta46	30×20	1940	2051	BV	2166	2226.1	8.5	1.1	628
ta47	30×20	1789	1934	BV	2036	2064.2	6.7	0.9	572
ta48	30×20	1912	1986	BV	2078	2117.8	6.6	0.8	595
ta49	30×20	1905	2013	Ta1	2102	2143.8	6.5	0.8	628
ta50	30×20	1807	1967	BV	2065	2103.4	6.9	0.8	612
ta51	50×15		2760	Ta1	2870	2927.5	6.1	0.9	926
ta52	50×15		2756	Ta1	2883	2932.9	6.4	0.9	873
ta53	50×15		2717	Ta1	2742	2780.1	2.3	0.7	852
ta54	50×15		2839	Ta1	2839	2852.3	0.5	0.5	958
ta55	50×15		2679	NS	2798	2853.9	6.5	0.8	935
ta56	50×15		2781	Ta1	2882	2920.8	5.0	0.8	907
ta57	50×15		2943	Ta1	2989	3036.9	3.2	0.6	945
ta58	50×15		2885	Ta1	2954	3001.3	4.0	0.7	898
ta59	50×15		2655	Ta1	2742	2817.0	6.1	0.9	937
ta60	50×15		2723	Ta1	2803	2826.8	3.8	0.4	922
ta61	50×20		2868	NS	3022	3056.3	6.6	0.6	1485
ta62	50×20	2869	2900	BV	3136	3171.6	9.4	0.6	1609
ta63	50×20		2755	NS	2898	2939.9	6.7	0.7	1576
ta64	50×20		2702	NS	2855	2897.2	7.2	0.7	1557
ta65	50×20		2725	NS	2872	2930.0	7.5	0.8	1536
ta66	50×20		2845	NS	3008	3044.0	7.0	0.6	1515
ta67	50×20	2825	2826	BP	3019	3066.5	8.5	0.9	1517
ta68	50×20		2784	NS	2898	2958.6	6.3	0.9	1603
ta69	50×20		3071	NS	3233	3277.5	6.7	0.7	1376
ta70	50×20		2995	NS	3240	3293.5	10.0	0.8	1476
ta71	100×20		5464	Ta1	5851	5944.2	8.8	0.8	4747
ta72	100×20		5181	Ta1	5434	5464.8	5.5	0.4	5717
ta73	100×20		5568	Ta1	5977	6031.2	8.3	0.5	4964
ta74	100×20		5339	Ta1	5523	5584.2	4.6	0.6	4886
ta75	100×20		5392	Ta1	5793	5868.1	8.8	0.7	5912
ta76	100×20		5342	Ta1	5574	5661.6	6.0	0.6	5994
ta77	100×20		5436	Ta1	5615	5691.2	4.7	0.7	6221
ta78	100×20		5394	Ta1	5723	5758.9	6.8	0.4	6347
ta79	100×20		5358	Ta1	5552	5602.0	4.6	0.5	6570
ta80	100×20		5183	Ta1	5547	5595.7	8.0	0.5	6259

8.2.3 Limitations of Adaptive Scheduling

For up to 150 operations in a JSP we obtain quasi-optimal results and almost negligible deviations from the mean makespan. Therefore runtimes of less than 1 minute suffice on typical workstation platforms. In spite of the fact, that for e.g. a 10×10 problem instance we have a search space of already $(10!)^{10} \leq 4 \cdot 10^{65}$, the GA3 guides the search properly towards quasi-optimal solutions by taking at most 10 000 samples of the search space.

For larger problem instances of up to 400 operations, the relative error slightly increases although still near-optimal results are obtained. The standard deviation of the makespan is still very low. This proofs the GA3 to be a robust optimization strategy. The runtime needed here does not exceed 5 minutes even in extreme cases.

For larger problem instances (> 400 operations) the relative error increases drastically. Surprisingly, the deviation of the makespan is still very low. Robust population based search obtains these small deviations at the expense of an increasing runtime. For very large problems of the order of 100×20 operations roughly 1.5 hours runtime are needed for a single run.

In spite of the encouraging results obtained for small and medium sized problems, we doubt whether genetic search can be applied either to problems of still larger size or to more difficult instances. We see limits of applicability because of the arising complexity "catastrophe", compare Kauffman (1993).

– The larger the problem instance, the smaller the fitness contribution of a single building block to the overall fitness becomes. The selective force tending to preserve building blocks in the gene pool becomes weaker, because building blocks cannot be easily identified by the fitness value of a solution. Since schemata are disrupted at the same rate in small and large problems but selection looses much of its power when the problem size increases, we see a limit of useful adaptation capability.
– The difficulty of a problem mainly depends on the number of conflicting constraints[2] involved. Conflicting constraints cause epistasis and epistasis in turn cause genetic operators to distort solution characteristics. Therefore an increasing degree of conflicting constraints leads to a less predictable fitness contribution of building blocks. Again, the selective force becomes weaker because building blocks cannot be identified properly by selection.

In conclusion, GAs are well suited for small and medium sized problems. For extremely large, highly constrained or difficult problems the results are reasonable, but not necessarily near-optimal.

---

[2] Potentially conflicting constraints do not necessarily conflict in the subset of promising solutions of the search space. For quadratic problem instances and/or instances where jobs tend to compete for machines, many potentially conflicting constraints become effective. Therefore these problems are extremely difficult to solve, although the number of potentially conflicting constraints does not differ to the one of instances which are easy to solve.

9. Conclusions and Outlook

Throughout this thesis, we iteratively describe the development of a Genetic Algorithm for the solution of the JSP, a hard combinatorial optimization problem of practical relevance.

First we evaluate the opportunities of the components of the GA separately, before we choose one of the alternatives for each component to be implemented. This "iterative" research finally leads us to the approach of behavior driven interactions of GA individuals in a structured population, introduced under the name GA3 in Chap. 7.

To our knowledge, the GA3 produces the best results of all GAs approaches reported in literature. Chap. 8 lists the results obtained for the GA3 on 162 available benchmark problems. In spite of the encouraging results for small and medium sized benchmarks, very large and difficult instances cannot be solved to a near-optimal solution in an acceptable runtime.

In order to assess whether Evolutionary Search can satisfy the requirements of manufacturing systems, in the following we discuss both, the properties of real world problems and the general properties of Evolutionary Search.

9.1 The Real World is Different

Challenging benchmarks are generated in a way that the various jobs tend to compete for the same machine. At a first glance, competing jobs obey the requirements of a manufacturing system, because products are often produced in a similar fashion and therefore jobs follow a similar processing order. In contradistinction to theory, real manufacturing is more of a "sustained pursuit" with release times and due dates for jobs. We assume jobs to be released continuously over time. From this viewpoint an extreme competition of jobs for machines seems unrealistic, because jobs are released at different points of time.

Recently, Bierwirth et al. (1995) decomposed a dynamic shop floor into subsequent static ones by means of a temporal decomposition. The resulting problems consist of operations, whose jobs are released but have not been processed so far. These problems are small and relatively easy to solve. In this more realistic situation a problem type like the one modeled in challenging benchmarks hardly occurs.

In real world applications we may face additional constraints which are neglected by the JSP model. But we will hardly find the peculiarities of benchmark problems in manufacturing systems. Therefore several objections about benchmark problems can be raised in accordance with Pinedo (1995):

– In benchmark problems the processing times are typically distributed uniformly over a large range. Processing times assigned at random are drastically different from the technical requirements of most shop floors. In real world applications we will find typical processing times of operations to be processed on one machine
– Often, benchmark problems are of quadratic type. Real world problems are rarely quadratic. Typically we will find many more jobs than machines in a manufacturing system. Even for short scheduling periods the number of jobs will exceed the number of machines involved.
– The technological constraints of jobs in benchmarks are either uniformly distributed or artificially constructed by model builders in order to obtain "challenging" problems. In shop floors we will find some work flow of jobs through the machines obeying "natural orders" of assembly sequences etc.
– In order to be a challenge for modern heuristic techniques benchmark problems up to 2 000 operations are proposed. In practice we have to deal with stochastic events like machine breakdowns. Therefore such large problems are typically decomposed into considerably smaller sub-problems in order to maximize reliability and to avoid expensive re-scheduling in case of a breakdown.

Recently, Taillard (1994) compared benchmark- and real world problems for the Quadratic Assignment Problem, occuring e.g. in location- and flow optimization. Taillard showed, that in benchmark problems the local optima are widely spread throughout the entire search space, whereas in real world problems local optima tend to populate certain small areas of the search space. Reeves (1993) reports a similar observation for the Vehicle Routing Problem. For the Flow Shop Problem Reeves argues that in real life there should be a gradient of job processing times across machines, or that there should be correlation between the processing times of jobs on the same machine.

For the JSP Amar and Gupta (1986) have shown that the distributions typically chosen for generating benchmark problems hardly result in problems which reflect the problem structure of real world problems. Amar and Gupta compared benchmark problems with problems taken from an existing job shop floor which they regard to be a typical representative of medium sized production factories in the United States. They showed in distinction to benchmark problems real world problems show a high degree of problem structure and consequently the performance of algorithms differs strongly over real world and benchmark problems.

A problem is said to have structure, if good (i.e. near-optimal) solutions of a problem share a considerable amount of solution characteristics, i.e. they have a small distance to each other in terms of the search space.

What makes JSP benchmarks hard to solve for any optimization strategy is that benchmark problems show almost no problem structure. In other words, the makespan of a solution (partial ones included) does hardly correlate with its distance to the argument of the optimal solution. Under this circumstances the heuristic search is easily misguided and a sophisticated control mechanism is needed.

The above considerations imply a substantial degree of problem structure and a relatively small size of real world problems. We therefore assume that the JSP benchmarks considered in this thesis are not typical for the type of problem we have to deal with in practice.

9.2 GAs and Real World Scheduling

Several attempts have been made to integrate GAs into an overall classification of heuristic search techniques. Attention is paid to the role of the genetic operators which produce neighboring solutions in analogy to Local Search techniques. Vaessens et al. (1995) describe the GA to perform a "hyper-neighborhood" search by means of crossover. Jones and Forrest (1995) introduce a state-transition graph model for genetic operators in order to describe the search process of a GA.

We also underline the important role of genetic operators for successful adaptation. But we primarily insist on the importance of the GA's control structure in order to assess the GA performance. This view has important impacts on the effective suitability of GAs for scheduling problems:

- Genes represent solution characteristics of the underlying optimization problem. Evolution either proliferates or drives out genes from the gene pool by means of selection. Thus, selection is responsible for evolving problem structure in terms of solution characteristics. If a problem has no structure, selection cannot work efficiently and genetic adaptation fails.
- Significant changes of gene frequencies in the gene pool take place slowly over the generations. Therefore spontaneous improvements due to genetic drift take a long time to influence the population. Whenever a specific direction of search is introduced, such that certain gene constellations dominate the gene pool, the direction of search is irrevocable.
- Frequency changes in the gene pool are caused by selection which in turn is driven by the fitness observed in the population. Since the fitness is a relative performance measure, the GA does not attempt to generate overall improving solutions. Instead it rather tends to converge at a level of inferior solution quality.

From the above considerations the following conclusions can be drawn. Genetic adaptation will work sufficiently well only in the presence of a high degree of problem structure. Even then genetic adaptation will be slow and the results obtained are not necessarily near-optimal.

In this thesis we have shown that genetic operators should be tailored in accordance with the properties of the underlying optimization problem. In the presence of epistasis due to problem specific constraints appropriate operators can hardly be found. Epistatic effects distort a proper recombination of parental solutions in order to assure the feasibility of offspring. A remedy is the incorporation of a base heuristic which uses domain knowledge in order to improve the average fitness. This causes an increase of selection pressure which in turn results in a persistent search for improved solutions.

The advantage of spatially isolated sub-populations is twofold. The problem structure of several promising regions of the search space is explored simultaneously. The adaptation process in small sub-populations is considerably faster comparable to larger populations. Nevertheless, progress is limited because of inbreeding within the sub-populations. The attitude inheritance model avoids local convergence and therefore maintains a successful gene flow between the various sub-populations. The individuals ability to react on specific environmental conditions provides a more effective control structure of the GA at almost negligible costs.

However, GAs guide the search loosely which results in a relatively inefficient search. More tailored control structures than the one provided by genetic adaptation are needed in order to obtain optimal solutions within an acceptable runtime. On the other hand more tailored control structures are hardly capable to cope with varying objectives or additional constraints.

The currently most efficient algorithms for solving the JSP combine Local Search with Partial Enumeration. Although both techniques have been successfully applied to many combinatorial problems their key features appear highly problem dependent. Therefore it remains questionable whether such tailored techniques can be applied to production scheduling dealing with more intricate constraints than considered in this thesis and other objectives than the reduction of the makespan.

In conclusion we regard genetic adaptation to be a weak but robust optimization technique which can meet the requirements of manufacturing systems. GAs are capable to handle real world problems because the genetic representation of precedence relations among operations fits the needs of real world constraints in production scheduling. Moreover, GAs are applicable to a wide array of varying objectives and therefore they are open to many operational purposes.

References

Aarts, E. H. L., Van Laarhoven, P. J. M., Lenstra, J. K., Ulder, N. L. J. (1994): A Computational Study of Local Search Algorithms for Job Shop Scheduling. ORSA Journal on Computing, vol. **6**, 118–125

Adams, J., Balas, E., Zawack, D. (1988): The Shifting Bottleneck Procedure for Job Shop Scheduling. Management Science, vol. **34**, 391–401

Amar, A. D., Gupta, J. N. D (1986): Simulated Versus Real Life Data in Testing the Efficiency of Scheduling Algorithms. IEE Transactions, vol. **18**, 16–25

Angeline, P. J., Pollack, J. B. (1993): Competitive Environments Evolve Better Solutions for Complex Tasks. In: Forrest (ed.), 264–270

Applegate, D., Cook, W. (1991): A Computational Study of the Job-Shop Scheduling Problem. ORSA Journal on Computing, vol. **3**, 149–156

Bäck, T., Hoffmeister, F., Schwefel, H. P. (1991): A Survey of Evolution Strategies. In: Belew and Booker (eds.), 2–9

Baker, J. E. (1985): Adaptive Selection Methods for Genetic Algorithms. In: Grefenstette (ed.), 101-111

Balas, E., Vazacopoulos, A. (1994): Guided Local Search with Shifting Bottleneck for Job Shop Scheduling. Management Science Research Report # MSRR-609, Graduate School of Industrial Administration, CMU, Pittsburgh

Barker, J. R., McMahon, G. B. (1985): Scheduling the General Job-Shop. Management Science, vol. **31**, 594–598

Barnes, J. W., Chambers, J. B. (1995): Solving the Job Shop Scheduling Problem Using Tabu Search. IIE Transactions, to appear

Beasley, J. E. (1990): OR-Library: Distributing Test Problems by Electronic Mail. Journal of the Operational Research Society, vol. **41**, 1069–1072

Belew, R. K. (1989): When Both Individuals and Populations Search; Adding Simple Learning to Genetic Algorithms. In: Schaffer (ed.), 34–41

Belew, R. K., Booker, L. B. (eds.) (1991): Proc. of the 4th Int. Conf. on Genetic Algorithms. Morgan Kaufmann Publishers, San Mateo, California

Błażewicz, J., Ecker, K., Schmidt, G., Węglarz, J. (1993): Scheduling in Computer and Manufacturing Systems. Springer Verlag, Berlin, Heidelberg

Błażewicz, J., Domschke, W., Pesch, E. (1995): The Job Shop Scheduling Problem: Conventional and new solution techniques. European Journal of Operational Research, to appear

Bierwirth, C. (1993): Flowshop Scheduling mit Parallelen Genetischen Algorithmen; Eine Problemorientierte Analyse Genetischer Suchstrategien. Deutscher Universitäts-Verlag, Wiesbaden

Bierwirth, C. (1995): A Generalized Permutation Approach to Jobshop Scheduling with Genetic Algorithms. OR Spektrum, vol. **17**, 87-92

Bierwirth, C., Kopfer, H., Mattfeld, D. C., Rixen, I. (1995): Genetic Algorithm based Scheduling in a Dynamic Manufacturing Environment. IEEE Conf. on Evolutionary Computation, Perth, to appear

Brucker, P., Jurisch, B., Sievers, B. (1994): A Branch and Bound Algorithm for the Job-Shop Scheduling Problem. Discrete Applied Mathematics, vol. **49**, 107–127

Carlier, J. (1982): The One Machine Sequencing Problem. European Journal of Operational Research, vol. **11**, 42–47

Carlier, J., Pinson, E. (1989): An Algorithm for Solving the Job-Shop Problem. Management Science, vol. **35**, 164–176

Carlier, J., Pinson, E. (1990): A Practical Use of Jackson's Preemptive Schedule for Solving the Job-Shop Problem. Annuals of Operations Research, vol. **26**, 269–287

Carlier, J., Pinson, E. (1994): Adjustments of Heads and Tails for the Job-Shop Problem. European Journal of Operational Research, vol. **78**, 146–161

Cartwright, H. M., Mott, G. F. (1991): Looking Around: Using Clues from Data Space to Guide Genetic Algorithm Search. In: Belew and Booker (eds.), 108–114

Černy, V. (1985): Thermodynamical Approach to the Traveling Salesman Problem. J. Optim. Theory Appl., vol. **45**, 41–51

Christofides, N. (1975): Graph Theory; An algorithmic approach. Academic Press Inc., London

Collins, R. J., Jefferson, D. R. (1991): Selection in Massively Parallel Genetic Algorithms. In: Belew and Booker (eds.), 249–256

Davidor, Y. (1991): A Naturally Occurring Niche and Species Phenomenon: The Model and First Results. In: Belew and Booker (eds.), 257–263

Davidor, Y., Yamada, T., Nakano, R. (1993): The ECOlogical Framework II: Improving GA Performance at Virtually Zero Cost. In: Forrest (ed.), 171–176

Davidor, Y., Schwefel, H. P., Männer, R. (eds.) (1994): Parallel Problem Solving from Nature III. Springer Verlag, Berlin Heidelberg

Davis, L. (1985a): Applying Adaptive Algorithms to Epistatic Domains. Proc. of the 9th Int. Joint Conf. on Artificial Intelligence, Morgan Kaufmann Publishers, Los Altos CA, 162–164

Davis, L. (1985b): Job Shop Scheduling with Genetic Algorithms. In: Grefenstette (ed.), 136–140

Davis, L. (ed.) (1987): Genetic Algorithms and Simulated Annealing. Morgan Kaufmann Publishers, Los Altos, CA

Davis, L. (ed.) (1991): Handbook of Genetic Algorithms. Van Nostrand Reinhold, New York

Davis, L. (1991): Hybrid Genetic Algorithms. In: Davis (ed.), 54–71

Dell' Amico, M., Trubian, M. (1993): Applying Tabu Search to the Job-Shop Scheduling Problem. Annals of Operations Research, vol. **41**, 231–252

Dorndorf, U., Pesch, E. (1995): Evolution Based Learning in a Job Shop Environment. Comput. Oper. Res., vol. **22**, 25–40

Dorndorf, U., Pesch, E. (1993): Combining Genetic- and Local Search for Solving the Job Shop Scheduling Problem. In: APMOD93 Proc. Preprints, Budapest, 142–149

Elshafei, A. E. (1977): Hospital layout as a quadratic assignment problem. OR Quarterly, vol. **28**, 167–179

Fandel, G., Gulledge, T., Jones, A. (eds.)(1992): New Directions for Operations Research in Manufacturing. Springer Verlag, Berlin Heidelberg

Fandel, G., Gulledge, T., Jones, A. (eds.)(1993): Operations Research in Production Planning and Control. Springer Verlag, Berlin Heidelberg

Fang, H. L., Ross, P., Corne, D. (1993): A Promising Genetic Algorithm Approach to Job-Shop Scheduling, Rescheduling and Open-Shop Scheduling Problems. In: Forrest (ed.), 375–382

Fisher, H., Thompson, G. L. (1963): Probabilistic Learning Combinations of Local Job-Shop Scheduling Rules. In: Muth and Thompson (eds.), 225–251

Fleurent, C., Ferland, J. (1994): Genetic Hybrids for the Quadratic Assignment Problem. Series in Discrete Mathematics and Theoretical Computer Science, vol. **16**, 173–188

Forrest, S. (ed.) (1993): Proc. of the 5th Int. Conf. on Genetic Algorithms. Morgan Kaufmann Publishers, San Mateo, California

Fox, M. S. (1990): Constraint-Guided Scheduling — A Short History of Research at CMU. Computers in Industry, vol. **14**, 79–88

French, S. (1982): Sequencing and Scheduling; An Introduction to the Mathematics of the Job-Shop. Ellis Horwood Limited, England

Garey, M. R., Johnson, D. S. (1979): Computers and Intractability; A Guide to the Theory of NP-Completeness. W. H. Freeman and Company, San Franzisco

Giffler, B., Thompson, G. L. (1960): Algorithms for Solving Production Scheduling Problems. Operations Research, vol. **8**, 487–503

Glover, F., Greenberg, H. J. (1989): New Approaches for Heuristic Search: A Bilateral Linkage with Artificial Intelligence. European Journal of Operational Research, vol. **39**, 119–130

Glover, F. (1989): Tabu Search–Part I. ORSA J. on Computing, vol. **1**, 190–206

Glover, F. (1990): Tabu Search–Part II. ORSA J. on Computing, vol. **2**, 4–32

Glover, F., Laguna, M. (1993): Tabu Search. In: Reeves (ed.), 70–150

Goldberg, D. E., Lingle, R. (1985): Alleles, Loci, and the Travelling Salesman Problem. In: Grefenstette (ed.), 154–159

Goldberg, D. E. (1989): Genetic Algorithms in Search, Optimization and Machine Learning. Addison-Wesley, Reading Massachusetts

Gorges-Schleuter, M. (1989): ASPARAGOS: An Asynchronous Parallel Genetic Optimization Strategy. In: Schaffer (ed.), 422–427

Gorges-Schleuter, M. (1992): Comparison of Local Mating Strategies in Massively Parallel Genetic Algorithms. In: Männer and Manderick (eds.), 553–562

Grefenstette, J. J. (ed.) (1985): Proc. of the 1st Int. Conf. on Genetic Algorithms and Their Applications. Lawrence Erlbaum Associates, Hillsdale

Grefenstette, J. J., Gopal, R., Rosmaita, B., Van Gucht, D. (1985): Genetic Algorithms for the Traveling Salesman Problem. In: Grefenstette (ed.), 160–168

Grefenstette, J. J. (ed.) (1987): Proc. of the 2nd Int. Conf. on Genetic Algorithms. Lawrence Erlbaum Associates, Hillsdale New Jersey

Grefenstette, J. J. (1987): Incorporating Problem Specific Knowledge into Genetic Algorithms. In: Davis (ed.), 42–60

Haupt, R. (1989): A Survey of Priority Rule-Based Scheduling. OR Spektrum, vol. **11**, 3–16

Herdy, M. (1990): Application of the Evolutionsstrategy to Discrete Optimization Problems. In: Schwefel and Männer (eds.), 188–192

Hoffmeister, F., Bäck, T. (1990): Genetic Algorithms and Evolution Strategies: Similarities and Differences. In: Schwefel and Männer (eds.), 455–469

Holland, H. J. (1975): Adaptation in natural and artificial systems. The University of Michigan Press, Ann Abor

Hurink, J., Jurisch, B., Thole, M. (1994): Tabu Search for the Job-Shop Scheduling Problem with Multi-Purpose Machines. OR Spektrum, vol. **15**, 205–215

Inayoshi, H., Manderick, B. (1994): The Weighted Graph Bi-Partitioning Problem: A Look at GA Performance. In: Davidor et al. (eds.), 617–625

Jones, T. C. (1995): One Operator, One Landscape. Santa Fe Inst. of Technology, submitted to the 12-th Int. Conf. on Machine Learning.

Jones, T. C., Forrest, S. (1995): Genetic Algorithms and Heuristic Search. Santa Fe Inst. of Technology, submitted to the Int. Joint Conf. on Artificial Intelligence.

De Jong, K. (1975): An Analysis of the Behaviour of a Class of Genetic Adaptive Systems. Dissertation, University of Michigan.

Kahn, A. B. (1962): Topological Sorting in Large Networks. Communication of the ACM, vol. **5**, 558–562

Kargupta, H., Kalyanmoy, D., Goldberg, D. E. (1992): Ordering Genetic Algorithms and Deception. In: Männer and Manderick (eds.), 47–56

Kauffman, S. A. (1993): The Origins of Order; Self-Organization and Selection in Evolution. Oxford University Press, New York, Oxford

Kirkpatrick, S., Gelatt, C. D., Vecchi, M. P. (1983): Optimization by Simulated Annealing. Science vol. **220**, 671–680

Kirkpatrick, S., Toulouse, G. (1985): Configuration Space Analysis of Travelling Salesman Problems. J Physique, vol. **46**, 1277–1292

Kusiak, A., Chen, M. (1988): Expert Systems for Planning and Scheduling Manufacturing Systems. European Journal of Operational Research, vol. **34**, 113–130

Lageweg, B. J., Lenstra, J. K., Rinnooy Kan, A. H. G. (1977): Job-Shop Scheduling by Implicit Enumeration. Management Science, vol. **24**, 441–450

Lawrence, S. (1984): Resource Constrained Project Scheduling: An Experimental Investigation of Heuristic Scheduling Techniques. Technical Report, Graduate School of Industrial Administration, Carnegie Mellon University

Liepins, G. E., Hilliard, M. R. (1989): Genetic Algorithms: Foundations and Applications. Annals of Operations Research, vol. **21**, 31–57

Lin, S., Kernighan, B. W. (1973): An Efficient Heuristic for the Traveling Salesman Problem. Operations Research, vol. **21**, 498–516

Lipsitch, M. (1991): Adaptation on Rugged Landscapes Generated by Iterated Local Interactions of Neighboring Genes. In: Belew and Booker (eds.), 128–135

Männer, R., Manderick, B. (eds.) (1992): Parallel Problem Solving from Nature II, North-Holland, Amsterdam

Manderick, B., De Weger, M., Spiessens, P. (1991): The Genetic Algorithm and the Structure of the Fitness Landscape. In: Belew and Booker (eds.), 143–150

Matsuo, H., Suh, C. J., Sullivan, R. S. (1988): A Controlled Search Simulated Annealing Method for the General Jobshop Scheduling Problem. Working paper 03-04-88, Dept. of Management, Graduate School of Business, University of Austin, Texas 1988

Mattfeld, D. C., Kopfer, H., Bierwirth, C. (1994): Control of Parallel Population Dynamics by Social-Like Behavior of GA-Individuals. In: Davidor et al. (eds.), 15–25

Mehlhorn, K., Näher, S. (1989): LEDA, A Library of Efficient Data Types and Algorithms. Technical Report **A 05/89**, University of Saarbrücken, Germany

Mitchell, M., Holland, J. H. (1994): When Will a Genetic Algorithm Outperform Hill-Climbing? In: Cowan, J., Tesauro, G., Alspector, J. (eds.): Advances in Neural Information Processing Systems. Morgan Kauffman, San Mateo, CA

Morton, T. E., Pentico, D. W. (1993): Heuristic Scheduling Systems; With Applications to Productions Systems and Project Management. John Wiley & Sons Inc., New York, Chichester, Brisbane, Toronto, Singapore

Mühlenbein, H., Gorges-Schleuter, M., Krämer, O. (1988): Evolutionary Algorithms in Combinatorial Optimization. Parallel Computing vol. **7**, 65–85

Mühlenbein, H. (1990): Parallel Genetic Algorithms and Combinatorial Optimization. Internal paper of the Dept. of Electrical and Computer Engineering, CMU, Pittsburg.

Mühlenbein, H. (1991): Evolution in Time and Space – The Parallel Genetic Algorithm. In: Rawlins (ed.), 316–337

Mühlenbein, H. (1992): How Genetic Algorithms Really Work: I. Mutation and Hillclimbing. In: Männer and Manderick (eds.), 15–25

Mühlenbein, H., Schlierkamp-Voosen, D. (1994): The Science of Breeding and its Application to the Breeder Genetic Algorithm BGA. Evolutionary Computation, vol. **1**, 335–360

Muth, J. F., Thompson, G. L. (eds.) (1963): Industrial Scheduling. Prentice-Hall, Englewood Cliffs NJ

Nakano, R., Yamada, T. (1991): Conventional Genetic Algorithm for Job Shop Problems. In: Belew and Booker (eds.), 474–479

Nakano, R., Davidor, Y., Yamada, T. (1994): Optimal Population Size Under Constant Computation Cost. In: Davidor et al. (eds.), 130–138

Nissen, V. (1994): Evolutionäre Algorithmen; Darstellung, Beispiele, betriebswirtschaftliche Anwendungsmöglichkeiten. Deutscher Universitäts Verlag, Wiesbaden

Nowicki, E., Smutnicki, C. (1995): A Fast Taboo Search Algorithm for the Job Shop Problem. Management Science, to appear

Oliver, L. M., Smith, D. J., Holland, J. R. C. (1987): A Study of Permutation Crossover Operators on the Traveling Salesman Problem. In: Grefenstette (ed.), 224–230

Pearl, J. (1984): Heuristics: Intelligent Search Strategies for Computer Problem Solving. Addison-Wesley, Reading, Massachusetts

Pesch, E. (1993): Machine Learning by Schedule Decomposition. Research Report, University of Limburg, Netherlands

Pesch, E. (1994): Learning in Automated Manufacturing; A Local Search Approach. Physica Verlag, Heidelberg

Pinedo, M. (1995): Scheduling; Theory, Algorithms, and Systems. Prentice Hall, Englewood Cliffs, New Jersey

Radcliff, N. J. (1993): Forma Analysis and Random Respectful Recombination. In: Belew and Booker (eds.), 222–229

Raman, N., Rachamadugu, R. V., Talbot, F. B. (1989): Real-Time Scheduling of an Automated Manufacturing Center. European Journal of Operational Research, vol. **40**, 222–242

Rawlins, G. J. E. (ed.)(1991): Foundations of Genetic Algorithms, vol. **1**, Morgan Kauffman, San Mateo, CA

Rechenberg, I. (1973): Evolutionsstrategie: Optimierung Technischer Systeme Nach Prinzipien der Biologischen Evolution. Friederich Frommann Verlag, Stuttgart

Reeves, C. R. (ed.) (1993): Modern Heuristic Techniques for Combinatorial Problems. Blackwell Scientific Publications, Oxford

Reeves, C. R. (1993): Genetic Algorithms. In: Reeves (ed.), 151–196

Schaffer, D. J. (ed.)(1989): Proc. of the 3rd Int. Conf. on Genetic Algorithms. Morgan Kauffman Publishers, San Mateo CA

Scheer, A.-W. (1989): Enterprise-Wide Data Modelling; Information Systems in Industry. Springer Verlag, Berlin Heidelberg

Schull, J. (1990): The View from the Adaptive Landscape. In: Schwefel and Männer (eds.), 415–427

Schwefel, H. P. (1975): Evolutionsstrategie und Numerische Optimierung. Dissertation, Technical University Berlin

Schwefel, H. P., Männer, R. (eds.) (1990): Parallel Problem Solving from Nature I. Springer Verlag, Berlin, Heidelberg

Smith, J. M (1987): When Learning Guides Evolution. Nature, vol. **329**, 761–762

Smith, J. M. (1989): Evolutionary Genetics. Oxford University Press, Oxford

Spiessens, P., Manderick, B. (1991): A Massively Parallel Genetic Algorithm; Implementation and First Results. In: Belew and Booker (eds.), 279–286

Staats, A. W. (1975): Social Behaviorism. The Dorsey Press, Illinois

Stender, J. (ed.) (1993): Parallel Genetic Algorithms: Theory and Applications. IOS Press, Amsterdam, Oxford, Washington, Tokyo.

Stöppler, S., Bierwirth, C. (1992): The Application of a Parallel Genetic Algorithm to the $n/m/P/C_{max}$ Flowshop Problem. In: Fandel et al. (eds.), 161–171

Storer, R. H., Wu, S. D., Vaccari, R. (1992a): New Search Spaces for Sequencing Problems with Application to Job Shop Scheduling. Management Science, vol. **38**, 1495–1509

Storer, R. H., Wu, S. D., Vaccari, R. (1992b): Local Search in Problem and Heuristic Space for Job Shop Scheduling GAs. In: Fandel et al. (eds.), 149–160

Storer, R. H., Wu, S. D. (1993): Genetic Algorithm in Problem Space for Sequencing Problems. In: Fandel et al. (eds.), 584–597

Suh, J. Y., Van Gucht, D. (1987): Incorporating Heuristic Information into Genetic Search. In: Grefenstette (ed.), 100–107

Syswerda, G. (1989): Uniform Crossover in GAs. In: Schaffer (ed.), 2–9

Syswerda, G. (1991): Schedule Optimization Using Genetic Algorithms. In: Davis (ed.), 332–349

Taillard, E. D. (1993): Parallel Taboo Search Techniques for the Job Shop Scheduling Problem. ORSA Journal on Computing, vol. **6**, 108–117

Taillard, E. D. (1993): Benchmarks for Basic Scheduling Problems. European Journal of Operational Research, vol. **64**, 278–285

Taillard, E. D. (1994): Comparison of Iterative Searches for the Quadratic Assignment Problem. Technical Report CRT-989, Centre de recherche sur les transports, Université de Montréal.

Vaessens, R. J. M., Aarts, E. H. L., Lenstra, J. K. (1992): A Local Search Template. In: Männer and Manderick (eds.), 65–74

Vaessens, R. J. M., Aarts, E. H. L., Lenstra, J. K. (1994): Job Shop Scheduling by Local Search. Memorandum COSOR 94-05, (2. revised version), Eindhoven University of Technology, Netherlands

Van Dyke Parunak, H. (1992): Characterizing the Manufacturing Scheduling Problem. Journal of Manufacturing Systems, vol. **10**, 241–259

Van Laarhoven, P. J. M., Aarts, E. H. L. (1987): Simulated Annealing: Theory and Applications. Kluwer Academic Press, Dodrecht, Netherlands

Van Laarhoven, P. J. M., Aarts, E. H. L., Lenstra, J. K. (1992): Job Shop Scheduling by Simulated Annealing. ORSA Journal on Computing, vol. **40**, 113–125

Weinberger, E. (1990): Correlated and Uncorrelated Fitness Landscapes and How to Tell the Difference. Biological Cybernetics, vol. **63**, 325–336

White, K. P., Rogers, R. V. (1990): Job-Shop Scheduling: Limits of the Binary Disjunctive Formulation. International Journal of Production Research, vol. **28**, 2187–2200

Whitley, D., Starkweather, T., Fuquay, D. (1989): Scheduling Problems and Travelling Salesmen: The Genetic Edge Recombination Operator. In: Schaffer (ed.), 133–140

Whitley, D. (1989): The GENITOR Algorithm and Selection Pressure: Why Rank-Based Allocation of Reproductive Trials is Best. In: Schaffer (ed.), 116-121

Whitley, D. (1993): A Genetic Algorithms Tutorial. Technical Report, No. CS-93-103, Colorado State University, USA

Whitley, D., Gordon, S., Mathias, K. (1994): Lamarckian Evolution, The Baldwin Effect and Function Optimization. In: Davidor et al. (eds.), 6–15

Yamada, T., Nakano, R. (1992): A Genetic Algorithm Applicable to Large-Scale Job-Shop Problems. In: Männer and Manderick (eds.), 281–290

Yamada, T., Nakano, R. (1995): Job Shop Scheduling by Simulated Annealing Combined with Deterministic Local Search. Metaheuristics International Conference, Hilton Breckenridge, Colorado USA, 344-349

Springer-Verlag
and the Environment

We at Springer-Verlag firmly believe that an international science publisher has a special obligation to the environment, and our corporate policies consistently reflect this conviction.

We also expect our business partners – paper mills, printers, packaging manufacturers, etc. – to commit themselves to using environmentally friendly materials and production processes.

The paper in this book is made from low- or no-chlorine pulp and is acid free, in conformance with international standards for paper permanency.

Printing: Weihert-Druck GmbH, Darmstadt
Binding: Theo Gansert Buchbinderei GmbH, Weinheim